Breaking the Heartland

MERCER
UNIVERSITY PRESS

Endowed by
TOM WATSON BROWN
and
THE WATSON-BROWN FOUNDATION, INC.

Breaking the Heartland

The Civil War in Georgia

Edited by

John D. Fowler and David B. Parker

MERCER UNIVERSITY PRESS
MACON, GEORGIA

MUP/H824

© 2011 Mercer University Press
1400 Coleman Avenue
Macon, Georgia 31207
All rights reserved

First Edition

Books published by Mercer University Press are printed on acid-free paper that meets the requirements of American National Standard for Information Sciences—Permanence of Paper for Printed Library Materials.

Mercer University Press is a member of Green Press Initiative (greenpressinitiative.org), a nonprofit organization working to help publishers and printers increase their use of recycled paper and decrease their use of fiber derived from endangered forests. This book is printed on recycled paper.

Library of Congress Cataloging-in-Publication Data

Breaking the heartland : the Civil War in Georgia / edited by John D.
Fowler and David B. Parker –1st ed.
p. cm.
Includes bibliographical references and index.
ISBN 978-0-88146-240-1 (hardcover : acid-free paper)
1. Georgia--History--Civil War, 1861-1865--Social aspects. 2.
Georgia--Politics and government--1861-1865. 3. Georgia--History-
-Civil War, 1861-1865--Campaigns. I. Fowler, John D., 1965-
II. Parker, David B., 1956-
F290.B74 2011
975.8'03--dc22
2011003183

Contents

Introduction

by John D. Fowler

In 1960, noted Civil War historian Bell Irvin Wiley wrote a booklet for the Georgia Department of State Parks entitled *Why Georgia Should Commemorate the Civil War*. In a short but detailed twenty-three pages, Wiley sketched out a list of persuasive reasons why Georgians should participate in the war's centennial. He emphasized the importance of the conflict to American history, the key role Georgians played in organizing and administering the Confederate government, and the decisive battles that took place in Georgia. Now, as the state approaches the sesquicentennial, the reasons Wiley outlined are still as relevant.[1]

The Civil War was a watershed event in the history of the United States, forever changing the nature of the Republic and the relationship of individuals to their government. The war ended slavery and initiated the long road toward racial equality. Those reasons alone make the conflict vital to understanding the nation's turbulent past, its problematic present, and its beckoning future, and few states had a greater impact on the outcome of the nation's greatest calamity than the Empire State of the South. Georgia provided 125,000 soldiers for the Confederacy as well as thousands more for the Union cause. Also, many of the Confederacy's most noted generals and statesmen hailed from the state. Georgia was critical to the Confederate war effort because of its agricultural and industrial output. The Confederacy had little hope of winning without the farms and shops of the state. Moreover, the state was critical to the Southern infrastructure because of the river and rail links that crossed it and connected the western Confederacy to the eastern half. Perhaps most importantly, the war was arguably decided in North Georgia with the Atlanta Campaign and Lincoln's subsequent reelection. This campaign was the last forlorn hope for the Southern Republic and the Union's greatest triumph.

---

[1] Bell Irvin Wiley, *Why Georgia Should Commemorate the Civil War* (Atlanta: Department of State Parks, 1960).

Despite the state's importance to the Confederacy and the war's ultimate outcome, not enough has been written concerning Georgia's experience during those turbulent years. The essays that follow are an attempt to redress this dearth of scholarship. They present a mosaic of events, places, and people, exploring the impact of the war on Georgia and its residents and demonstrating the importance of the state to the outcome of the Civil War.

The essays included cover a wide variety of topics, but they can be organized broadly by subject and time frame. The first two works explore the effects of disaffection on the Georgia home front. Robert Scott Davis's essay, "War on the Edge: Civil War Era Politics and Its Legacy in an Appalachian County," focuses on Pickens County. The author proposes that the white population of Pickens County, as in most Appalachian counties, did not solidly support secession. Indeed, a significant portion of the populace opposed the Confederacy and remained loyal to the old Union throughout the war. Moreover, as the war continued, Confederate governmental policies such as conscription and impressment caused widespread disaffection even among secessionists. This eventually led to desertion, and isolated North Georgia counties such as Pickens were prime locations for deserter bands to hide out. Davis's work clearly demonstrates the divisive nature of secession for many of Georgia's people.

David Williams's essay, "Bitterly Divided: Georgia's Inner Civil War," covers many of the same issues as Davis's, although Williams focuses on the state as a whole. The author maintains that the Confederacy actually fought a two-front war, one against the Federal government and one against disaffected Southerners. His provocative essay posits that from the beginning the majority of Georgians opposed secession and were in effect led into war by undemocratic political maneuverings on the part of Governor Joseph E. Brown and the planter elite, who controlled the state government. Williams goes on to declare that as wartime conditions deteriorated, food shortages, resentment of the draft, desertion, impressment, and tax-in-kind measures led to a collapse of the already weak Confederate sentiment among the common whites of the state. Taken together, these two essays demonstrate a lack of cohesive support for the Confederacy in Georgia, especially among non-slaveholding whites of the lower and middle classes.

In "States of Dependence and Independence in Civil War Georgia," author Joseph P. Reidy investigates how Georgia families dealt with the realities of war in their daily lives. Like David Williams, Reidy finds that the growing burdens of the prolonged struggle eroded Southern morale. Faced with shortages of food and essential household items, spirits sagged. He points to the central role played by white women in attempting to keep families together and households functioning in the face of economic ruin. To further complicate matters at home, the slave population began exploiting the situation for additional compensation or concessions from masters. Moreover, black Georgians often joined the Federal invaders as laborers or soldiers to gain their freedom.

"Georgia Lowcountry Battlegrounds during the Civil War," by Jacqueline Jones, continues to examine the plight of African Americans. She finds an inner civil war occurring along the Georgia coast. While Union and Confederate forces fought for control of the Georgia coastline on one level, African Americans complicated these efforts as they struggled to assert their independence on another level. Thus, the war was a social revolution as well as a political one. She points out that while many blacks eagerly served the Union war effort as seamen, soldiers, pilots, spies, laborers, and scouts, they resisted the racism and stereotypes placed on them by the Federal forces and Northern white civilians. In effect, blacks wanted control of their labor and destiny and struggled mightily to achieve it.

The theme of the "proper" role for African Americans in a white society is taken up by David B. Parker in "'To the Youth of the Southern Confederacy': Georgia's Confederate Textbooks." Parker reveals the desire by Georgia whites to produce textbooks for the Southern Republic. Since the Confederates viewed themselves as engaged in a revolution to protect their superior way of life, they needed textbooks that conveyed their values to the future generations of the young nation. In reality, few substantive changes emerged in Southern texts. Parker shows that through the use of Bible verses and Judeo-Christian ethics, Georgians followed their fellow Confederates in extolling the virtues of slavery and proper Southern morals. In the end, the texts were more about justifying the peculiar institution than anything else.

In his innovative "'Wars and Rumors of Wars': Hearsay as Information on Georgia's Civil War Home Front," Chad Morgan explores how hearsay and rumor affected morale on Georgia's home front. Morgan contends that Georgians received fairly accurate information during the war's first three years because of letters from the front and newspapers from around the South. However, with the Atlanta Campaign, Union forces cut the communication lines for most Georgians leading to widespread rumors as the primary basis for information. If the rumors were positive morale improved, but if they were negative morale plummeted. Moreover, as reliable information became harder to obtain, many Georgia troops deserted to return home and protect their families from suspected and rumored Yankee atrocities. Thus, Morgan views rumor and hearsay as a destabilizing force on the battlefield and homefront and an area for future scholarly investigation.

The next three essays focus on the Atlanta Campaign. "'The Bottomless Pit of Hell': The Confederate Home Front in Bartow County, Georgia, 1864–1865," by Keith S. Hébert, takes an intriguing look at how the Atlanta Campaign affected the home front of one North Georgia county. He examines the hardships experienced by civilians caught in the wake of war as armies moved through their villages and farms. Hébert vividly illustrates that the county faced anarchy as armed bands of deserters, brigands, and Union and Confederate guerillas battled for control. Interestingly, unlike Davis and Williams, this author found that initially Confederate sympathy was present in Bartow County but waned over the course of the war. He finds, however, that Federal occupation reignited pro-Confederate sentiments if only out of disgust for the enemy.

In "From Gate City to Gotham: Sam Richards Chronicles the Civil War in Atlanta," Wendy Hamand Venet tells the story of Atlanta's Civil War through the eyes of English immigrant Sam Richards. Richards's rich diary offers insights into Southern wartime morale, economic conditions, the transformation of Atlanta into a major Confederate logistics center, and the impact of the war on the civilian population. Venet's essay captures the home front from the point of view of a unique person—a Southern urban dweller, a man whose loyalty to Southern independence ebbed and flowed with the tide of war. She illustrates that perhaps Confederate morale is best understood in light of Confederate success or failure.

John Fowler's essay, "'I Cannot Give the History of This Campaign Language to Describe Its Suffering': The Confederate Struggle for Atlanta," is the only full military study in the volume. In it, he explores the historiography of the Atlanta Campaign, focusing on six key questions: Was Joseph E. Johnston the best choice to head the Army of Tennessee in 1864? Why did Johnston not fight harder to defeat or stall William T. Sherman in the North Georgia Mountains? What really happened at Cassville? Should Johnston have been removed? Why did John B. Hood fail? Could the Confederates have won the Atlanta Campaign? The answers reveal that the Confederacy had little hope of winning the campaign in the Western Theater in 1864 given the personalities and events. Neither Jefferson Davis, Johnston, nor Hood could direct the Army of Tennessee to victory. By 1864, the war belonged to the Union. The South could win it only if the North chose to lose it.

The volume's last two essays cover the state government's efforts to bolster the Southern image during and after the war. The hardships of war and eventual defeat severely tested Georgia's people and their socio-economic and political ideology. Jennifer Lynn Gross's contribution, "Buttressed Patriarchs and Substitute Patriarchs: Aid to Georgia's Confederate Families during and after the Civil War," focuses on the effects of war on patriarchy. She maintains that through wartime and postwar aid and the Confederate pension system, the Georgia legislature sought either to buttress the veteran in his traditional role as head of household or, in the case of widows and orphans, assume the role of patriarch. She views the social welfare system as a key part of an effort by Southern males to perpetuate traditional gender roles.

In the last essay, "Buried at Savannah: Confederate Plain Folk Widows, Children, and the Civil War's Lost Memories," Mark V. Wetherington also examines how war affected widows and orphans. By examining the case of one family, that of Elizabeth Watson, he attempts to answer several important and intriguing questions such as what options were available to Confederate widows; what was the wartime responses of Confederate, state, and local authorities to the plight of widows; what was the fate of widows and orphans in the immediate postwar period; and what role did such families play in the remembrance of the war. He concludes that the wives and children of Confederate war dead faced new economic realities based on growing industrialization and the transformation of a new Southern economy. Despite the loss of the war and the reshaping of Georgian and Southern society, however, white Georgians clung fiercely to an exalted view of the Confederacy and their sacrifices. Given how much these families lost, it is little wonder they chose to remember the war and their dead loved ones as part of a noble struggle.

These essays reflect the latest attempts by scholars to understand and uncover Georgia's Confederate past. While many of the volume's eleven chapters focus on different individuals, households, communities, situations, events, and particular regions of Georgia, they are united in attempting to get at what poet Walt Whitman called the "real war"—the ugly realities inherent in a struggle as brutal and transforming as the American Civil War.[2] The essays highlight the variety of circumstances Georgians faced over the course of the Civil War era and call for future generations of historians to mine and sift the stories of Georgians facing the nation's greatest tragedy.

---

[2]Walt Whitman, "The Real War Will Never Get in the Books," *Prose Works, 1892: Specimen Days*, ed. Floyd Stovall, vol. 8 of *The Collected Writings of Walt Whitman*, ed. Gay Wilson Allen and Scully Bradley (New York: New York University Press, 1963) 115–18.

War on the Edge:
Civil War Era Politics and Its Legacy in an Appalachian County

by Robert Scott Davis

Historian Michael Johnson argued that the delegates to Georgia's Secession Convention listened to shouts for state independence instead of the whispers of doubt expressed by many of their other constituents.[1] In rural Pickens County, however, citizens spoke out above the din. Newspapers across the nation reported on an anti-secession meeting held there on 4 December 1860, wherein the participants announced "that we are opposed to the secession of Georgia from the Union and we will never consent, without a struggle lamely to consent to give up to the abolition traitors of the North, all of our rights under the Constitution of the United States."[2] Upon hearing that the state convention had voted to secede on 19 January 1861, this community made more protests and raised a United States flag as a symbol of dissent.[3] A story published decades later had a politically pragmatic Gov. Joseph E. Brown stating in answer to the news of this action: "By no means; let it float. It floated over our fathers, and we all love the flag now. We have only been compelled to lay it aside by the injustice that has been practiced under its folds. If the people of Pickens desire to hang it out, and keep it there, let them do so. I will send no troops to interfere with it."[4] The banner

---

[1]Michael P. Johnson, "A New Look at the Popular Vote for Delegates to the Georgia Secession Convention," *Georgia Historical Quarterly* 56/2 (Summer 1972): 271. The author acknowledges the help provided by Rev. Charles O. Walker and Dr. Keith Bohannon.

[2]"Pickens County," *Daily Chronicle and Sentinel* (Augusta GA) 15 December 1860.

[3]"Georgia State Convention," *Macon* (GA) *Telegraph*, 25 January 1861; "Important Demonstrations," *Southern Banner* (Athens GA) 30 January 1861; [no title], *Berkshire County Eagle* (Pittsfield MA) 14 February 1861.

[4]Isaac W. Avery, *The History of the State of Georgia from 1851 to 1881* (New York: Brown & Derby, 1881) 187–88; Keith S. Bohannon, "The Northeast Georgia Mountains during the Secession Crisis and Civil War" (Ph. D. diss., Pennsylvania State University, 2001) 67. Pickens County politico Lemuel J. Allred likely supplied Avery with the

reportedly flew on a 60-foot pole in front of the courthouse. Armed citizens guarded it until a wind from a sudden storm cloud shredded the flag and it vanished.[5]

The North Georgians who raised this standard, and their neighbors who would have taken it down, would famously represent the deep conflicts among their state's population over the war and for generations that followed. Both Confederate and pro-Union companies marched out from their numbers and the civilians among them suffered from deprivations committed by both armies. They would remain politically divided into the twenty-first century. Dissent occurred elsewhere across the state but widespread notoriety made this Appalachian people first a symbol of opposition to secession, then to war, later to the Confederate States, and finally to the Georgia's post-war reputation for political solidarity. Those deep conflicts support Anthony Gene Carey's thesis that only a combination of many historical, economic, and social factors explains the Civil War era politics of any community.[6]

At 232 square miles and as one of the smallest counties in the Georgia, Pickens also had one of the state's smallest populations: 4,951, or less than 0.5% of the state's total in 1860. According to William Tate, the county's census taker for that year, 94 percent of its heads of household were almost evenly divided among persons born in Georgia, North Carolina, and South Carolina. Other heads of household were natives of Tennessee, Virginia, Ireland, France, Holland, Kentucky, Alabama, England, Scotland, Louisiana, Pennsylvania, Massachusetts,

---

account of the flag incident and Allred may also have been the source for the news stories at the time about the flag raising. The Brown quote may also be typical literary license of the period by Allred, a man widely regarded for his storytelling abilities.

[5]"Important Demonstrations," *Southern Banner* (Athens GA) 30 January 1861; claims of Samuel [sic, Lemuel] J. Allred, Lemuel J. Allred deposition in Hosea Hopkins claim, and Robert B. McCutchen claim, *Barred and Disallowed Case Files of the Southern Claims Commission, 1871–1880,* National Archives microfilm M1407, fiche 594 and 1158, Records of the United States House of Representatives, Record Group (hereafter RG) 233, National Archives and Records Administration (hereafter NARA); Southern Historical Association, *Memoirs of Georgia,* 2 vols. (Atlanta: Southern Historical Association, 1895) 2:678.

[6]Anthony G. Carey, *Parties, Slavery, and the Union in Antebellum Georgia* (Athens: University of Georgia Press, 1997) 247.

Connecticut, and Vermont. Aside from farmers, they included coopers, millwrights, mechanics, blacksmiths, carpenters, wagon makers, clock makers, cobblers, hatters, brick masons, distillers, lawyers, tailors, seamstresses, and teachers.[7]

These people lived around a few small communities, the largest of which a visitor described in 1867: "Jasper is a small town and the county site of Pickens County. It is situated in a little poor elevation containing three or four brick houses (one of which is the Courthouse) and a few stores and liquor shop."[8] The county's other large settlement centered on the old tavern of Harnageville on Long Swamp Creek. The building had been taken over by the Tate family for whom the settlement would come to be named. John Azor Kellogg would remember it in 1864 as consisting of a store, a blacksmith shop, and a few houses.[9] Pickens's other villages of Hinton, Ludville, and Talking Rock would hardly have been much different.

In latitude, altitude, rainfall, and temperature, this land would prove to be on the margin of profitable cotton production. Without rivers or railroad, it lacked transportation for that crop. In 1860, it had half of its southern neighbor Cherokee County's population and roughly half of the same agriculture except that it ginned only ten bales of cotton and on a total of five farms to Cherokee's 978 bales produced by 1,244 slaves. Ten years later, only 25 percent of Pickens County had been cultivated. This hilly plateau between two mountain ranges also lacked more than seasonal water power for its Talking Rock/Price and Long Swamp creeks.[10]

---

[7]Pickens County GA (1860) *Eighth Census of the United States (1860)* National Archives microfilm M653, roll 133, Records of the Bureau of the Census, RG 29, NARA. A copy of the 1860 census of Pickens County appears in Tate, *History of Pickens County*, 94–199.

[8]Robert Riley Berry memoirs, in the possession of Jeff Daniel, Mountain Brook AL.

[9]Robert S. Davis, "Into the Wilderness: John Kellogg's Journey through Civil War North Georgia," *Chattanooga Regional Historical Journal* 7/2 (December 2004): 220.

[10]Joseph C. G. Kennedy, *Preliminary Report on the Eighth Census. 1860* (Washington DC: Government Printing Office, 1862) 250–51; *Agriculture of the United States in 1860: Compiled from the Original Returns of the Eighth Census* (Washington DC: Government Printing Office, 1864) 22–23, 26–27.

Tate counted only 246 slaves and 37 slaveholders in 1860. Of the latter, Samuel Tate, William's father, owned thirty-two people of various ages and William owned twenty-five; the two men were the only persons in the county who could have been classed as "planters." The local economy produced little in the way of products for markets elsewhere. Pork and wool made up almost all of its cash crops, but only some two dozen farmers produced enough of either to have been more than self-sufficient. In 1860, Samuel Tate had the largest farm operation with 250 pigs, 60 sheep, 42 cattle of all kinds, and 5 horses. He alone had a herd of hogs in triple digits and he produced by far the largest amount of corn: 3,500 bushels.[11]

The politics of Pickens County also reflected both isolation and insulation from the rest of the South. As early as 1838, a visitor wrote of hearing conflicting arguments on nullification of federal laws in the local taverns.[12] In the years that followed, debates raged in the newspapers on the question of the loyalty of such Appalachian people to Southern nationalism in the case of secession. Whether or not these whites had been driven into the mountains by the plantation economy, however, they certainly opposed economic competition from freedmen. North Georgia voters in general rejected politics that could have led to secession in 1833, 1843, and 1850.[13] Pickens County's dissenters of 1860 had stated

---

[11]Pickens County (1860) slave schedules, *Nonpopulation Census Schedules, Georgia, 1850–1880,* National Archives microfilm T1137, roll 6, RG 29, NARA.

[12]George Featherstonhaugh, *A Canoe Voyage up the Minnay Sotor,* 2 vols. (London: Richard Bentley, 1847) 2:226.

[13]Carey, *Politics, Slavery, and the Union,* 19, 240–47; [no title], *Southern Recorder* (Milledgeville GA) 13 September 1853; John Van Houten Dippel, *Race to the Frontier: "White Flight" and Western Expansion* (New York: Algora, 2005) 39–64; Steven Hahn, *The Roots of Southern Populism: Yeoman Farmers and the Transformation of the Georgia Upcountry, 1850–1890* (New York: Oxford University Press, 1983) 16–18, 20; David F. Weiman, "The Economic Emancipation of the Non-Slaveholding Class: Upcountry Farmers in the Georgia Cotton Economy," *Journal of Economic History* 45/1 (March 1985): 74–75, 82–82; Jacqueline Jones, *The Dispossessed: America's Underclasses from the Civil War to the Present* (New York: Basic Books, 1992) 55, 57; Morton Rothstein, "The Antebellum South as a Dual Economy," in *The Slave Economics,* ed. Eugene D. Genovese, 2 vols. (New York: John Wiley & Sons, 1973) 2:143–56, 157–69. For more on the attitudes of these people with regards to race and the Civil War, see John C. Inscoe, *Race, War, and Remembrance in the Appalachian South* (Lexington:

that they would keep their rights as citizens of the United States in spite of Northern calls for emancipation. Among them, Robert B. McCutchen claimed that when he unsuccessfully ran as a candidate for delegate to the secession convention, he opposed leaving the Union because it would result in the freeing of slaves and thereby "ruination." He later became a Civil War officer in the United States Army.[14]

By 1852, Georgia's organized statewide opposition to secession included Lemuel James Allred, a local land speculator and politician whose efforts created Pickens County on 5 December 1853, largely as a political fiefdom for him, his brothers, and eventually his brother-in-law, Robert McCutchen. At that time, the pro-Union, largely secretive, Native American "Know Nothing" Party found converts across North Georgia, and much of America, by pushing aside the issue of slavery in favor of xenophobia for the sake of national unity. In 1855, Pickens County entrepreneur and postmaster James Simmons tried to take political power as a Know Nothing. Samuel Tate supported Allred in defeating that effort on behalf of Cherokee and Pickens County Superior Court Circuit Judge Joseph E. Brown's successful campaign for governor. Brown beat out the Know Nothing candidate Benjamin Harvey Hill by 593 to 228 in Pickens in 1857. This electorate held a rally to support the new governor during the national panic of 1857 in his famous efforts to force the state's banks to continue making specie payments. The county also overwhelmingly endorsed his reelection in 1859 by 759 to 75 votes but then chose against him, 415 to 305, in 1861 when he championed secession. In 1863, Brown carried both the civilian and the army's vote while splitting the counties in North Georgia. In Pickens County, however, he received fifty-five votes to peace candidate Hill's 426. The

---

University Press of Kentucky, 2008) 13–64, and Richard B. Drake, "Slavery and Antislavery in Appalachia," in *Appalachians and Race: The Mountain South from Slavery to Segregation*, ed. John C. Inscoe (Lexington: University Press of Kentucky, 2001) 16–26.

[14]Robert S. Davis, "'The Business of Life': A Case Study of Using Credit Reports in a Community History in Pickens County, North Georgia," *Chattanooga Regional Historical Journal* 5/7 (July 2002): 60, 67–68. McCutchen may have been playing to fears raised by rumors of slave revolt conspiracies in Northwest Georgia. Herbert Aptheker, *American Negro Slave Revolts* (1943; rpt., New York: International Publishers, 1993) 354–55.

governor also failed to carry his home county, neighboring Cherokee, by 170 to 385 votes.[15]

Many Pickens Countians did accept the decision of the 1860–1861 state convention to secede. Even as a show of unity after the majority decided the issue, James Simmons of Pickens County and five other delegates refused to vote for secession, but they did sign a statement to defend the state against any enemy. Simmons remained an active and life-long Democrat. L. A. Simmons, the secessionist son of James, however, despaired of success in raising even one Confederate volunteer company in Pickens without the threat of conscription in spring 1861.[16] Enough men did come forward soon after to form Tate's Guards, on the same ground where the dissenters' banner had only recently flown. These men had a formal Confederate flag presentation that likely became the inspiration for a patriotic love poem by "Kate" of Jasper to her soldier that appeared a month later in the *Atlanta Intelligencer*. Members of Company E, and also Company D from Pickens County, 23rd Georgia Infantry, would see much of the deadliest fighting in the East.[17] The county also contributed significantly to at least four companies that served in Georgia and the West. Grand juries of 1861 and 1862 made presentments in support of the Southern Cause and noted that some one hundred of its citizens had enlisted in adjoining counties. At least 500

---

[15]Tad Evans, comp., *Macon, Georgia, Newspaper Clippings (Messenger)* 9 vols. (Savannah: T. Evans, 1997–2001) 6:49–51; F. C. Tate to Farish Carter, 26 January 1855, Farish Carter Papers, Southern Historical Collection, University of North Carolina at Chapel Hill; Davis, "The 'Business of Life,'" 59, 70–71; Avery, *History of the State of Georgia*, 26–27, 65–67; *Southern Confederacy* (Atlanta) 17 November 1861, "Election Returns, *Southern Recorder* (Milledgeville) 20 October 1857 and 17 November 1863.

[16]L. A. Simmons to Governor Joseph E. Brown, 2 May 1861, Georgia Confederate Miscellaneous 1861, Telamon Cuyler Collection, mss. 1170, Hargrett Rare Book and Manuscripts Library, University of Georgia Libraries, Athens; Michael P. Johnson, *Toward a Patriarchal Republic: The Secession of Georgia* (Baton Rouge: Louisiana State University Press, 1990) 118.

[17]Tate, *History of Pickens County*, 209; T. Conn Bryan, *Confederate Georgia* (Athens: University of Georgia Press, 1964) 213–14; "New Regiments," *Weekly Georgia Telegraph* (Macon) 23 August 1861.

Pickens Countians enlisted or were conscripted into the Confederate and state military.[18]

Many men, however, "served" only in the local reserves, at least two companies of state troops, and Col. A. K. Blackwell's 107th Georgia Militia Regiment. The latter still had 572 members on 4 March 1862. By 25 July 1863, at least 95 of its members had still declined to enlist in any other military unit and 132 men served only in the county's three home defense companies. Pickens County and North Georgia became renowned for desertions from the Confederate army but especially after the exceptionally bloody and nearby battle of Chickamauga in 1863. The total number of Pickens Countians who served in the United States Army and Navy, including deserters from the Southern military, likely totaled nearly 100 men who contributed largely to at least three companies.[19]

Many families found themselves divided by the war. Brothers Sam and Steve Hammontree, for example, joined Capt. Samuel Tate's previously mentioned Tate's Guards, which the sixty-four-year old patrician would actually command through to Virginia before he finally resigned his commission. Steve would die at the battle of Chancellorsville. Sam, however, survived capture and wounds to become one of the celebrated last Confederate veterans. He would adopt the name of Sam "Tate" Hammontree in honor of his old commander. Decades after the war, he publicly denounced state pensions based upon claims of Confederate service by men known to have served or supported the Union. Of his brothers, however, William Nelson Hammontree served in Pickens County's Company B of the 1st Georgia Battalion, United States Army, although he deserted to return home to protect his elderly parents from the deprivations of local gangs. Sylvestus M. Hammontree escaped the war by traveling north of the Ohio River. Upon his return, he found too many children in his household and divorced his spouse. Whatever their pasts, the Hammontree brothers and their in-laws would later suffer arrest for operating a moonshine still together without

---

[18]"Pickens County," *Southern Confederacy* (Atlanta) 13 March 1862; Tate, *History of Pickens County*, 93, 205–209, 227–29.

[19]Bryan, *Confederate Georgia*, 146–47; Pickens County 107th Regt. Ga. Militia file, 5 March 1862 and 25 July 1863, Adjutant General, RG 22-1-64, DOC 238, box 3, Georgia Archives, Morrow GA.

a license.[20] Similarly, the Jackson family of the Ludville community had Edmund in the 60th Georgia Confederate Infantry while his brothers John and Avery served in the Union army's 10th Tennessee Cavalry. Isaac Burleson petitioned for a federal pardon after the war for having been the postmaster for the Burnt Mountain Post Office. No military service records survive for two of his three sons who reportedly died during the war and outside of the state. The third sibling, William Washington Burleson, served in Tate's Guards before he deserted to join Pickens County's companies of both the 1st Georgia Cavalry and the 1st Georgia Infantry of the United States Army.[21]

Resistance to and avoiding the war took many forms in Pickens County. Whole families hid in isolated areas such as the overhang on Talking Rock Creek known as the Indian Hot House. Before he finally gave up, one farmer wore out six of his wife's dresses as a disguise to avoid conscription. Atlanta Provost Marshal George W. Lee discovered that the Pickens County's militia surgeon falsely declared men unfit to serve in the military. Gov. Brown provided exemptions to more than 5,000 officials, militia officers, government employees, and others across the state, including former Pickens County census taker William Tate.[22] Thomas Haley and other Pickens Countians organized an elaborate

---

[20]"The Civil War Memoirs of Sam Tate Hammontree, Company E, 23rd Regiment, C.S.A., Pickens County," *Northwest Georgia Historical and Genealogical Society Quarterly* 16/3 (Summer 1984): 39–41; "Uncle Sam Hammontree Sees Lawmakers at Work," *Macon* (GA) *Weekly Telegraph,* 7 July 1914; "Pickens County Confederates Visit Atlanta," *Atlanta* (GA) *Constitution,* 29 July 1927; Consolidated File Relating to William N. Hammontree, Enlisted Branch 5511-B-1883, Records of the Adjutant General, RG 94, NARA; *Sylvestus M. Hammontree vs. Nancy C. Hammontree,* 3 April 1869, Pickens County Superior Court microfilm, Heritage Room, Pickens County Public Library, Jasper; *US v. S. T, Hammontree et al,* case 1696, Northern District of Georgia, Atlanta, 1872–1911, box 66, Acc 52A177, RG 21, US Circuit Court, Civil, Criminal, Equity & Others, National Archives Southeast Region, Morrow GA.

[21]"Ludville Family Split by Civil War," *Marble Valley Historical Society Newsletter* 2 (January 1998): 1; *Pickens County Heritage Book 1853–1998* (Jasper GA: Pickens County Heritage Book Committee, 1998) 120–22.

[22][No title], *Coshocton* (OH) *Age,* 9 May 1885; John F. Andrews to Henry C. Wayne, 5 August 1863, Incoming Correspondence of the Adjutant General, RG 22-01-17, Georgia Archives; William Tate to Brown, 18 June 1862, box 57, Telamon Cuyler Collection.

"underground railroad" to help neighbors to escape to safety and well-paying civilian jobs behind the federal lines. They also provided information to the Union army. Other families, including the Tates, moved hundreds of miles deeper into the Confederacy to escape the war.[23]

These people had much to leave behind. A writer in 1859 told of some one hundred of their neighbors preparing to join an equal number of their Cobb County neighbors in moving to Texas. William Tate, in his 1860 census, wrote glowingly of the people's healthfulness and the area's climate, water, and mineral resources. He also recorded, however, that the crops had declined by two-thirds below the usual level and that more than 10 percent of the houses he visited had been abandoned.[24] The area's diverse mining operations ceased due to concerns over the coming war. As early as December 1861, James Simmons warned Gov. Brown of salt being unavailable within 15 miles of Pickens County due to speculation and wartime shortages. Without the means to preserve meat, he warned, farmers would release their hogs rather than butcher them as a winter food source. A group of his neighbors gathered at the courthouse and tried unsuccessfully to persuade him to lead them on a march on Marietta or Atlanta to press for their need for salt. An ongoing drought made all food scarce, but distillers contributed to the shortages by refusing to sell corn in order to profit from making alcohol. Jasper Smith wrote in late 1863 that government impressments of food and livestock in Pickens County had deteriorated to open robbery by anyone

---

[23]Bohannon, "Northeast Georgia Mountains," 205; deposition of George R. Mullins, 4 December 1874, in claim of George W. Campmire, 5875 (Pickens County 8) claim of Joseph Stover, 29 June 1871, 6454 (Pickens County 13) deposition of Harrison Pendley, 29 May 1873, in James Howell, 11511 (Pickens County 10) *Southern Claims Commission Approved Claims, 1871–1880*, Georgia (National Archives microfilm 658) Records of the Accounting Officers of the Department of the Treasury, RG 217, NARA; Jonathan D. Sarris, *A Separate Civil War: Communities in Conflict in the Mountain South* (Charlottesville: University of Virginia, 2006) 112.

[24]"The Georgia Press," *Charleston* (SC) *Tri-Weekly Courier*, 8 October 1859; Pickens County (1860) *Federal Mortality Schedules, 1850–1880*, National Archives microfilm T655, roll 8, social schedules, *Nonpopulation Census Schedules Georgia, 1850–1880*, National Archives microfilm T1137, roll 24, and population schedule, *Eighth Census of the United States (1860)* National Archives microfilm M653, roll 133, RG 29, NARA.

claiming to be a Confederate agent. Men declined even joining the state troops from the fear of leaving their property and families unprotected from war refugees who, with slaves, had moved into the county. In June 1863, the local justices could only afford to purchase an inadequate 800 bunches of yarn from the state for the needy as what remained of their funds was needed to buy bread for the destitute. Two months later, when A. J. Glen left his home at Talking Rock to enlist in a home defense unit called the Pickens Raid Repellers, eleven women robbed his tannery. He heard that they and their neighbors had declared themselves Yankees, would welcome the arrival of the Union army, and intended to steal rather than work for the rest of the war so that they could live as well as others.[25]

Early on Gov. Brown received warnings of serious opposition to the war in the Appalachian counties. In September 1861, James W. Dobson of Pickens County wrote to him asking what could be done about people acting or talking against the Confederacy. Twice in 1863, Brown dispatched state and Confederate troops into the mountains to crush flag-waving antiwar revolts by draft evaders, deserters, and Unionists. The government suspended conscription in most of North Georgia, although not in Pickens County, and Brown worked to end the impressments of food from the drought-stricken area. The state of Georgia, in response to the Federal invasion of 1863, however, conducted a census of men not in the army. North Georgians, including in Pickens County, protested this threat of a draft by burning down their jails. Samuel Wilson, a miner turned federal spy, returned to his pre-war home near Jasper in March 1864 to receive a welcome by a large antiwar crowd of his former neighbors. They complained of the impressments of their crops and livestock.[26]

---

[25]Bohannon, "Northeast Georgia Mountains," 86–92, 98, 113n.51, 115; Justices of the Inferior Court to Joseph E. Brown, 6 June 1863, and A. J. Glen to Joseph E. Brown, 7 August 1863, box 58, Telamon Cuyler Collection.

[26]Bohannon, "Northeast Georgia Mountains," 178; William Harris Bragg, *Joe Brown's Army* (Macon GA: Mercer University Press, 1987) 17–23; deposition of J. B. Crumly, 13 February 1864, Intelligence Reports, entry 961, Department of the Cumberland, Records of the US Army Continental Commands, 1821–1920, RG 393, pt.

Subsequent to the Federal invasion in spring 1864, Brown and the Confederate government created several local organizations, popularly called "home guards," to patrol for slave revolts and, in the mountain counties, for deserters. Even some Confederates claimed that the men of such units as Capt. Benjamin F. Jordan's company, which operated in Pickens and surrounding counties, were often deserters themselves and murderous brigands.[27]

In July 1864, federal Captain John P. Cummings led a cavalry raid into Pickens County to try to end partisan attacks on the Union army's nearby railroad supply line by Jordan's band. Local men took Cummings's command to the enemy camp near the community of Talking Rock. In the resulting battle, although wounded, Jordan escaped. He left eight of his men dead on the field, including a former captain from a Michigan regiment. The Yankees also captured four members of this company and burned four of the homes of the home guard members. Union soldiers may have also executed some of their prisoners in the Jasper town cemetery. When the troopers returned to the county seat, they were greeted as liberators by a crowd of more than 1,000. Cummings's men escorted local families to safety behind the federal lines, as well as a five-man delegation that sought help for their county from the Federal army. He also organized a company of 125 men under the county's sheriff David S. McCravey. A Union soldier, however,

---

i, and Samuel Wilson File, Spies, Guides & Scouts, entry 36, Records of the Provost Marshal, RG 110, NARA.

[27]"Terrible State of Affairs in North Georgia," *Southern Watchman* (Athens GA) 21 December 1864; "Tom Polk Edmundson," *Atlanta Constitution*, 1 May 1888; Joseph E. Brown to Howell Cobb, 5 May 1864, and Joseph E. Brown to James A. Seddon, 14 November 1864, Governor's Letterbook, 1861–1865, pp. 653, 726–27, microfilm reel 61/79, Georgia Archives; A. W. Reynolds to Cobb, 22 January 1865, in US War Department, comp., *The War of the Rebellion: A Compilation of the Official Records of the Union and Confederate Armies*, 128 vols. (Washington, DC: Government Printing Office, 1880–1901) ser. 1, 49 (1): 1:963–64 (hereafter cited as *OR*). Incomplete rosters of the pro-Confederate Georgia home guard units have been published as "A Partial Roster of the Georgia Confederate Home Guards," *Georgia Genealogical Society Quarterly* 31/3 (Fall 1995): 146–55.

wrote that Cummings's men had sunk to the level of the most notorious of the Confederate guerillas in Missouri.[28]

The situation for Pickens County's people, however, continued to deteriorate. English-born James George Brown of Murray County became the federal civilian chief of scouts. In early June 1864, he led a foray into Pickens County to kidnap James Simmons and other Confederate sympathizers while seizing private property, including slaves. Simmons escaped and the Union men suffered a punishing pursuit by twenty-five men of Jordan's company. From 13 to 15 August 1864, Gen. Joseph Wheeler's Cavalry Corps traveled through the area and routed the Unionists. In their wake, these Confederates left men whom they labeled as bushwhackers and deserters hanging from the trees.[29] J. G. Brown subsequently formed the Georgia Cavalry, USA, with Sheriff McCravey and his neighbors as Company D. After numerous defeats and heavy casualties, the Pickens County Unionists tried to reassemble the following September but reportedly some thirty of their number were eventually imprisoned for their role in the Federal burning of Canton, the county seat of Cherokee County, in October. Reports appeared in the Confederate press that President Lincoln had created a new state of North Georgia with Atlanta as its capital, James G.

---

[28]Davis, "Into the Wilderness," 221–22, 227; W. W. Lowe to D. F. How, 14 July 1864, *OR*, ser. 1, 53:867; John P. Cummings to E. H. Murray, 31 July 1864, in *OR*, vol. 52 (1):107; Green B. Raun to S. B. Moe, 29 July 1864, in *OR*, vol. 38 (5):299; "Note Book and Skraps [sic] from a Diary Kept by M. H. Brown," *Civil War Times Illustrated* Collection, US Army Military History Institute, Carlisle PA; "Federal Raid in Pickens County," *Columbus* (GA) *Ledger Enquirer*, 12 June 1864; "Disloyalty," *Southern Watchman* (Athens) 17 August 1864; Sherman Duckett, interview with author, 12 June 1985, cassette tapes, in the author's possession; "Woodrow Taylor," *Pickens County Progress*, 4 August 1983; Robert Winn to "Dear Sister," 27 July 1864, Winn-Cook Family Papers, Mss. A W776 8, Filson Club, Louisville KY. David Steward McCravey had been the doorkeeper to the Georgia state senate and a lieutenant in the 794th Georgia militia district. He resigned his commission as first lieutenant in Company L of the 36th Georgia Confederate Infantry to serve as the newly elected sheriff of Pickens County. Davis, "Into the Wilderness," 221–22, 227.

[29]Faye Stone Poss, comp., *The Southern Watchman, Athens, Georgia Civil War Home Front Coverage 1861–1865* (Snellville GA: self-published, 2008) 344; Lewis A. Lawson, *Wheeler's Last Raid* (Greenwood FL: Penkeville Publishing Co., 1986) 123; John E. Smith to W. T. Sherman, 15 August 1864, Thomas T. Heath to John E. Smith, 16 August 1864, *OR*, ser. 1, 38 (5):514, 539.

Brown as its new governor, and Baptist Rev. Elias W. Allred of Pickens County as its congressman. The latter would subsequently suffer arrest on charges of helping to form McCravey's home guard/posse, for sending his family to safety in the North, and for helping Federal soldiers to escape. Allred claimed that the charges had been at least misrepresented and that he served in the state troops. Although a member of Georgia's Confederate state legislature, he avoided prosecution only by Gov. Joseph E. Brown's intercession through the influence of his brother, Lemuel J. Allred, and the war coming to an end. Federal troops sent to Pickens County in an attempt to recover captured Federal cattle reported that the Unionists around Jasper were being hunted down and killed. A visitor to the area in late January 1865 described the desolation as so bad that to travel the region required bringing rations for rider and horse.[30]

Into this dire environment came escaped Federal Capt. John Azor Kellogg in October 1864. He would later plead with his government to come to the aid of McCravey's company/posse in their deadly battles with Jordan's company. The captain reported that the farmers there had to tend their fields armed and post scouts to keep from being murdered. Kellogg, however, likely also told how he had witnessed the wedding in Jasper of a Federal deserter to a local belle, that McCravey's men raided farms of pro-Confederate families, and that these men declined Capt. Jordan's call for a truce.[31]

The official end of the war failed to immediately bring peace to Pickens. Revenge killings took place across the county. Confederate sympathizers, for example, murdered Henry Leadford on the streets of

---

[30]Robert S. Davis, "The Curious Civil War Career of James George Brown, Spy," *Prologue: The Quarterly of the National Archives* 26/1 (Spring 1994): 24–25; Olivia Newton Cobb to Mary Ann Cobb, 11 November 1864, in Kenneth Coleman, cd., *Athens, 1861–1865, as Seen through Letters in the University of Georgia Libraries* (Athens: University of Georgia Press, 1969) 110; Poss, *Southern Watchman*, 339, 353, 365–66; "Mr. Aldred of Pickens County," *Daily Intelligencer* (Atlanta) 2 March 1865; "Terrible State of Affairs in North Georgia," *Southern Banner* (Athens GA) 15 February 1865; William T. Wofford to Joseph Brown, 8 February 1865, box 59, Telamon Cuyler Collection.

[31]Davis, "Into the Wilderness," 215–32; "Escape of Union Prisoners," *New York Herald*, 10 November 1864.

Jasper in September 1865. He had escaped to north of the Ohio River where he then joined the 144th Indiana Infantry Regiment.[32] That same month, the Nally brothers, having been duped into serving in the 1st Georgia Confederate Cavalry Regiment until they and most of their company deserted to become the 10th Tennessee Cavalry Regiment, United States Army, returned home to Hinton and killed members of Capt. Benjamin McCollum's Confederate home guards who had stolen their family's cow. Subsequently, this family became involved in the killings of civilians and a brawl with United States troops.[33] The first court after the war could only be held with the protection of Capt. Levi M. Hess's Company I of the 29th United States Infantry Regiment. Juries in 1865 through 1867 indicted the men of the Confederate home guard for murder and robbery. As late as 1867, the grand jury lamented that citizens had to carry guns for protection.[34]

The issue of race illustrates the exceptional nature of the postwar politics of this place. Its small and shrinking African-American community proved to be little or no competition for jobs. Specific racial incidents did not include lynching and but little Ku Klux Klan-like activity. Lemuel J. Allred and ex-federal Civil War officer Sion Darnell claimed connections to the 1860 flag-raisers, and both were seen as allies of Georgia's "carpetbagger," "black" Republican Governor Rufus Bullock. In 1867, however, Allred published a letter claiming that a meeting of Darnell and other Pickens County Republicans that included Allred's brothers actually represented a group of ex-Confederate opportunists calling for the disenfranchisement of former Rebels and the enfranchisement of ex-slaves.[35] Despite the prewar fears of the white

---

[32]Civil War pension claim of Henry Leadford, application 557,201, General Records of the Department of the Interior, RG 48, NARA.

[33][No title], *Daily Mississippian* (Jackson) 23 September 1865; [no title], *Union and Dakotaian* (Yankton, Dakota Territory) 7 October 1865; Robert S. Davis, "The Shooting at Scarecorn Campground," *North Georgia Journal* 15/3 (Autumn 1998): 12–16.

[34]Tate, *History of Pickens County*, 213; Pickens County Superior Court Minutes, book A (1854–1867) n.p., microfilm reel 97/65, Georgia Archives.

[35]Robert S. Davis, "Memoirs of a Partisan War: Sion Darnell Remembers North Georgia, 1861–1865," *Georgia Historical Quarterly* 80/1 (Spring 1996): 102, 104–105; Lemuel J. Allred, *Address of Lemuel J. Allred to the People of Pickens County Georgia and to the Public Generally* (Marietta GA: Marietta Journal Book & Job Office, 1868)

population, the 1870 census shows that the number of local African Americans actually declined after emancipation from 246 slaves to 129 freedmen. A year later, at a time when African Americans elsewhere suffered lynching for voting Republican, a mob of Pickens Countians assaulted freedman Andy Gwin for voting Democrat. In 1897, these fractious Republicans narrowly voted to protest federal patronage jobs going to blacks. Eighteen years later, prominent Democrat Sam Tate, the grandson of the Confederate Capt. Samuel Tate, organized a company of his white workers to protect the members of the county's small African-American community, many of whom worked in Tate's marble quarries, from threatened violence by unemployed, desperate whites in nearby counties. The Civil Rights Movement came late to Pickens and it made gains only with the nation as a whole. Even today many jobs are still denied members of the black community. In 1985, the county's one African-American small businessman, a printer who had recently moved to the county, went out of business, in part, from threats made against his white drivers by Ku Klux Klansmen from outside of the county acting at the request of a local citizen. Members of that group subsequently held a public event on the courthouse square.[36]

Pickens County's families would include staunch Democrats, but what remained of the 1860 dissenters' United States flag reportedly hung on public display in the courthouse until 1947 when the building burned. At various times, Pickens had the only white Republican newspaper in Georgia (operated by native son William Stephens Clayton, a veteran of the 10th Tennessee Cavalry, USA); a post office and several sons named for General William Tecumseh Sherman; and a Jasper chapter of the Grand Army of the Republic, a federal veteran's organization.[37] Only in

n.p., copy in the Pickens County Folder, Vertical Files, Georgia Archives. Darnell countered that Allred had been a Confederate agent who rode with the home guard. Lemuel would soon after return to the Democrat Party, as would Joseph E. Brown, but Darnell and the other Allred brothers would remain Republicans for life.

[36]*Statistics of the Population of the United States at the Tenth Census (June 1, 1880)* (Washington DC: Government Printing Office, 1883) 386; [no title], *Atlanta* (GA) *Constitution*, 20 May 1871; [no title], *The Morning Herald* (Lexington KY) 1 August 1897; Charles O. Walker to author, 21 November 2004, in the author's possession.

[37]"Pickens," *Macon Daily Telegraph*, 5 June 1886; Dallas Byess, interview with author, 10 September 1983, cassette tapes, in the author's possession; Tate, *History of*

a few instances since 1865 have the voters of Pickens County voted in the majority for a Democrat for president even while, occasionally, voting for local Democrats such as Farish Carter Tate of Jasper, the son of the 1860 census taker, in his ventures into "the enemy's country" to successfully run for Congress.[38]

Over time, Pickens County's unusual heritage drew notice as something odd and quaint. Mentions of the 1860 flag protest appeared in broad histories and on television quiz shows. National news services occasionally reported on how Pickens County candidates for public office ran as independents to avoid offending relatives and neighbors.[39] Whereas a typical American courthouse square has a monument to its Civil War veterans, the war memorial in Pickens begins with the dead of World War I. Until recently, even the choice of undertaker depended upon the politics of the deceased. Today Jasper holds the oldest continuous Fourth of July festivities in Georgia.

The people of Pickens County had begun the Civil War both distressed and with public opposition to secession. Years of violence, deprivation, and tragedy followed, which fostered complex and conflicted local politics. Economic progress, however, did encourage reconciliation, at least among the white families what historian Robert M. Calhoon has termed for America's whole history as "moderation." The English-born Atherton brothers rebuilt their wool-manufacturing complex on Talking Rock Creek that had been destroyed during the war and began spinning cotton, even for markets as far away as Philadelphia. Crops were good and, despite Pickens Countians like Sheriff McCravey moving to Texas and the West, the white population increased from 4,705 to 5,188 persons of both sexes and all ages from 1860 to 1870. Children from families of both parties intermarried.

Pickens County, 89, 207–208; Southern Historical Association, *Memoirs of Georgia*, 1:677.

[38]"Strange Combination," *Republican* (Jasper GA) 5 November 1896. Pickens County has sent two other men to the House of Representatives, Phil Landrum and Ed Jenkins, both Democrats. Roscoe Pickett, Sr., served as chairman of the state Republican Party and as his party's candidate for governor.

[39]John Harman, "Pickens County Keeps Peace since Civil War by Voting Independent," *Atlanta Journal-Constitution*, 2 November 1988, p. 1.

On 17 September 1882, a railroad finally reached Jasper and it did far more than finally make Pickens County a northernmost province of the Cotton Kingdom. Cheap, practical transportation also revived the area's marble and gold mining; promised more manufacturing; promoted tourism; and otherwise brought in progress on a grand scale. Local patriarchs Lemuel J. Allred and James Simmons served as the senior masters of ceremony at the celebration of the arrival of the first train where in 1860 Pickens Countians had protested secession. In 1889, Henry W. Grady, the famed champion of the New South, would use Pickens County as the basis for his most famous call for industry and education to be brought to such rural communities. Sam Tate created a marble empire in the early 1900s that supplied stone to many of America's greatest buildings and which became the area's economic engine until the Great Depression. His Georgia Marble Company employed men of different races, religions, and politics.[40] The county's various Republican newspapers (and later the single Democratic paper) came to be replaced, in 1899, by just the *Pickens County Progress*. Only in the twenty-first century, however, with the passing of time and the presence of newcomers (who now outnumber the members of old families) has the county's traditional political eccentricities dissipated.

The Lost Cause sentiment of the New South eventually swept away most of the county's divisive Civil War past even while leaving its cultural consequences. Luke Tate, a Democrat and Sam Tate's brother, wrote the county's history in 1934 wherein he proudly proclaimed that one-eighth of the 1860 population of the county served in the Confederate forces and that Pickens had no Federal companies, distortions of facts that merited qualifications that he chose not to make. Through interviews with older local citizens and documentary research in previously unknown sources outside of the county, another view of the county's past has been found but that heritage has never been commemorated or publicly recognized in any way, even by an historical

---

[40]Robert S. Davis, "An American Woman Faces the Gallows: The Campaign to Save Kath-Kate Southern's Neck," *Chattanooga Regional Historical Journal* 2/2 (December 1999): 150–85, and Davis, "The Story of the Georgia Marble Dynasty," *Georgia Historical Quarterly* 89/3 (Fall 2005): 368–88; "Jasper," *Atlanta Constitution*, 26 March and 29 September 1882.

marker. James Simmons's Civil War home, built ca. 1830 and the last tie to that past, had to be demolished after decades of neglect. Recently, an article in the local newspaper repeated and expanded upon the misstatements in Tate's history to even deny that the county had any political past with the Republican Party at all.[41]

Demographic studies have largely failed to satisfactorily explain the reasons why and to what degree such a community supported either or both sides in the American Civil War. Research into Pickens County's history does, however, illustrate something of the mechanism of how complex political structures can become when people find themselves taking stands in a murderously dangerous environment. Over time, their legacy became more enduring than the public memory or its understanding. In 1898, for example, *Atlanta Constitution* editor Clark Howell reported on a North Georgia farmer enlisting his only son to serve in the Spanish American War. The old man stood solemnly, his head uncovered, through the whole ceremony of unfurling the national flag and the playing of the *Star Spangled Banner*. In a state still lamenting the Confederacy's defeat in 1865, this action seemed inexplicable. When asked about "his silent exhibition of patriotism and loyalty," this "soul as rugged but as placid as the great blue mountains which gave it birth" replied, "I am from Pickens County."[42] Howell asked for no further explanation.

[41]Tate, *History of Pickens County*, 254–55; Davis, "Memoirs of a Partisan War," 93–116, and Davis, "Into the Wilderness," 215–32; Mimi Jo Butler, "The Town of Jasper—The 1860s War Years Part 2," undated newspaper clipping from the *Pickens County Progress*, in author's possession.
[42]Lucian Lamar Knight, *Reminiscences of Famous Georgians*, 2 vols. (Atlanta: Franklin-Turner, 1907–1908) 1:725.

Bitterly Divided
Georgia's Inner Civil War

by *David Williams*

"It is a certain fact that the Southern people are fast becoming as bitterly divided against each other as the Southern and Northern people ever has been." At the height of the Civil War, while battles raged on distant fields, a southwest Georgia man named Samuel Knight wrote these words to Governor Joseph E. Brown as he outlined the many ways in which Southerners were working against the Confederacy. He concluded his observations by insisting, "I have not written this letter to exaggerate these things. I only write such as I know to be true."[1]

Knight saw clearly what generations of Americans have too often neglected—that during its brief existence, the Confederacy fought a two-front war. There was, of course, the war it waged with the North, the war so familiar to almost every school child. But, though school children have rarely heard of it, there was another war. Between 1861 and 1865, the South was torn apart by a violent inner civil war, a war no less significant to the Confederacy's fate than its more widely known struggle against the Yankees.

From its very beginnings, the Confederacy suffered from a rising tide of internal hostility. Ironically, it was a hostility brought on largely by those most responsible for the Confederacy's creation. Planters excused themselves from the draft in various ways, then grew far too much cotton and not nearly enough food. Soldiers went hungry, as did their families back home. Women defied Confederate authorities by staging food riots from Richmond, Virginia, to Galveston, Texas. Soldiers deserted by the tens of thousands, and draft evasion became commonplace. By 1864 the draft law was practically impossible to enforce and two-thirds of the Confederate army was absent with or without leave. Many deserters and draft evaders joined anti-Confederate

---

[1]Samuel D. Knight to Joseph E. Brown, 22 February 1864, Governor's Incoming Correspondence, Georgia Department of Archives and History, Morrow GA.

"tory" or "layout" gangs that controlled vast areas of the Southern countryside.[2]

Even before the Confederacy came into being, signs that a slaveholders' republic might have difficulty maintaining popular support, not to mention an effective fighting force, were clear. A majority of Southern whites, most of whom owned no slaves, opposed secession. The vote for delegates to Georgia's secession convention was almost evenly divided, with a likely majority of 42,744 to 41,717 rejecting secession. Nevertheless Georgia's secession convention, like other state conventions across the South, all of them dominated by slaveholders, ignored popular will and took their states out of the Union.[3]

---

[2]For an in-depth treatment of dissent in Civil War Georgia, see David Williams, Teresa Crisp Williams, and David Carlson, *Plain Folk in a Rich Man's War: Class and Dissent in Confederate Georgia* (Gainesville: University Press of Florida, 2002). See also Jonathan Sarris, *A Separate Civil War: Communities in Conflict in the Mountain South* (Charlottesville: University of Virginia Press, 2006); Thomas G. Dyer, *Secret Yankees: The Union Circle in Confederate Atlanta* (Baltimore: Johns Hopkins University Press, 1999); J. William Harris, *Plain Folk and Gentry in a Slave Society: White Liberty and Black Slavery in Augusta's Hinterlands* (Middletown CT: Wesleyan University Press, 1985); Mark A. Weitz, *A Higher Duty: Desertion among Georgia Troops during the Civil War* (Lincoln: University of Nebraska Press, 2000). For some of the most recent general studies of dissent in the Civil War South, see David Williams, *Bitterly Divided: The South's Inner Civil War* (New York: The New Press, 2008); David C. Downing, *A South Divided: Portraits of Dissent in the Confederacy* (Nashville: Cumberland House, 2007); James Alex Baggett, *The Scalawags: Southern Dissenters in the Civil War and Reconstruction* (Baton Rouge: Louisiana State University Press, 2003); William W. Freehling, *The South vs. the South: How Anti-Confederate Southerners Shaped the Course of the Civil War* (New York: Oxford University Press, 2001); *Enemies of the Country: New Perspectives on Unionists in the Civil War South*, ed. John C. Inscoe and Robert C. Kenzer (Athens: University of Georgia Press, 2001); *Guerrillas, Unionists, and Violence on the Confederate Home Front*, ed. Daniel E. Sutherland (Fayetteville: University of Arkansas Press, 1999). Older but still valuable studies include Georgia Lee Tatum, *Disloyalty in the Confederacy* (Chapel Hill: University of North Carolina Press, 1934) and Carl N. Degler, *Southern Dissenters in the Nineteenth Century* (New York: Harper and Row, 1974).

[3]In his seminal study (and still the leading authority) of secession in Georgia, Michael Johnson says of the popular vote for delegates that "Using the most generous estimate of the vote for immediate secession, the result of the election was 44,152 to 41,632 victory for the secessionists, a popular majority of just over 51 percent. A less generous and more realistic estimate of the vote for immediate secession yields a 42,744 to 41,717 cooperationist [anti-secession] victory, a majority of just over 50 percent." See Michael

Secessionist leaders like Robert Toombs had openly expressed their determination to see the South out of the Union whether a majority of the people supported the move or not. "We demand at your hands the sword," Toombs blustered in a speech before the Georgia legislature. "If you will not give it to us, we will take it." Responding to Toombs's threat, an anti-secession newspaper editor in Upson County wrote: "Let him take it, and, by way of doing his country a great service, let him run about six inches of it into his left breast."[4]

Following the convention's meeting, many of its anti-secession delegates insisted that the secession ordinance be ratified by Georgia voters. An Augusta editor joined the call by reminding its readers that previous conventions recommending alterations to the state constitution had sought the people's approval by ratification. But fearing the results of such a move, Joseph E. Brown, the pro-secession governor, refused. Georgia, like other seceding states, left the Union without submitting its secession ordinance to voter ratification.[5]

Despite their general reluctance to secede, there was some enthusiasm for the war among Southern whites after the firing on Fort

---

P. Johnson, *Toward a Patriarchal Republic: The Secession of Georgia* (Baton Rouge: Louisiana State University Press, 1977) 63. As for popular will among white Southerners generally, David Potter looked at the delegate vote throughout the South and concluded: "At no time during the winter of 1860–1861 was secession desired by a majority of the people of the slave states.... Furthermore, secession was not basically desired even by a majority in the lower South, and the secessionists succeeded less because of the intrinsic popularity of their program than because of the extreme skill with which they utilized an emergency psychology, the promptness with which they invoked unilateral action by individual states, and the firmness with which they refused to submit the question of secession to popular referenda." See David M. Potter, *Lincoln and His Party in the Secession Crisis* (New Haven CT: Yale University Press, 1942) 208. Potter's conclusions are supported by Paul D. Escott's more recent study, *After Secession: Jefferson Davis and the Failure of Confederate Nationalism* (Baton Rouge: Louisiana State University Press, 1978) 23–28, 42–44.

[4]"Robert Toombs's Secessionist Speech," in William W. Freehling and Craig M. Simpson, eds., *Secession Debated: Georgia's Showdown in 1860* (New York: Oxford University Press, 1992) 46; *Upson Pilot*, 8 December 1860.

[5]Allen D. Candler, comp., *The Confederate Records of Georgia*, 6 vols. (Atlanta GA: State Printing Office, 1909–1911) 1:349–61; *Augusta Chronicle and Sentinel*, 3 January 1861; *Columbus Sun*, 23 January 1861; *Milledgeville Southern Recorder*, quoted in *Thomasville Southern Enterprise*, 30 January 1861.

Sumter and Lincoln's call for an invasion of the South. But Confederate enlistments declined rapidly after the first major battle at Manassas that summer. In October, word came from Greene County to the governor's office that "our people don't seem to be inclined to offer their services." That same month, Captain Edward Croft of the Columbus Artillery reported that it was almost impossible to find volunteers. In February 1862, W. H. Byrd of Augusta wrote to Governor Brown that he had been trying for two weeks to raise a company in what he called "this 'Yankee City,' but I regret to say every effort has failed." That failure did not result from a lack of potential recruits. The *Augusta Chronicle and Sentinel* had noted a week earlier that "one who walks Broad street [sic] and sees the number of young men, would come to the conclusion that no war...was now waging."[6]

In April 1862, the Confederate congress responded to the recruitment problem by passing the first national conscription act in American history. Like the North's later draft, men of wealth could avoid military service by hiring a substitute or paying an exemption fee. And planters could have themselves or any other draft age white male, such as sons or overseers, exempted at a rate of one for every twenty slaves owned. This twenty-slave law was perhaps the most widely resented act ever imposed by the Confederacy, especially for poor soldiers already in the ranks. Said one Southern private, "It gave us the blues; we wanted twenty negroes. Negro property suddenly became very valuable, and there was raised the howl of 'rich man's war, poor man's fight.'"[7] Not surprisingly, desertion became an even greater problem for the Confederacy than for the Union. By 1864, Jefferson Davis himself admitted that "two-thirds of

---

[6]Green Moore to Joseph E. Brown, 4 October 1861, Talemon Cuyler Collection, Felix Hargrett Rare Book and Manuscript Library, University of Georgia, Athens; *The Papers of Jefferson Davis*, ed. Lynda Lasswell Crist and Mary Seaton Dix, 12 vols. (Baton Rouge: Louisiana State University Press, 1971–) 7:361; W. H. Byrd to Joseph Brown, 20 February 1862, Cuyler Collection; *Augusta Chronicle and Sentinel*, 12 February 1862.

[7]Sam R. Watkins, *Co. Aytch* (1882; rpt., Wilmington NC: Broadfoot Publishing, 1987) 69.

our men are absent...most of them without leave." That number ultimately included 60 percent or more of Georgia's troops.[8]

When one Georgia farmer was drafted, he complained bitterly to a neighbor: "They've got me in this war at last. I didn't want to have any thing to do with it any how. I didn't vote for Secession—but them are the ones who have to go & fight now—and those who were so fast for war, stay out."[9] Resentment toward conscription was evident throughout Georgia. A report from Franklin County made it clear that there were so many deserters and draft dodgers in the county that conscription efforts were useless. One conscript officer was nearly killed when he tried to enforce the draft law at Fort Gaines. Threats to his life became so serious that he fled the state. Resistance to the draft was rampant all across the South. Howell Cobb thought it would take the whole Confederate army to enforce conscription.[10]

Another practice that helped turn thousands of Southerners against the Richmond government was impressments, the confiscation of private property. They resented the fact that their families back home were forced to give up a portion, sometimes a major portion, of their meager produce while the more politically influential planters were left alone. That they had to sell at prices set by the government was even more galling. But it usually did not matter what the prices were. All farm families got in exchange were promissory notes, usually unredeemable, or inflated paper currency that was nearly as worthless. Very often they got nothing at all. One Georgia woman complained bitterly that "the country is plum full of [Confederate] cavalry just...stealing all the time." John Hagan, a soldier from Southwest Georgia, confirmed that assertion in a letter to his wife: "I believe our troops are doing as much harm in this country as the Yankees...and in fact where this army goes the people

---

[8]*Athens Southern Watchman*, 28 September 1864; James A. Riley, "Desertion and Disloyalty in Georgia During the Civil War" (M.A. thesis, University of Georgia, 1951) 106–107.

[9]Miss Abby's diary, 20 January 1864, Felix Hargrett Rare Book and Manuscript Library, University of Georgia, Athens.

[10]Riley, "Desertion and Disloyalty," 84; Emma J. Slade Prescott reminiscences, Atlanta Historical Society Archives; T. Conn Bryan, *Confederate Georgia* (Athens: University of Georgia Press, 1953) 90.

is ruined." He was certain that the Confederacy could never survive while handling its own people so roughly.[11]

Poor and middling farm families bore the brunt of impressment mainly because they were easier targets than the planters. Smaller farmsteads tended to grow more food products anyway, which was what the impressment agents wanted. For the planters, old habits were hard to break. They continued to devote much of their acreage to cotton at a time when thousands of soldiers and civilians were starving. Food riots, mostly involving women, occurred in cities throughout the South, Richmond, Galveston, Mobile, and Atlanta among them. Other Georgia cities that saw such disturbances included Columbus, Macon, Savannah, Augusta, Marietta, Forsyth, Cartersville, Hartwell, Blackshear, Colquitt, and Valdosta.[12]

In spring 1863, Confederate soldier Daniel Snell of Harris County wrote home to his wife Sarah: "You spoke of a riot in Columbus.... it is no more than I expected. I understand there was also one in Augusta.... What will become of the women and children with the food situation?"[13] Indeed, thousands of soldiers wondered how their families would get along in their absence. With government impressment stripping their farms bare and the planters unwilling to help, many began to question whether the Confederacy was worth preserving at all, much less fighting for. As the war lumbered on and conditions worsened, more and more soldiers decided it was not.

Presenting their rifles as furloughs to anyone who dared challenge them, deserters made their way over hundreds of rugged miles to help their starving families. Some never made it. Many of those who did were dragged back to the army in chains. Sergeant William Andrews of Clay

---

[11]Stephen E. Ambrose, "Yeoman Discontent in the Confederacy," *Civil War History* 8/3 (September 1962): 263; John Hagan to Amanda Roberts Hagan, 23 July 1863, in "The Confederate Letters of John W. Hagan," ed. Bell I. Wiley, *Georgia Historical Quarterly* 38/2 (June 1954): 196.

[12]For a comprehensive look at women's riots in Georgia, see Teresa Crisp Williams and David Williams, "'The Women Rising': Cotton, Class, and Confederate Georgia's Rioting Women," *Georgia Historical Quarterly* 86/1 (Spring 2002): 49–83.

[13]Louise Calhoun Barfield, *History of Harris County, Georgia, 1827–1961* (Columbus GA: Columbus Office Supply Co., 1961) 758.

County wrote that it was "an everyday occurrence for men to get letters from home stating that their families are on the point of starvation. Many a poor soldier has deserted and gone home in answer to that appeal, to be brought back and shot for desertion."[14]

The way the soldiers saw it, they had very little choice. If the government could not care for their families, the soldiers had to. Their first duty was to the survival of their wives and children. Even those with no families starving at home had great sympathy for those who did. William Andrews, a bachelor, insisted that he too, faced with the same situation, would desert. "Thank God," he wrote, "I have no wife and children to suffer on account of an ungrateful government."[15]

Soldiers deserted at an ever-increasing rate soon after conscription went into effect and they usually enjoyed the sympathy of their friends and neighbors—which encouraged even more men to desert. In September 1863, from North Georgia's Fannin County, deserter John Hopper wrote telling his brother who was still in the army, that "the people here are nearly all unanimously against [the] war holding on any longer." Hopper further assured him that "there is no dificulty now in staying at home [and] no opposition from the citizens. I can tell you if you can only get here with out being took up it is all right—for in the place of opposition you will have protection."[16]

Some deserters put themselves out of the Confederacy's reach by joining the Federals. Thomas A. Watson of Fannin County, William Fife of Harris County, Cornelius Dawson of Clinch County, and Andrew T. Harris of Murray County, all Confederate deserters, were among more than 2500 white Georgians who joined Union forces. Baldwin County native David R. Snelling had deeply personal reasons for his Union service. David's father William, a man of modest means, died of fever when David was five. His mother Elizabeth Lester Snelling, whose family had never approved of her marriage, was forced onto a small plot of land adjoining the Baldwin County plantations her brothers owned.

---

[14]William H. Andrews, *Footprints of a Regiment: A Recollection of the First Georgia Regulars, 1861–1865* (Atlanta GA: Longstreet Press, 1992) 39.

[15]Ibid.

[16]William C. Davis, *Look Away!: A History of the Confederate States of America* (New York: Free Press, 2002) 233, 448n.25.

When Elizabeth died a few years later, young David was taken in as a farmhand by his uncle, David Lester. While his cousins were sent away to school, David was put to work in the fields along with Lester's slaves. In May 1862, under threat of conscription, he joined the Confederate army. That summer he deserted and signed up with the Federals. Two years later, as a lieutenant in General William T. Sherman's cavalry escort during the March to the Sea, David went out of his way to lead a raid against his uncle's plantation a few miles from Milledgeville. His troops seized provisions and livestock, then burned the gin house.[17]

The increasing reluctance of Southerners to serve in the Confederate army reflected a much broader discontent. From its beginnings, many poor whites saw the conflict as a rich man's war. That view became more widely held among plain folk as the months dragged by. Planters brought the Confederacy into existence but would not grow corn enough to feed its soldiers or their families. Speculators were driving prices of even the most basic necessities far beyond the reach of most Southerners. The burdens of taxation and impressment fell heaviest on the small farmers, as did the brunt of conscription. That disparity produced a class-based political consciousness among plain folk that made itself felt in the 1863 elections. Southern voters ousted nearly half their congressional representatives that year.[18]

---

[17]Thomas A. Watson, Small Print Collection, box 18, no. 79, Georgia Department of Archives and History; William Fife file, Compiled Service Records, National Archives, Washington DC; Folks Huxford, *Pioneers of Wiregrass Georgia: A Biographical Account of Some of the Early Settlers of That Portion of Wiregrass Georgia Embraced in the Original Counties of Irwin, Appling, Wayne, Camden, and Glynn*, 11 vols. (Homerville GA: Huxford Genealogical Society, 1951–) 8:82; Andrew T. Harris file, Murray County GA, archives 004 143B, Southern Claims Commission Approved Claims, National Archives, Washington DC; Robert S. Davis, "Forgotten Union Guerrilla Fighters from the North Georgia Mountains," *North Georgia Journal* 5/2 (Summer 1988): 347–74. Robert S. Davis, "Black and White in Blue: The Recruitment of Federal Units in Civil War North Georgia," *Georgia Historical Quarterly* 85/3 (Fall 2001): 348; Robert S. Davis, "Memoirs of a Partisan War: Sion Darnell Remembers North Georgia," *Georgia Historical Quarterly* 80/1 (Spring 1996): 113; Bonner, "David R. Snelling: A Story of Desertion and Defection in the Civil War" *Georgia Review* 10/3 (Fall 1956): 275–82.

[18]Kenneth C. Martis, *Historical Atlas of the Congresses of the Confederate States* (New York: Simon and Schuster, 1994) 87.

Disaffected as most plain folk had become by fall 1863, Georgia's 7 October election results could hardly have surprised any careful observer. Milledgeville's *Confederate Union* reported of the General Assembly: "but few of the old members have been returned." The news was even worse for Georgia's congressional incumbents. Georgia voters sent nine new legislators to Congress, eight of them elected on platforms opposing the Davis administration. Julian Hartridge of Southeast Georgia's First District was the only member of the state's House delegation to retain his seat. Georgia's 90-percent freshman rate was the greatest of any Confederate state. Little wonder the new members were much more attuned to the concerns of plain folk than their predecessors. Most Georgia delegates to the First Confederate Congress had supported both conscription and impressment. In the Second Congress, only three backed conscription. One supported impressment.[19]

Plain folk were active in local elections as well. In Columbus, they offered their own slate of candidates for city office on the "Mechanics' and Working Men's Ticket." According to the *Columbus Enquirer*, the new party "prevailed by a very large majority" in the 7 October balloting. Its success sent shock waves through the ranks of the city's political establishment. Some went so far as to suggest excluding common folk from future elections by reinstituting extensive property qualifications for voting and office holding.[20]

The *Enquirer*'s editor gave voice to elitist fears just two days after the vote when he chastised plain folk for their "antagonistic" attitude and condemned the "causeless divisions of our citizens into classes."[21] Reaction to the *Enquirer*'s criticism was swift and direct. On 13 October, a competing city paper, the *Columbus Sun*, ran a letter it received from a local man signing himself "Mechanic."

Voting by Classes

Editor Daily Sun:—I notice in the Enquirer, of Friday evining, an article complaining bitterly of the people voting by classes.... He says,

---

[19]*Milledgeville Confederate Union*, 3 November 1863; Martis, *Historical Atlas of the Congresses of the Confederate States*, 87, 110–13.

[20]*Columbus Enquirer*, 9 October 1863; *Columbus Sun*, 13 October 1863.

[21]*Columbus Enquirer*, 9 October 1863.

"there is certainly no ground for any antagonism in the city." In this the Enquirer is mistaken; for any man, woman or child can see that the people are dividing into two classes, just as fast as the pressure of the times can force them on. As for example: class No. 1, in their thirst for gain, in their worship of Mammon, and in their mighty efforts to appropriate every dollar on earth to their own account, have lost sight of every principle of humanity, patriotism, and virtue itself, and seem to have forgotten that the very treasures they are now heaping up are the price of blood, and unless this mania ceases, will be the price of liberty itself; for we know something of the feeling which now exists in the army, as well as in our work-shops at home. The men know well enough that their helpless families are not cared for, as they were promised at the beginning of the war.... They know, too, that every day they remain from home, reduces them more and more in circumstances, and that by the close of the war a large majority of the soldiery will be unable to live; in fact, many of them are ruined now, as many of their homes and other effects are passing into the hands of speculators and extortioners, for subsistence to their families. Thus you see, that all the capital, both in money and property, in the South, is passing into the hands of class No. 1, while class No. 2 are traveling down, soon to take their station among the descendants of Ham. You can easily see who are class No. 2. The soldiery, the mechanics, and the workingmen, not only of Columbus, but of all the Confederate States. In view of these things, is it not time that our class should awake to a sense of their danger, and in the mildest possible manner begin the work of self-defense.... Then we claim the right, as the first alternative, to try and avert the great calamity, by electing such men to the councils of the nation as we think will best represent our interests. If this should fail, we must then try more potent remedies.

Efforts to find "more potent remedies" had already given rise to a loosely organized movement, widely known as the Peace Society, to end the conflict with or without Southern independence. The Peace Society was one of perhaps a dozen or more secret or semi-secret organizations that sprang up across the South to oppose the war. Little is known of the society's early days. It probably formed in North Alabama or East Tennessee during spring 1862 and later spread to Georgia. The society's activities included spreading dissent among soldiers as well as civilians.

James Longstreet, Lee's senior corps commander, said that "the large and increasing number of desertions, particularly amongst the Georgia troops, induces me to believe that some such outside influence must be operating upon our men."[22]

Closer to home, an insurrection plot was discovered among troops at the Rose Dew Island batteries south of Savannah. Spurred by local citizens connected with the Peace Society, the soldiers took an oath never to fight the Yankees, to desert at the earliest opportunity, and encourage others to do the same. Though the Peace Society was composed mostly of those who wanted nothing more than an end to the fighting, Unionists were at the heart of the organization and remained its principal advocates throughout the war.[23]

From the very outset of the Civil War, Unionism had considerable support in the South, even to the point of taking up arms against the Confederacy. Approximately 300,000 Southern whites served in Union armies during the war, not counting those in irregular units who numbered many more.[24] In Georgia, Unionism found its greatest strength among whites in areas with few slaves such as the northeast mountains and the pine barrens of the southeast. But even in Black Belt regions, where slaves made up over half the population, there were significant numbers of white anti-Confederates.

As early as March 1862, John O'Connor of Fort Gaines warned Governor Brown of "spies and traitors" operating all along the lower Chattahoochee River. General Howell Cobb was so concerned about anti-Confederate sentiment in Southwest Georgia that he began censoring the postal service later that year. E. H. Grouby noted in the *Early County News* that there were deserters "in every direction." One

---

[22]James Longstreet, *From Manassas to Appomattox: Memoirs of the Civil War in America* (Philadelphia: J. B. Lippincott, 1896) 651.

[23]US War Department, comp., *The War of the Rebellion: A Compilation of the Official Records of the Union and Confederate Armies*, 128 vols. (Washington, DC: Government Printing Office, 1880–1901) ser. 1, 35 (1): 529–32 (hereafter cited as *OR*); *OR*, ser. 1, 36 (2): 551–52.

[24]About 200,000 of the Southern whites who served in Union armies were from the border slave states. Another 100,000 came from the Confederacy. See Frehling, *The South vs. the South*, xiii.

officer called the wiregrass "one of the greatest dens for Tories and deserters from our army in the world."[25]

The situation was no better to the east. A Lowndes County resident warned Governor Brown of local deserters and draft dodgers throughout the piney woods of South Georgia. In October 1863, a Savannah man wrote that troops in Southeast Georgia were demanding peace and would soon turn to mutiny or desertion if they did not get it. There were already more than a thousand deserters hiding in the Okefenokee Swamp alone.[26]

Antiwar feeling in Georgia was so strong by 1863 that state and Confederate officials could do little against it. Popular support and innumerable hiding places made it nearly impossible to track down deserters and draft dodgers. The Bureau of Conscription's superintendent admitted that public opinion made it difficult to enforce the draft act. There was, he lamented, no disgrace attached to desertion or draft evasion. One band of deserters quietly set up camp on an island in the Chattahoochee River. Family and friends kept them supplied with food and other necessities until the war was over. Some deserters were more outspokenly defiant. In Stewart County, several men of the 3rd Georgia Regiment openly declared that they had no intention of returning to the army.[27]

Even when deserters and draft dodgers were captured, there was no guarantee of punishment. When a conscript company in Franklin County captured several deserters, the local jailor would not lodge them. So great was popular antiwar sentiment that judges refused to hold court on draft evaders without a military escort. Even when trials were held, convictions were rare. Juries consistently refused to return guilty verdicts against those who opposed the war. General Howell Cobb conceded in

---

[25]John O'Connor to Joseph E. Brown, 10 March 1862, Governor's Incoming Correspondence; Edward Mueller, *Perilous Journeys: A History of Steamboating on the Chattahoochee, Apalachicola, and Flint Rivers, 1828–1928* (Eufaula AL: Historic Chattahoochee Commission, 1990) 109; *Early County News*, 20 January 1864; Bessie Martin, *Desertion of Alabama Troops from the Confederate Army: A Study in Sectionalism* (New York: AMS Press, 1966) 52.

[26]*OR*, ser. 1, 28 (2): 411.

[27]*OR*, ser. 4, 3:1119–20; W. R. Houghton and M. B. Houghton, *Two Boys in the Civil War and After* (Montgomery AL: Paragon Press, 1912) 237–41; John W. Riley to Joseph E. Brown, 22 July (no year) Governor's Incoming Correspondence.

August 1863 that to drag antiwar men into court was "simply to provide for a farcical trial." Later that year two Lumpkin County men, John Woody and John A. Wimpy, were tried on charges of treason. In the face of strong evidence against them, and after Woody confessed his opposition to the war, local juries acquitted both men. Soon after, Woody left for Tennessee and joined the Union army.[28]

Despite empathy from local residents and their growing numbers, life for deserters hiding out in the mountains and bottomlands was precarious at best. They were harassed by army patrols, and sympathizers often had little food to give them. Some became so desperate that they fled to the Yankees. When Sherman's army entered North Georgia in spring 1864, hundreds of Confederate deserters greeted the invaders—so many that officials could not process them fast enough. Some were put to work as support troops for front-line Federal soldiers. They even helped the Yankees dig entrenchments in preparation for the assault on Rebel lines at Kennesaw Mountain.[29]

With Sherman's troops bearing down on Atlanta and Confederate forces drained too weak by desertion to stop them, Governor Brown issued a proclamation ordering home guards and state and local officials to rally at the city and hurl the Yankees back. Few answered the governor's call. Some avoided duty by claiming protection from the central government, saying they had been "mustered into Confederate Service for local defense." In a desperate letter to the secretary of war, Brown protested that "the thousands who have such details cannot be permitted to hide behind them when the State is being overrun."[30]

---

[28]Riley, "Desertion and Disloyalty," 69; *OR*, series 1, 28 (2): 273; Jonathan D. Sarris, "An Execution in Lumpkin County: Local Loyalties in North Georgia's Civil War," in *The Civil War in Appalachia: Collected Essays*, ed. Kenneth W. Noe and Shannon H. Wilson (Knoxville: University of Tennessee Press, 1997) 141–42; William S. Kinsland, "The Civil War Comes to Lumpkin County," *North Georgia Journal* 1/2 (Summer 1984): 23–24; Sarris, *A Separate Civil War*, 95–96.

[29]*OR*, ser. 1, 38 (4): 594.

[30]Joseph Brown to Jefferson Davis, 19 July 1864, governor's letter book, Georgia Department of Archives and History; J. A. Seddon to Joseph Brown, 21 July 1864, governor's letter book, Georgia Department of Archives and History.; Brown to J. A. Seddon, 22 July 1864, ibid.

Others claimed exemption as county office holders. D. A. Johnson, a bailiff in Berrien County, was one of many who refused to go. A more patriotic neighbor, who anonymously signed his letter "Over Fifty," wrote to Governor Brown that Johnson was "a Tory, and ought to be in front of some good man." Hall County Justice of the Peace William O'Kelley had two brothers who had already deserted from the Georgia Militia. Hardly a Brown supporter to begin with, O'Kelley refused to take up arms. An acquaintance wrote to Brown of O'Kelley: "I have heard him say myself that he had rather shoot you than a deer."[31]

After Sherman captured Atlanta in September, hundreds of soldiers and civilians remained in the city and aided the Federal army. Some went further than that. One gang of Georgia ex-Confederates led by Alonzo Rogers and Porter Southworth formed themselves into a battalion and called it the "Volunteer Force of the United States Army from Georgia."[32]

In Georgia's wiregrass region, deserters sometimes turned to the Union blockade fleet on the Gulf Coast for help. In early 1863, John Harvey, representing a group of 500 wiregrass deserters and draft dodgers, met with Lieutenant George Welch of the USS *Amanda* at Apalachicola, Florida, to discuss placing the men under protection of Federal authorities. Armed only with shotguns, they had been skirmishing with conscript companies for some time and their ammunition was running low. They preferred to be declared under protective custody either as prisoners or refugees but, according to Welch, added "that they would follow me or any other leader to any peril they are ordered to rather than leave their families and go north." Welch was sympathetic but declined, saying he did not have enough manpower to guarantee safe passage for that many men from that deep in enemy territory. However, as Confederate strength along the Apalachicola

---

[31]Anonymous to Joseph Brown, 6 June 1864, Governor's Incoming Correspondence; Moses W. Finger to Joseph Brown, 14 May 1864, Governor's Incoming Correspondence; Henry Collom to Joseph Brown, 27 May 1864, Governor's Incoming Correspondence.
[32]*OR*, ser. 1, 44: 977; Riley, "Desertion and Disloyalty," 64.

declined, the Federals did begin running ammunition and other supplies upriver to anti-Confederate partisans.[33]

As their ranks grew, some deserters and other anti-Confederates formed armed guerrilla bands. They raided plantations, attacked army supply depots, and drove off impressment and conscript officers. A Confederate loyalist in Fort Gaines begged Governor Brown to send a company of cavalry for protection against these raiders. Another deserter band known as Colquitt's Scouts terrorized residents of Floyd County until its leader, "Captain Jack" Colquitt, was finally killed. When authorities in Fannin County arrested members of one deserter gang in June 1863, some of their comrades, along with local sympathizers, mounted a violent rescue. Several pro-Confederates were killed in the bloody gun battle. So brutal had Georgia's internal civil war become by fall 1863 that the editor of Milledgeville's *Confederate Union* wrote: "We are fighting each other harder than we ever fought the enemy."[34]

As early as September 1862, forty men in West Georgia's Marion County "secured and provisioned a house and arranged it in the manner of a military castle." Well armed and supplied, they swore not only to prevent their own capture but to protect other Georgians who sought sanctuary in their makeshift fortress. While Confederate and state military officials attempted to drive them out, military assaults had little impact on men who held a "determination to resist to the last extremity."[35]

The situation was just as dangerous in the northern part of the state. From Gilmer County came news in July 1862 of "tories and traitors who have taken up their abode in the mountains." They were an ideal haven for such men. The terrain made it difficult to send troops in after them, and so did the attitudes of the mountain people. That same month, a letter

---

[33]Maxine Turner, *Navy Gray: A Story of the Confederate Navy on the Chattahoochee and Apalachicola Rivers* (Tuscaloosa: University of Alabama Press, 1988) 130–31, 325n.6.

[34][name illegible] to Joseph Brown, 5 October 1864, Governor's Incoming Correspondence; George M. Battey, Jr., *A History of Rome and Floyd County* (Atlanta: n.p., 1922) 197–99; G. W. Lee to Joseph Brown, 12 June 1863, governor's letter book; *Milledgeville Confederate Union*, 24 November 1863.

[35]*Macon Telegraph*, 15 September 1862.

arrived on the governor's desk from Fannin County, just north of Gilmer, warning that "a very large majority of the people now here perhaps two thirds are disloyal." A few months later, anti-Confederate resistance became so aggressive in Fannin that one man called it a "general uprising among our Torys of this County." Most of Northeast Georgia's tory bands wanted nothing more than to sit out the war. Others, especially those with no family ties in the region, were more prone to violence. September 1862 found Lumpkin County being overrun by Unionists and deserters, robbing local citizens of guns, money, clothes, and provisions. One Confederate sympathizer wrote that "the Union men—Tories—are very abusive indeed and says they will do as they please." The *Dahlonega Signal* estimated that one of Lumpkin County's tory bands, led by "the notorious Jeff Anderson," numbered between one and two hundred.[36]

One of the earliest formed and most active bands of Union men in Northeast Georgia was led by Horatio Hennion. A Northerner by birth, Hennion had moved to White County's Mossy Creek community in his early twenties and married a local girl. The other men in his band of at least two dozen were born in Georgia and the Carolinas. All were nonslaveholders, and some were tenants or day laborers who owned no land. Those who did own land held no more than a few hundred dollars worth of real estate and personal property.

Hennion worked as a wagon maker in Gainesville during the secession crisis and made his support for the Union clear. Even after war broke out, Hennion remained openly anti-Confederate even as other local Unionists were falling silent. Threats to his life forced him and his family back to Mossy Creek, where he lived in peace until local pro-Confederates tried to kill him. In August 1861, he fled to North Carolina, but returned a year later and organized a band of anti-Confederates that included men from White County and neighboring Hall County. They fought running battles with Confederate conscript companies, rescuing

---

[36]W. W. Findley to Joseph Brown, 26 July 1862, Governor's Incoming Correspondence; W. A. Campbell to Joseph Brown, 12 July 1862, and 28 February 1863, Governor's Incoming Correspondence; Josiah A. Woody to Joseph Brown, 6 September 1862, Governor's Incoming Correspondence; *Dahlonega Signal*, quoted in *Augusta Chronicle and Sentinel*, 30 January 1863.

one of their members from the White County jail after his arrest by a conscript officer. Hennion's band became even more effective when he and his men signed "an agreement of mutual protection" with deserters hiding out in the region.[37]

Soon after he got word of events in the mountains, Governor Brown issued a proclamation aimed at the "very considerable number of deserters and stragglers" and those who aided them. Brown knew "that numbers of these deserters, encouraged by disloyal citizens in the mountains of Northeastern Georgia, have associated themselves together with arms in their hands and are now in rebellion against the authority of this State and the Confederate States." He issued a proclamation "commanding all persons…to return to their respective commands immediately." Brown also warned "all disloyal citizens to cease to harbor deserters or encourage desertion…as the law against treason will be strictly enforced against all who subject themselves to its penalties."[38]

Brown's warning had little effect, and in late January 1863 he took action. Brown sent a mounted force under Colonel George Washington Lee, commandant of Atlanta, and Captain E. M. Galt to Dahlonega with orders to "secure the arrest of deserters and restore the public tranquility." By early February, around 600 deserters had been rounded up and marched back to the army. Fifty-three civilian Unionists had been arrested and sent to Atlanta, among them the tory leader Jeff Anderson. Only a month later, Confederate loyalists in Lumpkin County were begging Governor Brown for more troops. In June, the *Athens Southern Watchman* reported that "some of those who were forced into the army by the cavalry last winter have returned with Government arms and ammunition in their hands and are creating serious apprehensions of future troubles." Already anti-Confederates led by a Hall County man calling himself Major Finger had attacked a small ironworks in White County. They burned the coal, stole the tools, and broke the forge

---

[37]Keith S. Bohannon, "They Had Determined to Root Us Out: Dual Memoirs by a Unionist Couple in Blue Ridge Georgia," in *Enemies of the Country*, 98–106.

[38]*OR*, ser. 4, 2: 360–61.

hammer. In Fannin County, tories had attacked a group of Confederates sent to arrest deserters, killing one man and wounding several others.[39]

Fannin County was hit again in August when tories led by Soloman Bryan disarmed all the pro-Confederates. According to one pro-Confederate, they "robbed our people of every single gun and all the ammunition." Similar confrontations took place all over Northeast Georgia. A Union County man informed the governor that the "mountains are filling with deserters and disloyal men" and begged him to send arms and ammunition. Brown sought help from the Richmond government, telling Jefferson Davis that "tories and deserters in North Eastern Georgia are now disarming the loyal people and committing many outrages." Brown got no response, and the outrages continued. He finally sent another expedition to northeast Georgia in October 1863. It arrested "quite a number of deserters, stragglers, marauders," but had little effect on the general state of affairs.[40]

In early November, White County Confederates went after the tories themselves. They hid along a wooded roadside, posted a sentinel up the way, and waited for his signal. When it came, the men sprang from the woods and ordered their adversaries to halt. The tories responded with a hail of gunfire, wheeled their horses, and rode off, with their pursuers firing after them. One Confederate loyalist, Lewis Pitchford, died in the exchange. A few weeks later, pro-Confederate vigilantes apprehended Jake Wofford, believed to have fired the shot that killed Pitchford. The mob stood Wofford on a plank with a rope around his neck hoping to force a confession. But the condemned man refused to say a word.

---

[39]Henry C. Wayne to E. M. Galt, 17 January 1863, adjutant general's letter books, Georgia Department of Archives and History; *Atlanta Southern Confederacy*, 4 February 1863; G. W. Lee to Joseph Brown, 5 February 1863, Governor's Incoming Correspondence; Citizens of Dahlonega GA to Joseph E. Brown, 4 March 1863, Cuyler Collection; *Athens Southern Watchman*, 17 June 1863.

[40]W. A. Campbell to Joseph Brown, 4 August 1863, Governor's Incoming Correspondence; T. J. Haralson and others to Joseph Brown, 7 August 1863, Governor's Petitions, Georgia Department of Archives and History; Joseph Brown to Jefferson Davis, 25 August 1863, governor's letter book; G. W. Lee to Joseph E. Brown, 6 October 1863, Cuyler Collection.

Someone in the crowd finally jerked the plank away from Wofford's feet and sent him, with whatever secrets, to his death.[41]

Brown ordered yet another force to Northeast Georgia in early 1864, but it fared even worse than its predecessors. One Gilmer County Confederate wrote that "the Tories with their squirrel rifles, pick off our men from behind rocks and trees and all manner of hiding places. In this way they have killed six or eight of our soldiers." J. J. Findley of Dahlonega reported that "the District is overrun with Deserters, Tories, and Rogues...and that the condition of things is worse in that region than ever."[42]

Conditions were just as bad in Northwest Georgia, and had been for some time. As early as October 1862, deserters led by a man named Crawford terrorized the citizens of Marietta and Cobb County. Early the next spring in Walker County, tories threatened to destroy the crops of any man who sided with the Confederacy. In March, a group of Confederate loyalists wrote to Governor Brown begging him for assistance. One pro-Confederate had already been shot at, and another's house had been robbed. Violence broke out in neighboring Dade County as well.[43] Brown sent a company of state troops to quell the tory uprising and asked for Confederate troops to help. In a letter to General Joseph E. Johnston, who commanded the Confederacy's western armies, Georgia's adjutant general Henry C. Wayne stressed the urgency of the problem but suggested a delicate handling. Both he and Brown knew that popular support for the Confederacy was unsteady to begin with. A heavy-handed invasion by Confederate troops might turn inactive layouts into active partisans. "As these misguided people are our own citizens, His Excellency [Governor Brown] desires that...you will deal with them as gently as the heinousness of their offense will permit. It is thought that some of the insurgents are deserters from your armies." Gentle response or not, military efforts did little but make matters worse for loyal Con-

---

[41]*Savannah Morning News*, 16 November 1863; *Athens Southern Watchman*, 25 November 1863.

[42]Henry C. Wayne to G. W. Lee, 23 January 1864, adjutant general's letter books.

[43]*Atlanta Confederacy*, quoted in *Augusta Chronicle and Sentinel*, 28 October 1862; *OR*, ser. 1, 23 (2): 738.

federates. Most had been driven out of LaFayette in Walker County by spring 1864.[44]

In the state's southern half, newspapers warned communities throughout the region to beware of deserters and other suspicious individuals. They suggested offering rewards to slaves, who often assisted deserters and tory gangs, if they would inform on their allies. The *Albany Patriot* advertised a $250 reward for the apprehension of George Martin, dead or alive, for uttering "treasonable sentiments against the Confederacy" and for the attempted murder of a lieutenant who had tried to arrest him. Doctor A. Blasdell, a Wilkinson County dentist, was reported to have been ridden out of town on a rail for displaying Union sympathies, but was suspected of still being in the area. He could probably have remained easily enough. Much of South Central and Southeastern Georgia was especially popular country for those evading military service. South of the Ocmulgee and Altamaha rivers, the swamps, bottomlands, and pine barrens provided ample cover from Confederate and state enlistment officers. Unlike the fertile, rolling hills of cotton-producing Southwest Georgia, piney woods and marshy lowlands dominated to the east. The land was less fertile, the people generally poorer. The farms were usually small and isolated. Cattle supplanted cotton, and slaveholding dropped off dramatically. In some Southeast Georgia counties, slaves accounted for only 10 percent of the population.[45]

Travel was difficult for those unfamiliar with the territory, making searches for deserters challenging for military officials sent into the region. Bridges were in a constant state of disrepair. Roads were scarce, "mere trails…a person not accustomed to them [could] scarcely follow them." The swamps and cypress hammocks dotting the region allowed draft evaders to "run from swamp to swamp & from one locality to

---

[44]*OR*, ser. 1, 23 (2): 737–38; *Augusta Constitutionalist*, 7 May 1864.

[45]*Albany Patriot*, 23, 30 May and 5 September 1861. For a concise treatment of draft evasion in South Georgia, see David Carlson, "The 'Loanly Runagee': Draft Evaders in Confederate South Georgia," *Georgia Historical Quarterly* 84/4 (Winter 2000): 589–615. See also David Carlson, "Wiregrass Runners: Conscription, Desertion, and the Origins of Discontent in Civil War South Georgia" (MA thesis, Valdosta State University, 1999).

another so quickly & easily that it is almost impossible to catch [them]."[46]

Some deserters formed mounted units and rode the wiregrass plains, pine barrens, and cypress swamps posing as impressment officers. One outraged editor wrote: "These scoundrels seek the fairest, fattest and most quiet portion of our territory for the theatre of their depredations. They pounce suddenly upon the prosperous plantations, and sweep them of their best laboring stock, and such stores of meat, grain and forage as they can carry off, under pretense of a legal impressment."[47]

Some sought only to lay low, building camps in the pine barrens of southeast Georgia where "no unfriendly soljier is perusin around and axin for papers. Here the melanckoly mind is soothed. Here the loanly runagee can kontemplate the sandy roads, the wiregrass woods, and the million of majestik pines."[48] Still others turned farmhouses into armored fortifications, such as those in Marion and Coffee counties, or hid at safe havens established on the lands of sympathetic neighbors.

In Coffee County, Ben Pearson, a small planter, accused one of the area's most active layout gangs headed by "Old Man" Bill Wall of stealing his produce and livestock. Trouble had been brewing between Pearson's and Wall's men for some time. At one point, Pearson found a grave dug outside his front door. He finally offered a cash reward and amnesty for Wall himself if the "Old Man" would come forward and turn his men in to local authorities. Wall, a school teacher and something of a poor man's poet, could not resist poking fun at Pearson's presumption that he might do such a thing.

> If it is my choice to stay at home,
> and the woods in beauty roam;

---

[46]Sumter County Superior Court, minute book, April 1861, Sumter County Courthouse, Americus GA; Richard Harwell and Philip N. Racine, eds., *The Fiery Trail: A Union Officer's Account of Sherman's Last Campaign* (Knoxville: University of Tennessee Press, 1986) 61; A. T. MacIntyre to H. C. Wayne, 21 April 1865, Adjutant and Inspector General's Incoming Correspondence, Georgia Department of Archives and History.

[47]*Milledgeville Confederate Union*, 3 January 1865.

[48]*Atlanta Southern Confederacy*, 21 June 1864.

Pluck the flowers in early spring,
and hear the little songsters sing!

Why, then, should I, for the sake of gain,
leave my conscience with a stain.
A traitor! who could hear the name
with no respect for age or fame;

Who, for the sake of a little gold,
would have his friends in bondage sold?
I would rather take the lash
than betray them for Confederate trash.

You say they kill your sheep and cows,
You say they take your hoss and your plows,
You say they took your potatoes away,
You say they dug your grave one day.
All this may be true;
It makes me sorry for you.

Yet, sir, if I, these men betray
and they were all taken away,
And they did not in the battlefield fall,
They would come back and kill
"Old Man Bill Wall."[49]

The rise of armed layout bands was only the most violent reflection of widespread discontent with the Confederacy and the war. And, as the war entered its final year, few expected the Confederacy to survive for very long. In a March 1864 *Early County News* editorial, E. H. Grouby wrote: "We cannot help thinking this is the last year of the war.... we

---

[49]Warren P. Ward, *Ward's History of Coffee County* (1930; rpt., Spartanburg SC: Reprint Company, 1985) 141–42. For more on Bill Wall, see Mark Wetherington, *Plain Folk's Fight: The Civil War and Reconstruction in Piney Woods Georgia* (Chapel Hill: University of North Carolina Press, 2005) 224–25.

have now entirely too many little jackass upstarts filling positions in our government." As Grouby's comment suggests, most Georgians were so disgruntled with the Confederacy by 1864 that they actually looked forward to its fall. In October of that year, Grouby wrote that the only people who still backed the war effort were those who held "fat Government contracts" and corrupt officials who were "not yet done fleecing the Government. Their voice," he said, "is still for war, war, war!"[50]

Lacking any direct political power, the voice of the common folk was expressed in local meetings throughout Georgia where declarations were drawn up demanding an end to the war. A Hart County assembly, attended by "a large number," asked Governor Brown to call a state convention to arrange "a speedy peace." Citizens in Lumpkin County did the same. "All most to a man," wrote James Findley, they were eager for peace. When Jackson County men tried to hold an antiwar meeting, Confederate cavalry broke it up. Undeterred, they met again a short time later to draw up resolutions urging an end to the "bloody and destructive war." They sent a list of their demands to Governor Brown and the *Athens Southern Watchman*. The *Watchman*'s editor published their demands and called the cavalry's action "an assumption of power unparalleled in any professedly free Government."[51]

Such demands were common in central Georgia's cotton belt as well. Asserting their "inalienable right of popular assemblage," Jasper County folk met at the courthouse to insist on an end to "the great sufferings of our people." Upson County citizens met at Thomaston and voted "to stop the war on any terms." According to one attendee, "some of the citizens go so far as to say that they will be glad to see Lincoln in possession of the state." One assembly in a rural district of Bibb County was especially aggressive in its demands. A crowd of about sixty voters, all but four of them antiwar men, met to elect local justices. After the balloting, one of the newly elected justices threatened to drive every

---

[50]*Early County News*, 30 March and 5 October 1864.

[51]*Athens Southern Watchman*, 25 January 1865; James Findley to Joseph Brown, 26 January 1865, Governor's Incoming Correspondence; *Augusta Chronicle and Sentinel*, 29 January 1865; *Athens Southern Watchman*, 18 January 1865.

Confederate official out of Macon and "pledged himself to raise 300 men in twenty-four hours for that purpose if required."[52]

In South Georgia, Echols County's citizens called for a state convention so that a "free discussion may be had relative to the situation of our bleeding country." An antiwar gathering in Wilcox County urged Governor Brown "to settle this Bloody conflict at once by negotiations before the whole white male population is butchered up." So did citizens in Berrien and Pierce counties. Tatnall and Liberty countians insisted that they would rejoin the Union whether Georgia did or not. A Union meeting in Thomas County turned violent when the assembly was forced to beat back an assault by pro-Confederates.[53]

By the time of the Thomas County incident, Sherman had completed his march to the sea and was heading north through the Carolinas. Some of his troops were left behind to hold Savannah, and other Federals occupied the rest of Georgia's coast. Most of what the Yankees did not control in Georgia, Unionists and deserters did. In southeast Georgia's first congressional district, the largest by area in the state, Lieutenant Alfred Prescott reported that "all law, both civil and Military seems to be overthrown." The region was, he said, "to a greater or lesser extent, disloyal.... No officer of the C. S. Army who is a stranger to the people can travel through these counties with safety." In an open letter, "the few loyal citizens" of Irwin, Berrien, Echols, and Coffee counties begged for help from the commanding general of the district. Deserters had stolen supplies from the government's storehouses at Blackshear and Homerville and had run conscript officers out of Berrien and Irwin counties. The district enrolling officer, Duncan Clinch, wrote General Cobb that "not only the deserters, but almost the entire

---

[52] *Augusta Chronicle and Sentinel*, 26 February 1865; W. A. Thomas to Howell Cobb, 18 January 1865, Howell Cobb Papers, Felix Hargrett Rare Book and Manuscript Library, University of Georgia, Athens; J. T. Smith to Joseph Brown, 25 February 1865, Governor's Incoming Correspondence.

[53] *Milledgeville Confederate Union*, 28 February 1865; Citizens of Wilcox County to Joseph Brown, 14 January 1865, Joseph E. Brown Papers, Felix Hargrett Rare Book and Manuscript Library, University of Georgia, Athens; *Augusta Chronicle and Sentinel*, 2 February 1865; Berrien County Inferior Court, Minutes, 18[?] January 1865, Georgia Department of Archives and History; *OR*, ser. 1, 47 (3): 262; *OR*, ser. 1, 44: 827–28; *Augusta Register*, quoted in *Sumter Republican*, 21 January 1865; *OR*, ser. 1, 47 (2): 31.

population" of Appling, Coffee, Pierce, Berrien, Clinch, Ware, Wayne, and adjacent counties were resisting Confederate authority. And, he wrote, they were determined to drive him off.[54]

In North Georgia, the conscript officer of Paulding County had to protect himself with posted guards. Further to the northeast, one Confederate loyalist wrote that the mountain region was in a "deplorable condition—desertions from the army, straggling to an incredible degree, and all kinds of irregularity." These irregularities were, he wrote, "not only tolerated, but I must say connived at by those whose duty it is to rectify these evils." Even those who did not support the tories usually turned a blind eye to their activities. Some state militia units, like the command at Dahlonega headed by Colonel James J. Findley, hardly bothered with an occasional muster. When General A. W. Reynolds went to investigate, he found Findley's men "scattered over the country, as if quartered at home." In January 1865, Richmond sent a detachment to the region under General W. T. Wofford with orders to arrest all stragglers and deserters. Findley warned that it would do little good. He knew his men could keep themselves well hidden in the hills. It would be impossible for Wofford's force to track them all down. Reynolds agreed that it was a wasted effort. Even if they could be captured and returned to the army, Reynolds knew they would simply go home again or desert to the Federals.[55]

Things were nearly as difficult for Confederate officials in the cotton belt. In December 1864, B. J. Fry reported to General Cobb from Augusta that "the whole country from here to the Ocmulgee [a stretch covering the eastern half the state] appears to be full of stragglers.... Complaints are made here almost daily from the surrounding counties of

---

[54]Alfred Prescott to P. Looney, 27 February 1865, Confederate Bible Records, United Daughters of the Confederacy, Georgia Department of Archives and History; *Albany Patriot*, 23 March 1865; B. F. White to Lamar Cobb, 6 January 1865, Cobb Papers; J. Williams to J. A. Davis, 26 February 1865, Cobb Papers; Clinch to Howell Cobb, April 4, 1865, Cobb Papers.

[55]Andrew J. Hansell to Howell Cobb, 10 January 1865, Cobb Papers; Joseph Henry Lumpkin to J. A. Campbell, 31 December 1864, Cobb Papers; *OR,* ser. 1, 49 (1): 963; *OR,* ser. 1, 45 (2): 805; James J. Findley to Joseph Brown, 26 January 1865, Incoming Correspondence; A. W. Reynolds to Howell Cobb, 22 January 1865, Cobb Papers.

their depredations." In Walton County, bands of armed deserters and Unionists controlled the countryside. The same was true in Morgan County. In the West Georgia counties of Marion and Chattahoochee, bands of deserters fought running battles with what Confederate authorities remained. Some state militia officers suggested abolishing conscription as a means of appeasing the disaffected. Enforcement efforts had become useless anyway. In March 1865, Georgia assemblymen adopted a resolution calling on Congress to repeal the Conscript Act.[56] It was a useless gesture. Time and tide were turning too quickly against the Confederacy.

In April 1865, the last major Confederate armies surrendered. On 10 May, Yankee troopers captured Jefferson Davis near Irwinville, Georgia, as he fled south in a vain effort to get out of the country and establish a Confederate government-in-exile. Other Rebel officials were soon in custody and the Confederacy ceased to be.

In a sense, though, the Confederacy as a nation never really existed at all. Eminent Georgia historian E. Merton Coulter, enamored as he was with the Lost Cause, could still admit that the Confederacy never became an "emotional reality" to most of its people.[57] Even at its beginning the Southern Confederacy lacked firm support. Less than half of white Southerners had favored secession in the first place. A majority of Georgians had opposed it. What support the Confederacy did have gradually eroded as the passions of 1861 faded under the realities of war.

To many, the Confederacy became the greater enemy. It conscripted their men, impressed their supplies, and starved them out. It favored the rich and oppressed the poor. It made war on those who dared withhold their support and made life nearly as miserable for the rest. That reality led plain folk across Georgia and the South to work against the Confederacy. Their actions and attitudes contributed in large part to Confederate defeat, a fact that was well known to Southerners at the

---

[56]B. J. Fry to Howell Cobb, 16 December 1864, Cobb Papers; T. T. Eason to Howell Cobb, 28 March 1865, ibid.; Bryan, *Confederate Georgia*, 264n.84; *Milledgeville Confederate Union*, 30 December 1864; James J. Findley to Joseph Brown, 26 January 1865, Governor's Incoming Correspondence; *Augusta Constitutionalist*, 10 March 1865.

[57]E. Merton Coulter, *The Confederate States of America, 1861–1865* (Baton Rouge: Louisiana State University Press, 1950) 105.

time. Some had even predicted it. In his November 1860 speech warning against secession, Georgia's Alexander Stephens, ironically soon-to-be Confederate vice president, prophesied that should the South secede, Southerners would "at no distant day commence cutting one another's throats." In fall 1862, an Atlanta newspaper put it just as bluntly: "If we are defeated, it will be by the people at home."[58] And so the Confederacy was defeated, not only by the Union army—in which 300,000 Southern whites served—but also by resistance on the home front.

---

[58]"Alexander H. Stephens's Unionist Speech," in *Secession Debated*, 68; *Atlanta Southern Confederacy*, 25 October 1862.

States of Dependence and Independence in Civil War Georgia

by Joseph P. Reidy

The Civil War affected Southern families much more than the military service of more than one million men, some 260,000 of whom never returned home, would suggest. Because of the family's central place in Western life and culture, the disruption and strains that families endured during the war reverberated throughout society. Moreover, because Southern families also provided the social framework for the master-slave relationship, the sectional tension over the future of slavery, which escalated throughout the 1850s and then exploded following Abraham Lincoln's election as president in November 1860, rocked the family to its foundation. Southern political theorists and elected officials had for years distinguished between the household and the society at large, particularly in the area of public policy. Government might legislate for the public good, but domestic affairs were the prerogative of the household head. The Civil War changed that.

Southern military and government officials began crossing the threshold of the home, first by enlisting men for military service and then by seizing animals, food, and other articles to support the war effort. In time, the reach extended to slaves. The household head's relationship to his dependents—based on his responsibility to provide and protect and his right to rule largely without challenge—began to change. When Northern political leaders declared their intent to undermine the Confederate war effort by destroying slavery, they opened a second front against Southern patriarchal authority, the effects of which touched non-slaveholding household heads no less than opulent planters. From all quarters, military mobilization worked to transform domestic relationships.

When looking backward from the present, it is tempting to presume that emancipation was an inevitable outcome of the war, at least after Lincoln issued the Emancipation Proclamation on 1 January 1863. Nothing could have been further from the truth. In the vortex of war, everything—from which side would prevail to the consequences of day-to-day actions—was uncertain. And even as the Union's triumph became clearer by fall 1864, the practical implications remained foggy. By situating slave emancipation within the framework of changes in domestic relationships initiated by the war, this essay will explore the dynamic interaction between broad social policy—particularly the steps the United States and the Confederate States took to mobilize for war and to achieve victory—and its manifestation in relationships of dependency within households and communities at the local level.

As war clouds gathered during spring 1861, families began feeling the changing barometric pressure almost immediately. The mobilization of men profoundly affected children. Departure scenes featured admonitions from fathers to behave in their absence. Fathers particularly exhorted their sons to assist their mothers and to compensate as much as possible for the paternal absence. In the early part of the war, letters from children to their fathers aimed to reinforce the impression of their conformity with these expectations of good behavior and growth into the new responsibilities, just as those from fathers to their children continued to encourage and, as required, to admonish. Yet as the war continued, the admonitions grew fewer and less intense, in part because the father could not enforce them. Households adjusted to the father's absence with the mother and children, relatives and neighbors all taking on pieces of his responsibilities. Many years later, J. W. Frederick recalled that at the age of twelve-and-a-half, while his father was away with the Georgia Home Guards, he and his mother managed the family plantation and made momentous decisions that affected their lives.[1]

Throughout the war, but particularly at its outset, the idealized Southern family served as propaganda both for rallying the faithful and for inspiring would-be recruits. Far from being the mere objects of this campaign, women played an important part in orchestrating it. Elite

---

[1]Gerald J. Smith, ed., "Reminiscences of the Civil War by J. W. Frederick," *Georgia Historical Quarterly* 59/5 (Supplement 1975): 154–59. More generally, see James Marten, *The Children's Civil War* (Chapel Hill: University of North Carolina Press, 1998) chap. 5.

women gave a patriotic makeover to their traditional obligation to perform charitable works, which derived from their domestic role as mothers and their public role as church and civic volunteers. During the initial rush of excitement, public-spirited women in Augusta formed the Ladies Volunteer Sewing Society to make uniforms; by 1862, as the war's impact took a different turn, they broadened their mission and restyled themselves as the Ladies Hospital and Relief Association. Mrs. J. C. C. Blackburn of Lamar County sent Governor Joseph Brown a gold watch with the request that it be used "to the best advantage" of the soldiers.[2]

The wives and other female relatives of the men who raised volunteer companies—and who, upon enlistment, were commissioned as captains of the companies—took this obligation especially seriously. Fueled by a sense of noblesse oblige, supplemented by community pride and Confederate patriotism, the women aimed to preserve on the home front the hierarchical relationship of responsibility and dependence that armed service institutionalized between officers and enlisted men. What is more, they maintained the tradition role of civic engagement, expanding its practice to meet the new circumstances. Over time, the spouses of enlisted men would appeal to the spouses of officers for assistance with a wide array of problems, just as the men themselves would appeal to the officers for help in varying circumstances. By the third year of fighting, as material privation intensified on the home front, these appeals increasingly focused on requests for furloughs. Given growing manpower shortages in the Confederate army, granting such

---

[2]LeeAnn Whites, "The Charitable and the Poor: The Emergence of Domestic Politics in Augusta, Georgia, 1860–1880," *Journal of Social History* 17/4 (Summer 1984): 601–16; see also the [Macon] *Georgia Journal & Messenger*, 31 July 1861, for analogous developments in Macon. Mrs. J. C. C. Blackburn to Joseph Brown, quoted in Mark A. Weitz, *A Higher Duty: Desertion among Georgia Troops during the Civil War* (Lincoln: University of Nebraska Press, 2000) 141. Bell Irvin Wiley, *The Life of Johnny Reb: The Common Soldier of the Confederacy* (Baton Rouge: Louisiana State University Press, 1943). Chap. 1 describes the rush to arms, including the varied roles of women in the mobilization.

requests became increasingly difficult, which, in turn, sparked growing rates of absence without leave and desertion.[3]

Confederate leaders could not have foretold how their own actions would undercut the very ideals they professed. War necessarily intrudes into domestic arrangements even when the battlefield is hundreds of miles away. In modern times, the nation-state leads the intrusion to satisfy its need for men, foodstuffs, and the supplies and implements of war. Over the course of the Civil War, government agents of the Confederate States and of the state of Georgia, at some times working in concert and at others in apparent opposition, resorted to impressment. This exercise of emergency authority appropriated prerogatives that otherwise would have been the sole domain of the male household head. Moreover, impressment officers often took flagrant advantage of the men's absence by seizing food and work animals and by interfering with the management of slaves. Taken together, these actions recast the landscape of domestic relations. They also created political divisions within the Confederacy, particularly between Richmond strategists who emphasized the need support the armies in the field and local authorities who witnessed the adverse impact on civilians at home.

Georgia Governor Joseph E. Brown championed government action to address the special needs of soldiers' families and entertained direct appeals for their relief. By the end of winter 1862–1863, the growing burden of subsistence prompted women in Georgia and in other Confederate states to engage in public demonstrations. From small towns such as Thomasville, Milledgeville, and Forsyth to the major cities of Atlanta, Columbus, Augusta, and Macon, women used force to gain access to subsistence goods and to punish identified speculators and hoarders by looting their establishments and seizing their stockpiles. In

---

[3]George C. Rable, *Civil Wars: Women and the Crisis of Southern Nationalism* (Urbana: University of Illinois Press, 1989); Drew Gilpin Faust, *Mothers of Invention: Women of the Slaveholding South in the American Civil War* (Chapel Hill: University of North Carolina Press, 1996); Edward D. C. Campbell, Jr., and Kym S. Rice, eds., *A Woman's War: Southern Women, Civil War, and the Confederate Legacy* (Charlottesville: University Press of Virginia, 1996); Laura F. Edwards, *Scarlett Doesn't Live Here Anymore: Southern Women in the Civil War Era* (Urbana: University of Illinois Press, 2000).

time, women employed in Confederate government factories struck for
higher wages, appealing for relief from the rising cost of living and
expecting their neighbors to understand why they resorted to such
Yankee-like tactics. As soldiers' wives engaged in direct dialogue with
government officials and the public at large, they assumed an advocacy
role on behalf of their families—husbands included—which further
eroded the authority of the absent household heads.[4]

A newspaper editor who commented on these transgressions of "the
bounds of decorum" attributed them to female nature, arguing that "with
reason somewhat weaker, they have to contend with passions somewhat
stronger" than those of men. Pressing beyond this appeal to the
conventional thinking of male readers, the editor identified a profound
threat to domestic order. Although scarcity helped to explain the
women's desperation, taking matters into their own hands cut their social
moorings; "by one transgression," he argued, "a female...forfeits her
place in society forever."[5] The action of government officials had the
potential both to alleviate and to exacerbate this dynamic. Timely relief
could remove the need for indecorous behavior. But it also inserted a
third-party between traditional household heads and their families. Such
interventions not only created direct new lines of communication
between household dependents and government officials but also
spawned new expectations of mutual rights and responsibilities and for
even greater involvement by the state in domestic affairs.[6]

---

[4]Teresa Crisp Williams and David Williams, "The Women Rising: Cotton, Class, and
Confederate Georgia's Rioting Women," *Georgia Historical Quarterly* 86/1 (Spring
2002): 49–83. See also David Williams, Teresa Crisp Williams, and David Carlson, *Plain
Folk in a Rich Man's War: Class and Dissent in Confederate Georgia* (Gainesville:
University Press of Florida, 2002). For a notice of a strike by women employed at the
Confederate States' Central Laboratory at Macon in October 1864, see *Macon Daily
Telegraph and Confederate*, 19 October 1864.

[5]Williams and Williams, "Women Rising," 73.

[6]See Stephanie McCurry, "Women Numerous and Armed: Gender and the Politics of
Subsistence in the Civil War South," in *Wars within a War: Controversy and Conflict
over the American Civil War*, ed. Joan Waugh and Gary W. Gallagher (Chapel Hill:
University of North Carolina Press, 2009) 1–26. See also Mark V. Wetherington, *Plain
Folk's Fight: Civil War and Reconstruction in Piney Woods Georgia* (Chapel Hill:
University of North Carolina Press, 2005) chap. 5.

Notwithstanding the war's impact on domestic relationships derived from blood kinship, it had a much more lasting—indeed, in many respects, revolutionary—impact on the extended families that included slaves. By the mid-nineteenth century, Georgia slaveholders had extolled the virtues of slavery as an ideal type of domestic relationship for several generations. Enslaved laborers constituted the base of the family pyramid and the master the apex, with the owner's wife and children, along with other family members and unrelated dependents in between. The household served as the touchstone of political society: firmly established as the lord of his domain, the patriarch served as its official representative to the world at large. More broadly, defenders of slavery promoted a conservative image of pastoral family life in the South that contrasted sharply with their portrayal of urban life in the North. There the traditional family was eroding in the face of unbridled money-making, the growth in manufacturing, and an influx of foreign immigrants, coupled with the increasing popularity of abolitionism, feminism, and a host of other "isms." A potential threat—not to mention a frontal assault—on slavery threatened the stability of the household and, in turn, the entire social order.[7]

Although proponents of the ideology intended it for home consumption by their slaves and not strictly for export to the North and the rest of the world, the enslaved population of Georgia and the other slaveholding states was not buying. Instead, they viewed Abraham Lincoln's election as a signal event, perhaps even a sign of imminent deliverance from bondage, despite the secession of seven deep-South states, including Georgia, during the winter of 1860–1861. The storied escapes from the past—including that of William and Ellen Craft from Macon in 1848—took on fresh currency and rumors about imminent deliverance began to circulate. With the outbreak of hostilities in April 1861, the prospect of a Northern invasion became real, and "throughout

---

[7]See Eugene D. Genovese, *The Political Economy of Slavery: Studies in the Economy and Society of the Slave South* (New York: Pantheon Books, 1965); Genovese, *Roll, Jordan, Roll: The World the Slaves Made* (New York: Pantheon Books, 1974); Elizabeth Fox-Genovese, *Within the Plantation Household: Black and White Women of the Old South* (Chapel Hill: University of North Carolina Press, 1988); George Fitzhugh, *Sociology for the South, or, The Failure of Free Society* (Richmond: A. Morris, 1854).

the South," according to an observer writing from Macon, "the Blacks are already informed of the object of that invasion." Who could possibly believe, he wondered, "that a vast majority of the slaves would not with avidity escape from bondage if they felt there was a power near to secure them that Boon."[8]

Confederate strategists viewed slave labor in the aggregate as an asset that would support the material needs of the Confederacy. By not viewing the laborers as sentient beings and as members of domestic networks that encompassed both their own kinfolk, the masters' families—black and white—and the families of slaves and masters in their neighborhoods, they neglected to see the potential flaw in their strategy.[9] Raising an army strained familial relationships and the smooth operation of households. Enlistment necessarily created voids in the patterns of authority and production within households. Recruits from slaveholding households might also take a favored slave as a body servant, thereby further diminishing the domestic workforce. And whether the enslaved servant saw this opportunity as one that would result in further advantage within the antebellum model or one that might result in eventual freedom is immaterial, inasmuch as both white and black members of the family shared a joint concern about the safety of their loved ones.

Not all enslaved laborers viewed military mobilization, and specifically the master's absence, through that lens. Instead, they observed a power vacuum and began to take advantage of it. In response, local communities placed slave patrols on heightened alert. Even in the piney woods, where the African-American population was small, fears abounded. In 1862, W. B. Overstreet of Coffee County informed Governor Brown that the mobilization left soldiers' wives "Exposed to the Negroes," and he predicted "woe bee the women & children" in the

---

[8]S. T. Bailey to Howell Cobb, 4 May 1861, Erwin-Cobb-Lamar Family Papers, University of Georgia. On the importance of rumors, see Steven Hahn, *A Nation under Our Feet: Black Political Struggles in the Rural South from Slavery to the Great Migration* (Cambridge MA: Harvard University Press, 2003).
[9]On slave neighborhoods, see Anthony E. Kaye, *Joining Places: Slave Neighborhoods in the Old South* (Chapel Hill: University of North Carolina Press, 2007).

event of a general conscription.[10] An upward spike in unauthorized leaves from plantations after hours hinted at the loosened reins of power but did not tell the whole story. Instead, it was in the performance of daily chores that enslaved men and women demonstrated the full effect of their masters' absence, particularly when mistresses had to assume supervision over the field laborers as well as the household staff. From all over the state (and indeed from every slave state) came reports of slaves' slowing the pace of work, refusing to follow instructions, moving about at will, and generally attempting to assert control over their actions and their lives. As unsettling as these developments were during the first year of the war, the imposition of the Confederate draft in spring 1862 intensified the pressure.

These actions on the part of the enslaved prompted varying responses. Wives and teenaged sons attempted to assert control, generally with the assistance of neighbors or relatives. In Thomas County, for instance, when Duncan Curry went to war, his fifteen-year-old son assumed the role of slave driver. The laborers promptly ignored the son's authority—defying orders and leaving the plantation when they pleased—until Duncan's brother restored order and schooled his nephew in the use of the whip. Sallie Jackson of Clarke County reported to her husband Asbury, a lieutenant in the 44th Georgia Infantry, that his family was "doing as best we know" in his absence "or as good as we can get the Servants to do." With "no white man" to direct them, the slaves "learn to feel very independent."[11]

Broader signs of defiance on the part of the enslaved, such as stealing, dealing in illicit goods, traveling without a pass, and the like, drew the attention of county grand juries, which in turn led to increased vigilance on the part of sheriffs. So what in antebellum times constituted domestic unrest that the master would have addressed within the household overflowed the boundaries of the household and became the preoccupation of civil authorities. In part to remediate this problem, the

---

[10]Quoted in Wetherington, *Plain Folk's Fight*, 161.

[11]On Curry, see Susan Eva O'Donovan, *Becoming Free in the Cotton South* (Cambridge MA: Harvard University Press, 2007) 72–73; on Jackson, see T. Conn Bryan, *Confederate Georgia* (Athens: University of Georgia Press, 1953) 125. See also Marten, *Children's Civil War*, 171.

Confederate government in Richmond decreed in fall 1862 that for every twenty slaves on a plantation, one white man might be exempted from the draft to serve as overseer. Rebecca Bryan, a widow in Twiggs County, promptly petitioned Confederate authorities for such an exemption so that her farm manager might "oversee or control" her twenty-four field hands.[12]

Slave unrest was a byproduct of secession, war, and the resulting strains on household and community structures of discipline throughout the South. From the standpoint of the enslaved, these openings expanded the long-contested boundaries of the master-slave relationship. Slaves were able to move about with greater ease—though not without risk—and to exert greater control over their lives. Men enjoyed greater access to the customary practice of visiting wives on other plantations, and the incidence of "lying out" increased. However, as Georgia—and the surrounding states for hundreds of miles in every direction—assumed the character of an armed camp, aiming to achieve lasting freedom through flight remained a risky undertaking.[13]

All that changed with the coming of Union armed forces, beginning with the capture of Port Royal, South Carolina, in November 1861. From that time forward, naval vessels operated along the coast of Georgia. Recalling stories of the British fleet in the same waters during the American Revolution, planters well understood the potential for disruption deep into the interior. Accordingly, they began making plans to relocate (or in the terminology of the day, to refugee) their families to working plantations in the piedmont or in Southwest Georgia or to summer cottages in the Appalachian Mountains.[14] With people and lives

---

[12]Statement of Rebecca Bryan, 3 November 1862, M-2754 1862, Letters Received, Adjutant and Inspector General, Records of Confederate War Department Staff Departments, War Department Collection of Confederate Records, RG 109, National Archives, Washington DC. See Armstead L. Robinson, *The Bitter Fruits of Bondage: The Demise of Slavery and the Collapse of the Confederacy, 1861–1865* (Charlottesville: University of Virginia Press, 2005) 179–82, for treatment of the so-called Twenty Negro Law.

[13]The best general treatment of wartime slavery in Georgia remains Clarence L. Mohr, *On the Threshold of Freedom: Masters and Slaves in Civil War Georgia* (Athens: University of Georgia Press, 1986).

[14]O'Donovan, *Becoming Free*, 82–85.

thus cast into motion, the slaves' disciplinary boundaries both expanded and contracted: expanded in the sense that those who refused to participate in the forced migration might seek shelter with family members or friends still on the coast or seek protection and freedom under the Union flag; and contracted in the sense that masters tightened the screws to prevent exactly such possibilities.

The war also created new opportunities and constraints on the domestic relationships of enslaved men and women. Couples discussed their fate, hoping that a new day was dawning but uneasy about stepping fully into the light. Much of this uneasiness derived from past experience; the long struggle for freedom might be coming to some resolution, but it was not yet won. What were the advantages and disadvantages of fleeing slavery, for instance? Should men attempt to flee, leaving their wives to care for their children and their elderly relatives? If so, could they reasonably hope to return to help their families escape? The answer varied with a wide range of circumstances, beginning with geography. The presence of Union forces within striking distance might prove attractive, but only if the prospect of surpassing local slave patrols and Confederate Home Guards was realistic. By the same token, forced disruptions to routines—such as impressment—provided occasions for laborers or skilled slaves to escape, either for good to the Yankees or for a time to bargain for advantages with their masters.

Beginning in summer 1862, the impetus for enslaved men to seek refuge with the Yankees grew even stronger as Union commanders at Port Royal began recruiting black men to serve in the US army. By the fall, the recruits were taking part in amphibious operations along the coast of Georgia where they seized property, disrupted critical support operations such as saltworks, and liberated slaves.[15] Union forces soon established refugee camps on several islands where they relocated escaped slaves who then commenced growing provisions to support themselves. Federal strategists quickly grasped that providing protection

---

[15]See, for example, Brig. Gen. Rufus Saxton to Hon. E. M. Stanton, 25 November 1862, US War Department, comp., *The War of the Rebellion: A Compilation of the Official Records of the Union and Confederate Armies*, 128 vols. (Washington, DC: Government Printing Office, 1880–1901) ser. 1, 14: 192.

and material support to the fugitives undermined the Confederate war effort. But they could not have imagined the full impact of their actions on the stability of slaveholding households.

Not surprisingly, federal military advances prompted Confederate countermeasures. Early in summer 1862, Confederate General Hugh W. Mercer, commanding at Savannah, issued orders demanding the services of 20 percent of the enslaved men and teenaged boys to fortify the defenses around the city.[16] Although Mercer aimed to respect the property rights of the owners, not all agreed that the circumstances required a forced draft of laborers. Some masters went so far as to hide their slaves from the impressment officers; others wrote to Confederate officials in Richmond for relief. Such actions appeared to contradict the masters' oft-repeated admonitions to respect legitimate authority. One disgruntled slaveholder from Laurens County wrote to the Confederate secretary of war complaining that he and his neighbors were being required "to do more than our share" and seeking the return of the impressed laborers. "Is it right for a few poor counties to risk their slaves & do all the work, while the wealthier counties stand aloof & do nothing at all?" he asked. "We must have equality in this confederacy or it will blow up."[17]

If the division among masters were not enough for enslaved laborers to exploit, that between masters and government officials presented intriguing new possibilities. This mobilization differed from prior forced drafts of slave labor for the public good in its potential for indefinite service and its inherent risk of injury, death, escape, or capture by the Yankees. Impressment put people into motion, and not all reached the intended destination. Moreover, the work itself brought men and women into contact with others similarly situated whose lives were disrupted in the cause of Confederate liberty. With words of freedom in the air and prospects for achieving it on the ground, plots to escape took shape.

---

[16]O'Donovan, *Becoming Free*, 79–81.

[17]Joseph M. White to Hon. Geo. W. Randolph, 8 September 1862, in Ira Berlin et al., eds., *The Destruction of Slavery*, ser. 1, vol. 1 of *Freedom: A Documentary History of Emancipation, 1861–1867* (New York: Cambridge University Press, 1982–1993) 699–700.

As they pondered the implications of their deteriorating authority, slaveholders began seeking assistance from the very officials whose actions were contributing to their consternation in the first place. More than simply requesting an end to impressment or an equitable distribution of the toll, some sought radical measures to avert the further deterioration of social order. In August 1862, a group of Liberty County planters wrote to General Mercer proposing what would have been unthinkable even a year earlier. They were particularly troubled that an estimated 20,000 slaves fled their masters since the Yankees arrived, most having headed to the coast where the men enlisted in the Union army and navy, provided invaluable military intelligence, and served as guides to federal operations and liberators to slaves. Besides losses valued at $12–15 million, the flight produced "insecurity of the property along our borders & the demoralization of the negroes that remain…& may finally result in perfect disorganization and rebellion" if left unchecked. "Negroes will congregate from every quarter" along the seaboard, they predicted, "and become a lawless set of runaways, corrupting the Negroes that remain faithful, depredating on property of all kinds & resorting it may be to deeds of violence." The petitioners recommended summary execution for those "*taken in the act of absconding*, singly, or in parties," and, in light of the procedural constraints affecting the civil courts, they requested that Mercer order his troops to do the work.[18]

As the Liberty County planters wrestled with the logic of placing military law above civil law, they could not escape exploring the relationship between slaves and the state. This conundrum had been a centerpiece of Southern jurisprudence throughout the nineteenth century, as both judges and jurors contended with the dual nature of slaves as persons and property. Ideological pronouncements notwithstanding, planters understood that the master-slave relationship was never strictly a domestic affair. From long before the Civil War, the behavior of masters and slaves was subject to scrutiny—even censure—from multiple

---

[18]R. Q. Mallard et al. to Brig. Gen. Hugh W. Mercer, 1 August 1862, in Berlin et al., eds., *Destruction of Slavery*, 795–98. Spelling and punctuation in the quoted passages are as they appear in the original. Mercer forwarded the letter to the Confederate Secretary of war with a recommendation that the Confederate Congress consider appropriate legislation rather than putting the responsibility into the hands of military officers.

external sources. Some of these, such as neighborhood gossip, were informal, and others, such as the actions of church congregations or local and state government officials, were more formal. Perennially reluctant to concede household management to outsiders, slaveholders clearly perceived the circumstances of war as requiring nothing less. But as they puzzled through a solution to deteriorating order, the Liberty County petitioners had to concede a direct relationship between slaves and the government.

The planters reasoned that free white men engaging in treasonous behavior would be dealt with summarily, but "in the case of the Negroes, it would be hard to mete out a similar punishment under similar circumstances, because of their ignorance, pliability, credulity, desire of change, the absence of the political ties of allegiance & the peculiar status of the Race." As planters followed their own logic, they posited that the slaves "constitute a part of the Body politic, *in fact*, and should be made to know their duty" and that running away constituted "rebellion against the power & authority of their owners & the Government under which they live." Yet confining and punishing them "privately by owners or publicly by the Citizens of the County, will not abate the evil; for the disaffected will not thereby be reformed, but will remain a leaven of corruption in the mass & stand ready to make any other attempts that may promise success." Private correspondence also reflected the planters' public position. Charles C. Jones and his son exchanged letters pondering the future of "our entire social system" unless Confederate officials intervened forcefully. The circumstances of war required owners to cede what remained of their authority to military commanders; moreover, they said nothing about compensation to the owners of summarily executed slaves.[19]

Unlike the coastal regions, which experienced the Union presence from fall 1861 onward, inland regions of the state felt the pressure of invading

---

[19]Ibid., 797, punctuation modernized from original. The Jones correspondence is quoted in Peter W. Bardaglio, *Reconstructing the Household: Families, Sex, and the Law in the Nineteenth-Century South* (Chapel Hill: University of North Carolina Press, 1995) 116.

forces less consistently and directly. Indeed, until fall 1863, the entire central and southwestern parts of the state constituted precisely the safe haven that refugeeing planters from as far away as the Mississippi River valley were seeking. Yet in a curious twist, the movement of new people upset those regions as well. Persons coming from the Atlantic coast already experienced the demoralization that the Liberty County planters decried; and those coming from the west brought tales of dramatic advances by federal military and naval forces. Planters in rural districts with sufficient numbers of masters and overseers to maintain strict discipline and with little prospect of invasion might reasonably hope to contain the slaves' desire for radical change. But for masters living in cities, particularly manufacturing centers, or along railroads or navigable rivers, the prospects for conducting business as usual along the antebellum model diminished with each Union victory.

Hired and impressed slave laborers began to understand the new dynamics and exploit the opportunities that they presented. At the ordnance facilities in Macon, for instance, hired men gained the rights to earn additional compensation in the form of overtime payments and to keep gardens. Once having received those concessions, they pressed for even more, specifically the employment of wives and provision of quarters for wives and children. At the beginning of 1863, Captain J. W. Mallet, superintendent of the ammunition laboratory, agreed to permit the children of a slave couple he employed and housed to join their parents without charge provided that the master fed them or the parents shared their rations. The laborers soon drew the officials into the role of third-party advocates on their behalf in dealings with their masters. While far from a new phenomenon, this practice took on new features in wartime. Government officials could always flex their muscles, but the imperatives of home defense conferred additional power, which individual masters defied at the risk of official retribution and censure by patriotic neighbors.[20]

---

[20]Mallet to F. O. Rogers, 11 June 1863, Superintendent of Laboratories Letters Sent, 24:142, Records of the Ordnance Department, War Department Collection of Confederate Records, RG 109, National Archives, Washington DC. See also Joseph P. Reidy, *From Slavery to Agrarian Capitalism in the Cotton Plantation South: Central Georgia, 1800–1880* (Chapel Hill: University of North Carolina Press, 1992) chap. 5;

Depending on their personalities, the strength of their ties to local slaveholders, and the sheer numbers of enslaved workers they required, the superintendents took varying approaches to their work. More often than not, they sought amicable business deals with slaveholders. But as the pressures to produce the goods of war intensified and the ability to mobilize the necessary labor force deteriorated, the superintendents' relationships with hiring masters and their hired slaves took on new aspects. For more than a year, Captain Mallet negotiated with Dr. A. C. Rogers, a prominent planter and physician in Monroe County, over the terms of employment of Rogers's slaves. The slaves pleaded with Mallet to have Rogers furnish them additional clothing; similarly, they informed Rogers that they would run away if Mallet did not reassign them from the swamp where he had stationed them and furnish them with rations of bacon instead of beef.[21] This three-party dynamic upset the traditional balance of power between masters and slaves. With one of the contracting parties a government official, the other a private citizen, and the laborer an enslaved "part of the Body politic," the relationships between the citizen and the state and between the slave and the state took a new turn. Recent studies demonstrate how the legal system mediated the complex interrelations between masters and slaves and among the array of parties with interests of one kind or another in slavery.[22] In the heat of the wartime mobilization, government authorities exerted far greater influence over the master-slave relationship than antebellum jurists ever would have imagined. At the same time, slaves proved adept at changing their loyalties as the circumstances warranted.

Chad Morgan, *Planters' Progress: Modernizing Confederate Georgia* (Gainesville: University of Florida Press, 2005).

[21]See Reidy, *From Slavery to Agrarian Capitalism*, 124–25.

[22]See, for instance, Laura F. Edwards, *The People and Their Peace: Legal Culture and the Transformation of Inequality in the Post-Revolutionary South* (Chapel Hill: University of North Carolina Press, 2009); Ariela Gross, *Double Character: Slavery and Mastery in the Antebellum Southern Courtroom* (Princeton: Princeton University Press, 2000); and Christopher Waldrep, *Roots of Disorder: Race and Criminal Justice in the American South, 1817–80* (Urbana: University of Illinois Press, 1998).

By fall 1863, as Union military successes in Tennessee began to suggest the likelihood of an invasion of Georgia from the north, and as that movement began to materialize in spring 1864, inhabitants of the state became wary of the potential consequences. Newspaper advertisements for runaway slaves that appeared in the *Macon Daily Telegraph* demonstrate the wide-ranging impact of these developments. Henry ran from Americus, where his owner had refugeed from Tennessee. Ed, a carpenter and tanner brought from Savannah in 1861, headed home early in the new year of 1864. Andrew, who had recently been removed from Southwest Georgia to Macon for having attempted to reach the Yankees, was apparently making another try. Although John Sparrow and Nelson did not disguise their intention to flee to the Yankees above Atlanta when they ran in June 1864, the Crawford County native Jim was more circumspect. Having fled the service of an officer in an Alabama regiment, he bore papers permitting him passage to join General John Bell Hood's army.[23]

Even without resorting to flight, enslaved African Americans pushed against the traditional restraints. In August 1864, Julie Pope Stanley described the state of affairs in Clarke County to her husband Marcellus who was absent in the army. Because "there are so few white men in the neighborhood and they do not visit the plantation at all," she reported, "the Negroes do as they please."[24] As General William T. Sherman's forces moved toward Atlanta, authorities again impressed slave laborers to fortify defensive positions. In August 1864, slaves at work in the ordnance establishments in Macon were impressed into service at Atlanta. In a pattern magnified many times over in the midst of this frenzied mobilization, a number of the men made their way to the Yankees, frustrating the aims of Confederate strategists and further complicating the increasingly strained relationship between masters and the Confederate government. Several men left wives and children with

---

[23]See the advertisements in the *Macon Daily Telegraph*: for Henry, 25 November 1863; for Ed, 9 January 1864; for Andrew, 27 May 1864; for John Sparrow and Nelson, 13 June 1864; for Jim, 8 October 1864.
[24]Quoted in Weitz, *A Higher Duty*, 161–62.

the ordnance superintendents, and Captain James H. Burton at the armory continued to house those in his charge.[25]

When Atlanta fell in September 1864, residents of the central part of the state began bracing for the worst. Soon they experienced what an army bent on destroying property could do. Planters with properties in Southwest Georgia or ties to persons so situated packed their families and embarked on the now-familiar journey. Those who could not escape made contingency plans that included hiding valuables and provisions and reinforcing the stereotypical image of Yankees as devils incarnate for the benefit of their slave laborers. In his capacity as planter, Howell Cobb removed the able-bodied slaves from his wife's plantation near Milledgeville; in his capacity as commander of the defenses at Macon, he ordered a draft of 500 slave laborers to work on the fortifications. These tactics fell far short of stopping the ensuing demoralization. Quite simply, even rumors of the approaching Union army further destabilized slaveholding households.[26]

Regardless of their individual understandings of slavery and its place in national politics or of their personal prejudices toward persons of African ancestry, most of Sherman's soldiers believed implicitly that confiscating or destroying plantation property and disrupting agricultural production would help shorten the war, and they pillaged with gusto. The number of slaves who were effectively liberated in these operations numbered in the thousands. But their future was anything but certain. As Sherman's forces neared Milledgeville, the general occupied the plantation that Howell Cobb had recently evacuated, leaving behind, according to one of Sherman's staff officers, "some fifty old men—cripples—and women and children" to fend for themselves. Sherman himself doled out provisions "and assured them that we were their friends," reported the officer. "One old man answered him: 'I spose dat

---

[25]James H. Burton to A. Cobb, 13 December 1864, Macon Armory Letters Sent, 29:172, Records of the Ordnance Department, War Department Collection of Confederate Records, RG 109, National Archives, Washington DC.

[26]Reidy, *From Slavery to Agrarian Capitalism*, 132–33; Mohr, *On the Threshold of Freedom*, 93–95; Joseph Glatthaar, *The March to the Sea and Beyond: Sherman's Troops in the Savannah and Carolina Campaigns* (New York: New York University Press, 1985).

you'se true; but, massa, you'se 'll go way to-morrow, and anudder white man 'll come.'"[27] True and lasting freedom did not necessarily follow the master's departure or the Yankees' arrival.

Those who followed the Union army's march to the sea occupied a similar state of limbo: free from the slave past but now dependent upon men whose first objective was not necessarily securing for the formerly enslaved an independent future. As one of Sherman's corps neared Savannah in December 1864, they encountered the deep and swift-running Ebenezer Creek. The men built a pontoon bridge, crossed safely, and then—reportedly at the orders of the corps commander—destroyed the bridge before the escaped slaves who were following the army could cross, leaving them in a state of panic with raging waters before them and Confederates behind.[28] Yet, even with such a setback, de facto freedpeople made their way to Savannah after Sherman occupied the city, still hopeful that Lincoln's army would act the part and not just wear the costume of liberators and protectors.

Once having achieved the protection of the United States armed forces and government, however, the freedpeople found themselves in a new variant of dependence, which, though fundamentally different from the master-slave relationship, also differed from pre-Civil War relation-ships between the government and either household heads or their dependents. First, the key actors represented the federal government rather than state or local governments, and second, they exercised sweeping authority on matters that were beyond the pale of government action beforehand. The circumstances surrounding General William T. Sherman's famous January 1865 orders establishing a reservation for African-American refugees along the coast of South Carolina and Georgia illustrates the point. Following his arrival in Savannah, the general and US Secretary of War Edwin M. Stanton met with a delegation of leading black ministers from the city. In response to a series of questions, the group's spokesman, the Reverend Garrison

---

[27]George Ward Nichols, *The Story of the Great March: From the Diary of a Staff Officer* (New York: Harper & Brothers, 1866) 58–59.
[28]See Anne J. Bailey, *War and Ruin: Sherman and the Savannah Campaign* (Wilmington DE: Scholarly Resources, 2003) 91–94.

Frazier, explained his understanding that "the freedom…promised by the [Emancipation] proclamation, is taking us from under the yoke of bondage, and placing us where we could reap the fruit of our own labor, take care of ourselves and assist the Government in maintaining our freedom." To the follow-up question of how these objectives might be realized, Frazier replied "to have land, and turn it and till it by our own labor—that is, by the labor of the women and children and old men." By such means, Frazier predicted, "we can soon maintain ourselves and have something to spare"; but their true object was "to be placed on land until we are able to buy it and make it our own." Finally, he envisioned that the young men would "enlist in the service of the Government, and serve in such manner as they may be wanted."[29] Military service would strengthen the soldier's tie to the government, supplanting the master and creating an expectation of freedom—indeed, of citizenship—in exchange for the risk of life. The master-slave relationship of old stood on the brink of dissolution.

Special Field Order No. 15 set aside coastal lands for the exclusive occupation of former slaves and authorized "respectable negroes, heads of families" to establish "peaceable agricultural settlement[s]" consisting of individual homesteads not exceeding "forty acres of tillable ground" each. Recognizing the fragility of these proposed settlements, he placed them under the jurisdiction of a military officer and enjoined his supporting departments to help the settlers achieve success. Emphasizing that these arrangements were provisional and subject to higher approval, Sherman offered "possessory title[s]" to the land pending final disposition by the national government. Following Frazier's lead, he exhorted young men to enlist as soldiers "to contribute their share towards maintaining their own freedom, and securing their rights as citizens of the United States."[30] In a stroke, Sherman undercut the former master's dominion and elevated black male household heads to the place

---

[29]"Negroes in Savannah," *New-York Daily Tribune*, 13 February 1865, reprinted in Ira Berlin et al., eds., *The Wartime Genesis of Free Labor: The Lower South*, ser. 1, vol. 3 of *Freedom: A Documentary History of Emancipation, 1861–1867* (New York: Cambridge University Press, 1982–1993) 331–37, quotation on 334.

[30]Special Field Orders, No. 15, Headquarters Military Division of the Mississippi, 16 January 1865, in Berlin et al., eds., *Wartime Genesis of Free Labor*, 338–40.

formerly occupied by their masters. But he did more. He also elevated them to the status of citizens, thereby further undermining the former master's role as intermediary between his domestic dependents and the apparatus of the state.

In spring 1865, federal authorities placed Tunis G. Campbell, a Northern-born African-American missionary, in charge of land claims on St. Catherine's and several other sea islands in McIntosh County. In addition to the emphasis on self-support, Campbell also worked with the refugees to establish a government for the island, complete with a constitution, a legislature, and a court system. This government projected a level of civic engagement that presaged Radical Reconstruction and the establishment of manhood suffrage in the postwar years.[31] But until the war ended and the destruction of slavery was ratified in the Thirteenth Amendment, the men and women who gained nominal freedom under the Union flag continued to depend deeply on the government for protection.

Despite the success of St. Catherine's, an unintended outcome of Sherman's settlement plan played out during summer and fall 1865. When the planters and the families white and black who had refugeed to other parts of the state during the war returned to their coastal homes, they encountered strangers with Sherman's possessory titles. The planters appealed to President Andrew Johnson for restoration of their property; Johnson freely granted the enabling pardons, and the Freedmen's Bureau undertook the unenviable task of repossessing the possessory titles. In the end, the former slaves who remained with their masters through the turmoil of war returned to their homes but without possession of the land that their labor as slaves had made productive and that General Sherman's orders had promised. Their struggle to get free of their former masters' residual claims to patriarchal authority over their labor and their personal lives, not to mention to assert the rights of citizens, was only beginning.[32]

---

[31]Russell Duncan, *Freedom's Shore: Tunis Campbell and the Georgia Freedmen* (Athens: University of Georgia Press, 1986).

[32]William S. McFeely, *Yankee Stepfather: General O. O. Howard and the Freedmen* (New Haven: Yale University Press, 1968) chap. 7.

The Civil War redrew the lines of dependence and independence in Georgia and other slave states. The terminology of independence and freedom (and their opposites, dependence and slavery) suffused the politics of the Civil War era. What began with a bid for national independence on the part of the Southern states most strongly committed to slavery ended with freedom to the slaves. The original defense of homes and firesides produced a revolution in family relationships, particularly when viewed from the ideological perspective of slavery as a domestic relationship. But even within the households of non-slaveholders—whether yeoman farmers or unskilled workers—the war transformed traditional domestic relationships. When men departed for military service, women had to devise ways to fill the void, taking on both the labor and the decision-making responsibilities of the men. At the end of the war, men and women alike slipped back into their prewar patterns as much as possible. Although some women may have given up their new responsibilities grudgingly—except for the physically demanding chores, that is—most did so with a measure of relief. Widows were unable to avail themselves of such a luxury, and they carried their burdens into the postwar era if not also for the rest of their lives.

The civic accommodation was a different matter, in no small measure thanks to the unprecedented levels of government intervention into domestic life during the war. Of course, African Americans readily availed themselves of the protection that federal authority promised, particularly the officials of the Bureau of Refugees, Freemen and Abandoned Lands, which began operations in Georgia and the other Southern states during spring and summer 1865. Household dependents in white families—chiefly but not exclusively women—saw no reason to cease bringing their business before government officials and, more generally, the court of public opinion, to seek redress. Although these relationships continued to evolve, in some respects changing and in others remaining the same, as a result of the Civil War, the lines of authority and dependence in Southern households would never again look as they had before secession.

Georgia Lowcountry Battlegrounds
during the Civil War

by Jacqueline Jones

In early September 1862, nine pistol-wielding Southerners made their way onto Cumberland Island, off the coast of Georgia, and took control of the plantation owned by Robert Stafford, a wealthy slaveholder. A military report filed soon after the incident offered these details: The invaders—"their conduct being of riotous and threatening character, refusing to submit to any control"—seemed intent on "killing the cattle and overrunning the private dwelling with arms and clubs in their hands." Held hostage in his own home and fearing for his life, Stafford appealed for assistance to a local naval officer stationed in nearby St. Andrew's Sound. In response, a lieutenant-commander dispatched a steamer and armed troops to the island. They quickly overwhelmed the invaders and placed them in irons.[1]

The men who harassed Robert Stafford and killed his cattle left him deeply shaken but unharmed. They were, in the words of W. T. Truxtun, lieutenant-commander of the *USS Alabama*, "a number of strange negroes," some of whom had been enslaved by Stafford and others who were unknown to him. They had been armed by a Union officer in Fernandina, Florida, and then they had apparently traveled to the island with the sole purpose of seizing the plantation and impressing upon its owner his own powerlessness. James H. Stimpson, acting master of the *USS Alabama*, declared the black men "in a state of mutiny," thereby justifying their incarceration. Yet shortly after gaining control of the situation, Truxtun ordered the men released; Stafford had given "up all claim to them," and Truxtun proceeded to place them "on the ship's books as a portion of her crew." The blacks thus joined the more than 400 other fugitive slaves who would eventually serve as seamen on US

---

[1]*Official Records of the Union and Confederate Navies in the War of the Rebellion* (hereinafter *ORN*) 30 vols. (Washington DC: Government Printing Office, 1894–1922) ser. 1, 13:299.

naval vessels patrolling the Georgia coastline during the Civil War. Among these were several with the last name Stafford, hailing from Cumberland Island. In their struggle for freedom in the land of their forebears, black combatants complicated the Southern-Northern dynamic of the conflict; they would fight for the Union, but they would fight on their own terms.[2]

Far from the major military operations that engulfed the Mississippi Valley and the northern reaches of the Confederacy, the lush Georgia lowcountry and Sea Islands proved an unlikely battleground during the first three and a half years of the Civil War. United States military officials had assigned little strategic value to Georgia's 118-mile coastline, a tiny fraction of the Confederacy's total of 3,500 miles. In April 1861, President Lincoln had issued a blockade order in an effort to deprive the rebels of supplies via the sea and the Mississippi River. Within a year, Union forces had captured Fort Pulaski, at the mouth of the Savannah River, considerably diminishing the traffic of blockade-runners up and down the river and its tributaries. Nevertheless, throughout the war, combat troops and guerilla forces bitterly contested lowcountry swampland and marshy terrain, a contest that was ideological and political as well as military.

From spring 1861 onward, officials of the state of Georgia feared that eventually the Savannah River would prove to be the gateway through which Federal naval power and army troops would invade the state and capture the vast cotton-growing region that lay upriver. Yet when the river port of Savannah fell to Federal forces in December 1864, the assault came from the interior of the state, not from the sea. For their part, black people of the Gullah-Geechee culture viewed the lowcountry battleground as a place where black men could win the honor accorded all loyal seamen and soldiers and could demonstrate their prowess as guides, pilots, and spies for the Northern cause. Yet in their determination to fight for freedom and not just for the Union, blacks revealed their own deeply held ideas about the meaning of the war itself.

---

[2]Ibid., 13: 299, 300. See also National Park Service, "The Civil War Sailors Database," http://www.itd.nps.gov/cwss/sailorstrans.htm; Mary R. Bullard, *Cumberland Island: A History* (Athens: University of Georgia Press, 2005) 135, 155.

These ideas diverged from those of Confederates and white Union military officers and civilians. Indeed, the battle over this sliver of coastline constituted a microcosm of the larger conflict and foreshadowed a new stage of that conflict after the cessation of hostilities in 1865.

Ever distrustful of the centralizing policies of Confederate leaders, Georgia's Governor Joseph E. Brown initially sought to deploy the state's soldiers to defend their home turf, the coastline first and foremost. Brown early called to arms the able-bodied white men of Georgia, exhorting them, "We are left to choose between freedom at the end of a desperate and heroic struggle[,] and submission to tyranny, followed by the most abject and degraded slavery to which a patriotic and generous people were ever exposed." In Brown's mind, "tyranny" welled from the Confederate capital of Richmond no less than from Washington DC. By summer 1861, however, officials of the Confederate States of America (CSA) had forced Brown to abandon his effort to prevent Georgia's fighting men from serving under CSA officers elsewhere in the South. Still, Brown maintained at best an uneasy working relationship with a variety of authorities jockeying for control of the state's mobilization efforts—President Jefferson Davis and the members of his cabinet, army and navy officers in the lowcountry, and Savannah municipal officials. Together these authorities reached a rough consensus about their priorities: early in the war, expedite the blockade runners that could deliver necessary military supplies; then later in the war, obstruct the Savannah River and prevent the incursion of Federal forces up the state's waterways. Lowcountry Confederates both military and civilian also aimed to safeguard the estimated 35,000 slaves (out of a total population of 60,000 blacks and whites) living on the coast and the islands. Forced to grow food and build fortifications, these bond men and women formed the backbone of the Southern mobilization effort. More to the point, slaves constituted the bulk of the wealth of the Confederate elite and embodied the principle upon which that elite had spearheaded secession—the right to hold people as property.[3]

---

[3]Allen D. Candler, ed., *State Papers of Governor Joseph E. Brown Relating to the Public Defense, the Organization and Equipment of Troops, Provision for the Family of*

Union generals and naval officials identified a diverse and expansive set of goals: seal the coastline against blockade runners; establish provisioning bases for their own forces; soften up the batteries lining the Savannah River and its tributaries; plug up the creeks and waterways that made the lowcountry a sieve for traffickers of all kinds; and appropriate foodstuffs, raw materials, and other resources useful to the war effort. Beginning in 1863, Union officers facilitated US treasury agents' efforts to seize cotton stockpiled on Sea Island and coastal plantations. Nevertheless, Union officers were not wholly united in either their objectives or their tactics, disagreeing among themselves about a host of issues, including the destruction of the enemy's private property, the employment of black people eager to contribute to the Union cause, and the timing of emancipation of the local enslaved population. The Union campaign to control the Georgia coastline also spurred a rivalry between navy and army forces. In March 1862, Flag-Officer (later Rear Admiral) Samuel Francis DuPont embraced his mission, with the official mandate that "the naval power that controls the seacoast of Georgia controls the State of Georgia," and he remained a rival of his land-based counterparts. In this impulse, he received encouragement from the assistant secretary of the navy, Gustavus V. Fox, who told DuPont in June 1862, "The crowning act of this war ought to be by the Navy.... I feel that my duties are two-fold; first, to beat our southern friends; and second, to beat the Army."[4]

Slaves and free people of color blurred the line between civilian and combatant. Black seamen and soldiers volunteered as early as spring 1862; they were among the first black servicemen for the Union. Yet as fugitives, black men and women transformed the whole region into a

---

Soldiers, etc., 1860 to 1865, vol. 2 of *The Confederate Records of the State of Georgia* (Atlanta: Chas. P. Byrd, 1909) 199. On Brown's states' rights views, see Candler, ed., *Official Correspondence of Governor Joseph E. Brown, 1860–1865,* vol. 3 of *The Confederate Records of the State of Georgia* (Atlanta: Chas. P. Byrd, 1910) 35–90; Joseph H. Parks, *Joseph E. Brown of Georgia* (Baton Rouge: Louisiana State University Press, 1977) 110–28.

[4]*ORN,* ser. 1, 12:575; *Samuel Francis DuPont: A Selection from His Civil War Letters,* Vol. Two: *The Blockade: 1862–1863* (Ithaca NY: Cornell University Press, 1969) 96.

staging ground for freedom-fighters. Self-sufficient colonies offered shelter for refugees, opportunities for former slaves to make money by supplying Union gunboats, and proof of black people's determination to live independently of whites of all kinds. Through their words and actions, black men and women also expressed the rage—and outrage—borne of generations of slavery, expressions that did not always comport with the standards of warfare shared by Confederate and Union officers alike. Lowcountry battlelines remained fluid, ever shifting with time, as more and more blacks seized their own freedom and in the process transformed the nature of the conflict. Reacting to these transformations, whites found themselves compelled to reconsider their own ideas about what they called the black "race." While some Union officers confronted and adjusted their own prejudices, others remained steadfast in preconceptions that had little to do with reality. Most dramatically, planters along the coast began to relinquish the generations-long ideology that held that black people were childlike, naturally dependent on and grateful to white people. In 1862, a group of Liberty County slaveholders stated the matter forthrightly—"that the Negroes, constitute a part of the Body politic, *in fact*; and should be made to know their duty; that they are perfectly aware that the Act which they commit is one of rebellion." That roiling and contentious lowcountry body politic, as defined over the course of the war and variously by Confederates, Union military officers, and slaves-becoming-freedpeople, is the subject of this essay.[5]

White Southerners and Northerners alike understood that they occupied alien territory along the Georgia coast. The sprawling cotton plantations on the Sea Islands and the rice plantations that lined the Savannah and Altamaha Rivers near the coast were among the most profitable of antebellum Southern staple-crop estates. Large slave holdings, combined with absentee owners, produced a region best described as the heart of Africa America, where West African folk traditions shaped the everyday lives of enslaved men, women, and children. (Here the Georgia

---

[5]Ira Berlin, Barbara J. Fields, Thavolia Glymph, Joseph P. Reidy, and Leslie S. Rowland, eds., *Freedom: A Documentary History of Emancipation, 1861–1867*, ser. 1, vol. 1, *The Destruction of Slavery* (Cambridge: Cambridge University Press, 1985) 797.

lowcountry is defined as the Sea Islands and the coastal counties of Chatham, Bryan, Liberty, McIntosh, Glynn, and Camden.) Rice planters relied on the forced labor of black workers to construct and maintain a complicated hydraulic system of rice cultivation: workers flooded the springtime fields with fresh water pushed upriver by the tides and onto the fields through canals and culverts. Planters organized their laborers according to the task system, which provided that, after slaves completed their assigned work in the field, they could devote the rest of the day to activities that benefited themselves and their families, such as tending gardens or keeping chickens, hogs, or bees. In fact, though, task labor amounted to a double burden imposed on men and women who were forced to grow their food as well as toil in the muck of the rice fields. One former enslaved rice hand named John Brown recalled the "awful work" carried out in foul-smelling, wet fields that were bitterly cold in winter and sweltering in summer. Sunstroke and insect and snake bites made planting, hoeing, and harvesting rice a physically dangerous ordeal. This heavy work performed by women, combined with waterborne illnesses produced by polluted water, caused horrific rates of child mortality on lowcountry rice plantations: on some holdings only one out of ten children lived to see their first birthday.[6]

For generations whites had told themselves that only people of African descent could live and labor in the area year-round; though contradicted by high mortality rates in the rice fields, the conventional

---

[6] *Slave Life in Georgia: A Narrative of the Life, Sufferings, and Escape of John Brown, a Fugitive Slave, Now in England,* ed. L. A. Chamerovzow, 2nd ed. (Freeport NY: Books for Libraries, 1971) 186–87. On lowcountry rice culture see also *Life and Labor on Argyle Island: Letters and Documents of a Savannah River Plantation, 1835–1867,* ed. James M. Clifton (Savannah: Beehive Press, 1978); Leslie A. Schwalm, *A Hard Fight for We: Women's Transition from Slavery to Freedom in South Carolina* (Urbana: University of Illinois Press, 1997); and Mart A. Stewart, *"What Nature Suffers to Groe": Life, Labor and Landscape on the Georgia Coast, 1680–1920* (Athens: University of Georgia Press, 2002). On high mortality rates and the particular productive and reproductive burdens of women rice hands, see Leigh Ann Pruneau, "All the Time Is Work Time: Gender and the Task System on Antebellum Lowcountry Rice Plantations" (Ph.D. diss., University of Arizona, 1997); William Dusinberre, "Them Dark Days: Slavery in the American Rice Swamps" (Athens: University of Georgia Press, 2000); and Marie Jenkins Schwartz, *Birthing a Slave: Motherhood and Medicine in the Antebellum South* (Cambridge: Harvard University Press, 2006) 129–30.

view was that blacks could survive the heat of the summer and the onslaught of mysterious fevers and maladies. The noted Savannah physician Richard D. Arnold wrote of "how utterly impossible it is for the white Race to do the outdoor work in this hot climate." Nevertheless, the reality was complicated. In the rice fields, enslaved workers of all ages succumbed in large numbers to gastrointestinal and respiratory diseases, but in general they maintained a relative (compared to whites) immunity to yellow fever and malaria, mosquito-borne illnesses. During the summer, many lowcountry planters sought cooler climes, either in the North or in upcountry Georgia. These whites remained indifferent to the plight of their enslaved labor forces. In the late 1850s some lowcountry planters and politicians called for a reopening of the African slave trade, to replace the chronically diminishing black population. Ignorant of the ways that bacteria and insects caused disease, whites knew only that lowcountry deadly fevers carried away many of their own community each year.[7]

A number of elite men expressed confidence early in the war that the lowcountry's climate and attendant dangers would work to the advantage of the South. A rice planter, Louis Manigault, believed that "no Yankee dare put his foot" in the region. Theodorick W. Montfort, an attorney, predicted that "Providence, sand flies, musquitoes & sickness" constituted the Confederacy's most effective weapon in repelling the Northern invaders. Yet Southern white men of varying ranks had little choice but to accept assignments along the coast and on the islands—this despite the fact that, in the words of a young officer, the Savannah attorney George Mercer, these were places of "low swampy fields, where the insects are terrible[,] the air close and fetid and full of miasma and death," where white men languished "in the rain & dew, [with] bad water to drink, amidst poisonous airs & rank weeds." For the majority of ordinary soldiers, the lowcountry was indeed a site of extreme discomfort, as they consumed unpalatable food and dirty water and

---

[7]Richard H. Shryock, *Letters of Richard D. Arnold, M.D., 1808–1876*, Papers of the Trinity College Historical Society, Double ser. 18–19 (Durham NC: Seeman Press, 1929) 71; Lillian Foster, *Wayside Glimpses, North and South* (New York: Rudd and Carleton, 1860) 105.

suffered from epidemics that swept through encampments and long hot days of inaction and boredom. In contrast, wealthy officers brought with them to riverbank batteries and Fort Pulaski enslaved men who served as personal cooks and valets; these officers received bundles of food and baskets of fresh laundry from loved ones living nearby, and they regularly slipped back into Savannah for a dinner party or a bath and a good night's sleep. Most Southern soldiers however could not shake the conviction that their occupation of the coast was unnatural to the degree that it defied the logic of slaveowners' ideology justifying the enslavement of large numbers of people of African descent in the lowcountry killing fields.[8]

Unencumbered by preconceptions of the coast and its supposed inhospitability to whites, Union officers and soldiers found the locale exotic, a veritable tropical paradise, especially in the winter, when roses bloomed and warm, soft breezes swept across the flat land and seascape. Nevertheless, the physical beauty of the area could not compensate for its many natural impediments to the successful prosecution of Federal war aims. Especially challenging for seamen was the navigation of narrow, winding, unmapped rivers and streams—waterways large and small clogged with submerged tree limbs, mud flats, man-made obstructions— all overrun by unpredictable tides and currents. Seeking to erect batteries on the Sea Islands and on the banks of inland creeks and rivers, Union engineers found "soft, unctuous mud, free of grit or sand, and incapable of supporting a heavy weight," rendering it difficult if not impossible to position cannon. Fatigue workers were forced to enclose their feet in sandbags to keep from sinking into the soft soil. Here then was a

---

[8] *Life and Labor on Argyle Island*, 327; Spencer B. King, "Rebel Lawyer: The Letters of Lt. Theodorick W. Montfort, 1861–1863," *Georgia Historical Quarterly* 49/2 (June 1965): 214; "Diary of George A. Mercer," p. 41 (23 June 1862), p. 45 (9 August 1862) Georgia Historical Society, Savannah GA. See also Mrs. E. F. Neufille in Susan M. Kollock, ed., "Letters of the Kollock and Allied Families, 1826–1884" (pt. 4), *Georgia Historical Quarterly* 34/3 (September 1950): 243; *The Children of Pride: A True Story of Georgia and the Civil War*, ed. Robert Manson Myers (New Haven CT: Yale University Press, 1972) 1096. For the perspective of foot soldiers, see W. H. Andrews, *Footprints of a Regiment: Recollections of the 1st Georgia Regulars, 1861–1865* (Atlanta: Longstreet Press, 1992) 9–10.

landscape that would prove a formidable barrier to the effective deployment of men and matériel.[9]

For the Gullah-Geechee, the lowcountry was neither a profitable machine for producing rice and cotton nor a hindrance to immediate war aims; rather, the coast was a sacred landscape that evoked their West African ancestral homelands and nourished a distinctive culture that shaped patterns of work, family life, and religious faith. As one black leader, James M. Simms, put it, enslaved men and women of the lowcountry claimed special "Relations for the Lands.... Their Fathers and Mothers cleared these Swamps and Marshes, and made them the Fruitful Rice Fields they are." Many blacks came to know intimately the waterways that laced the region; creeks, cuts, rivers, bays, marshlands, and isolated hammocks provided refuge for fugitives and also sustenance for persons skilled in fishing and trapping. Each plantation in the region depended upon boatmen and pilots to transport flatboats of rice to Savannah's port and skiffs and to ferry white people from one place to the other. In their knowledge of native flora and fauna and in their mastery of land and waterways, enslaved laborers possessed a command of lowcountry geography and resources and thereby directly shaped the course of the war.[10]

Patterns of trade and culture linked the river port of Savannah to the coastal region. Many wealthy planters kept a residence in the city, and elites there made their living by transporting and marketing the loads of rice, cotton, and lumber that came in from the countryside. Certain values and self-interests also linked black cotton and rice hands to black

---

[9]*Blue-Eyed Child of Fortune: The Civil War Letters of Colonel Robert Gould Shaw*, ed. Russell Duncan (Athens: University of Georgia Press, 1992) 341; US War Department, comp., *The War of the Rebellion: A Compilation of the Official Records of the Union and Confederate Armies*, 128 vols. (Washington, DC: Government Printing Office, 1880–1901) ser. 1, 14:321 (hereafter cited as *OR*).

[10]James M. Simms to O. O. Howard, Savannah GA, 3 February 1865, Washington Headquarters, Records of the Commissioner, ser. 15, Letters Received, S-97 1865, Freedmen and Southern Society Project A-5161, University of Maryland. See also Stewart, *"What Nature Suffers to Groe"*; William S. Pollitzer, *The Gullah People and Their African Heritage* (Athens: University of Georgia Press, 1999); Margaret Creel, *"A Peculiar People": Slave Religion and Community-Culture among the Gullahs* (New York: New York University Press, 1988).

urban workers, enslaved and free; throughout the lowcountry, black men and women demonstrated an entrepreneurial spirit that favored money-making through the production and marketing of goods and services. On plantations, the task system allowed many rice workers to raise chickens and vegetables for sale to their owners or to customers in Savannah's market. In the city, skilled slaves were able to hire out their own time as teamsters, carpenters, butchers, and bricklayers (for example), in the process demonstrating that the profit-seeking impulse was not the exclusive purview of white men. This impulse among slaves and freedpeople would also affect the war effort in surprising ways.[11]

Though fighting a defensive war, the Confederacy early recognized the demographic limitations of its manpower mobilization efforts. In 1860, in contrast to the North's population of 22 million people (a number growing by virtue of foreign immigration), the South could claim only 6 million whites, 3.5 million slaves, and less than half a million free people of color. Within a year of the start of the conflict, CSA officials sought to institute a military draft, the first on North American soil, to ensure a force of 500,000 fighting men, a number that amounted to 5 percent of the whole population, black and white. Even before that time a debate had erupted among Southern slaveholders and Confederate officials alike over the proper use of the millions of enslaved workers under their control. Some whites even suggested that black men be armed and readied for combat. In May 1861, John J. Cheatham, of Athens, Georgia, advocated incorporating a few black fighting men into each company: "In this way there [sic] number would be too small to do our army any injury, whilst they might be made quite efficient in battle, as there are a great many I have no doubt that they would make good soldiers and would willingly go if they had a chance." In August of that year, a Charleston slaveowner went further and suggested not only that the army use enslaved men as soldiers ("as the *Greeks, Spartans*, and

---

[11]Jacqueline Jones, *Saving Savannah: The City and the Civil War* (New York: A. A. Knopf, 2008); Dylan C. Penningroth, *The Claims of Kinfolk: African American Property and Community in the Nineteenth-Century South* (Chapel Hill: University of North Carolina Press, 2003); Philip D. Morgan, "The Ownership of Property by Slaves in the Mid-Nineteenth Century Low Country," *Journal of Southern History* 49/3 (August 1983): 399–420.

Romans did") but also as cooks, launderers, military police teamsters, and sentries—this in addition to laborers in the fields, growing food, and in factories, producing supplies for the would-be new nation.[12]

Nevertheless, initially Confederate political and military leaders rejected proposals to arm the slaves and instead concentrated on impressing blacks for service and on urging their owners to volunteer them for the cause. Southern officials called upon planters in the lowcountry and its environs to provide able-bodied enslaved men and women to erect fortifications in and around Savannah and otherwise free up white men for fighting. The strenuous efforts of General Hugh W. Mercer, Commander of the Third Division of the Confederate District of Georgia, to meet quotas of impressed black laborers provoked angry responses from the region's planters, men who recognized the irony of the CSA confiscating and otherwise depriving slaveholders of their property. Fumed Joseph M. White of Laurens Hill in September 1862, "A government that does not protect its subjects in the enjoyment of their property, so far as lies in its power, is not the kind of government to command respect, or encourage the feelings of patriotism." Whites and planters all over the South offered a litany of complaints over the baneful effects of the impressment scheme, charging (correctly) that large numbers of slaves died in Confederate hands. Many enslaved workers who did survive and return to the plantation were ill or injured, and prone to inducing their friends and family members to flee at the first opportunity. Some observers even began to charge that planters more willingly gave up their sons than their slaves for the cause of Confederate nationhood. CSA military officials in particular claimed that they wasted much precious time and energy addressing the complaints of planters determined to resist "press agents" at all costs, and others justifiably worried about the health of their impressed enslaved workers, and angry about the unfairness of the system in general. The Reverend Robert Q. Mallard, a Presbyterian minister in Liberty County, noted the irony that "planters,

---

[12]*OR*, ser. 4, 2: 132; Ira Berlin, Barbara J. Fields, Steven F. Miller, Joseph P. Reidy, and Leslie S. Rowland, eds., *Free at Last: A Documentary History of Slavery, Freedom, and the Civil War* (New York: New Press, 1992) 5; Berlin, et al., eds., *The Destruction of Slavery*, 695.

who cheerfully surrendered their sons to the army, protested against the use of their slaves in the trenches!"[13]

Southern military officials early settled on the idea that they should use impressed blacks in fairly narrow capacities—as fatigue workers, factory operatives, teamsters, and cooks. In contrast, over the course of the war their Northern counterparts took a broader view and welcomed black contributions to the war effort in myriad ways. Union efforts to recruit black men as soldiers originated in the lowcountry. By spring 1862, Federal forces had gained control of the entire Georgia coastline, and in May General David Hunter, commander of the Department of the South, made a startling announcement when he declared that that black people "heretofore held as slaves, are therefore declared forever free." This announcement turned out to be premature, for his fellow officers expressed alarm at this radical move, and President Abraham Lincoln rescinded it a few days later. Nevertheless, Hunter set about forcibly rounding up black men for service. His harsh "recruiting" tactics, his insistence that men so enlisted wear bright red uniforms in contrast to the blue ones worn by their white counterparts ("The rebels see us, miles away"), and his failure to pay black troops provoked anger and resentment among black men and women alike.[14]

In contrast, US naval officers eschewed such strong-armed tactics, instead welcoming volunteers from throughout the lowcountry—even those like the attackers of the Stafford plantation, who appeared resistant to military discipline. These black men hailed from every coastal county and all of the Sea Islands and represented a wide range of occupations, including waiters, cooks, coal heavers, millers, stewards, and laborers, as

---

[13]Berlin, et al., eds., *The Destruction of Slavery*, 700; Robert Q. Mallard, *Plantation Life before Emancipation* (Richmond: Whittet and Shepperson, 1892) 45; *OR,* ser. 1, vol. 14, pp. 869, 902; Jones, *Saving Savannah*, 158, 59; Clarence Mohr, *On the Threshold of Freedom: Masters and Slaves in Civil War Georgia* (Athens: University of Georgia Press, 1986); Bruce Levine, *Confederate Emancipation: Southern Plans to Free and Arm Slaves during the Civil War* (New York: Oxford University Press, 2007).

[14]Ira Berlin, Thavolia Glymph, Steven F. Miller, Joseph P. Reidy, Leslie S. Rowland, and Julie Saville, eds., *Freedom: A Documentary History of Emancipation, 1861–1867*, ser. 1, vol. 3: *The Wartime Genesis of Free Labor: The Lower South* (Cambridge: Cambridge University Press, 1990) 190; Susie King Taylor, *Reminiscences of My Life in Camp*, ed. Catherine Clinton (Athens: University of Georgia Press, 2006) 40.

well as seamen. The names on muster records suggest that they had absconded from some of the most prominent planters in the region— Spaulding, Cooper, King, Middleton, and Scarlet, as well as Stafford— and that these former slaves ran away and volunteered for naval service in kin groups with their fathers, sons, and brothers. Cyrus Parkman, born in Savannah and twenty-seven years old when he joined the navy, listed his slave occupation as laborer; between 1862 and 1864, he served on a series of Union vessels, including *Somerset, Rhode Island, Powhatan*, and *Ethan Allen*. Alexander Parland, born in Brunswick and age twenty-five when he volunteered, joined the *Gem of the Sea* in September 1862, but reenlisted on the *Norwich* ten different times between then and spring 1865.[15]

In summer 1862, a group of Liberty County planters petitioned the Confederate commanding officer of the region and raised an alarm over the "threat of an Army of trained Africans for the coming fall and winter's campaigns." These planters were eyewitnesses to startling developments along the Georgia coast and fearful of the revolutionary potential of the estimated 20,000 fugitive slaves who had fled their owners' coastal and interior plantations and gravitated toward the lowcountry, seeking work, refuge, and military service behind enemy lines. Though still unofficial, Union efforts to recruit black men as soldiers and seamen had introduced a new and, to local whites, wholly menacing element into the contest for the lowcountry. Yet the Liberty County petitioners also elaborated on other explicit ways that the fugitives furthered the Union effort:

> The absconding Negroes hold the position of Traitors, since they go over to the enemy & afford him aid & comfort, by revealing the condition of the districts and cities from which they come, & aiding him in erecting fortifications & raising provisions for his support: and now that the United States have allowed their introduction into their Army & Navy, aiding the enemy by enlisting under his branners [sic] & increasing his resources in men, for our annoyance & destruction. Negroes occupy the position of Spies also, since they are employed in

---

[15]Dorothy Elwood, comp., "Black Georgia-Born Sailors in the Union Navy," http://ftp.rootsweb.com/pub/usgenweb/ga/military/civilwar/sailors[1–3].txt.

secret expeditions for obtaining information, by transmission of newspapers & by other modes; and act as guides to expeditions on the land & as pilots to their vessels on the waters of our inlets and rivers.

The petitioners estimated that "the absconding Negroes" represented $12–15 million in lost property to their owners; moreover, among the costs borne by planters was "the demoralization of the negroes that remain, which increases the continuance of the evil & may finally result in perfect disorganization and rebellion." The petition, addressed to General Hugh Mercer and signed by three planters, including the Reverend Mallard, ended with a call for officers in the surrounding area to execute fugitives summarily, thus depriving the enemy of their services and rendering them (or their corpses) a warning to other would-be black "Traitors." Mercer acknowledged that the situation was dire and that "the evil & danger alluded to may grow into frightful proportions, unless checked." Still, he was unwilling to authorize the whole destruction of slaveowners' property (i.e., the killing of large numbers of their slaves): "the responsibility of life & death, so liable to be abused, is obviously too great to be entrusted to the hands of every officer, whose duties may bring him face to face with this question."[16]

The direct involvement of black people in the Union war effort did indeed "grow into frightful proportions." Fugitive slaves, sometimes identified in official military reports by name (Peter McIntosh and Louis Napoleon among them, but usually referred to as "contraband"), provided a wealth of information useful to the US army and navy alike. Some men pinpointed the location of docks, batteries, and vessels, while others gave firsthand accounts of skirmishes. Because many had worked on fortifications and on shipbuilding projects in the vicinity of Savannah, and others had worked as crewmembers of Confederate vessels, they were able to provide detailed information about the size and movement of Southern forces, their location, and the extent of their resources. This assistance was not proffered blindly to Northerners. One black man volunteered as a guide only after he heard the news of the Emancipation

---

[16]Berlin et al., *Destruction of Slavery*, 795–98.

Proclamation, in January 1863; then he offered the Federals "hearty aid."[17]

Military officers singled out black soldiers for special praise, citing, in the words of Brigadier General Rufus Saxton, "the greater facility with which they can effect landings through the marshes and thick woods which line the banks of the streams." DuPont described the pilot William "who knew every foot of the river as he does all the inland waters," a man "of the most intelligent and excellent character." Black men won praise from their superiors for navigating winding streams and rivers bordered at times by Confederate sharpshooters. Black men instructed Union seamen on ways to broaden and deepen muddy inland channels and delivered to Union lines boats that belonged either to their masters or themselves.[18]

Former slaves such as Isaac Tatnall combined the roles of scout, spy, and pilot. In December 1861, Tatnall informed DuPont that in Savannah, support for the Confederacy was already eroding among German and Irish immigrants. (A few days earlier, William Barr, age twenty-two, a native of Ireland and formerly of Philadelphia, had deserted from Fort Pulaski and made his way to Union lines, where he too struck Federal officials as "particularly intelligent and anxious to be useful": he provided estimates of CSA troop strength in and around Savannah.) Tatnall, put to work as a pilot for the CSA's *St. Marys* navigating the Georgia coastline, was, according to Union officials, "thoroughly acquainted" with local batteries and waterways, a pilot who could be "perfectly relied upon" to guide gunboats through the obstructions and narrow channels of the Savannah River. Tatnall and other black pilots had proved instrumental in helping the Federals plan and execute the capture of Fort Pulaski.[19]

---

[17]Bullard, *Cumberland Island*, 155; *ORN*, ser. 1, 15:469; *OR*, ser. 1,14: 197.

[18]*OR*, ser. 1, 14: 190; Bullard, *Cumberland Island*, 154; Samuel F. DuPont, *A Selection from His Civil War Letters*, ed. John D. Hayes, 3 vols. (Ithaca NY: Cornell University Press, 1969) 1:306; Thomas Wentworth Higginson, *Army Life in a Black Regiment* (1870; rpt., New York: Collier Books, 1962) 95; *OR*, ser. 1, 14: 323.

[19]*ORN*, ser. 1, 12:432; *ORN*, 12:432–33; *OR*, ser. 1, 14: 324–25; DuPont, *Civil War Letters*, 1:306; *ORN*, scr. 1, 12:487. The 1860 Federal manuscript census for Georgia,

Within the context of armed conflict, news of a group of black men and women peacefully tilling the soil could strike fear in the hearts of lowcountry planters; such was the case when black refugees and fugitives established a colony on St. Simons Island in summer 1862. Union officials encouraged the effort; wrote Commander S. W. Godon (aboard the *Mohican* in St. Simons Sound) to his superior Flag-Officer DuPont, "such a colony, properly managed, would do much good." And indeed the colonists set about growing corn and other vegetables and marketing foodstuffs and their own services to seamen in the area. (Noted DuPont of the "contrabands": they "work for us in many ways and are very useful, and we pay them ten dollars a month and a ration.") A list of "tariff of prices" charged to customers reveals black people *qua* provisioners for the Union navy and entrepreneurs in their own right. The tariff also suggests the eagerness among former slaves to put a specific price on goods and services they had had provided their masters free of cost and under duress. Among the foodstuffs they sold were milk (4 cents a quart), corn (5 cents per dozen), terrapins (10 cents each), watermelons (10–15 cents each), chicken eggs (12 cents a dozen), turtle eggs (5 cents per dozen), as well as okra, beans, whortleberries, cantaloupes, and squash. The St. Simons colonists also raised chickens, caught rabbits, and fished for shrimp and fish, all of which they marketed to seamen. Black laundresses charged 50 cents per dozen articles of clothing ("when soap and starch furnished"). By midsummer the colony consisted of 600 men, women, and children.[20]

At the same time, the significance of St. Simons went beyond the obvious mutual advantage to both parties, buyers and sellers of goods and services. The colonists chose a leader from among themselves, Charles O'Neal; he was later killed in a skirmish with rebels on the island. In their attempts to establish a self-sufficient settlement, the colonists also reunited family members separated during slavery and the war. Union chaplain Mansfield French solemnized long-standing

Chatham County, Savannah (p. 288) lists a William Bar, age twenty-two, a laborer and native of Clare, Ireland, boarding with an Irish-born grocer and his family.

   [20]*ORN*, ser. 1, 12:634; George Alexander Heard, "St. Simons Island during the War between the States," *Georgia Historical Quarterly* 22/3 (September 1938): 249–72; DuPont, *Civil War Letters*, 1:336.

relationships as legal marriages and presided over baptism ceremonies that included not only nuclear families but also "children presented by relatives or strangers, the parents being sold." Susie Baker, a literate fourteen-year-old refugee from Savannah, started a school on the island: "I had about forty children to teach, besides a number of adults who came to me nights, all of them so eager to learn to read, to read above anything else." French made periodic appearances in the school to lecture the pupils on "Boston and the North," among other subjects.[21]

Yet the industriousness of the colonists did not always mesh with Federal officials' notions of black people's labor. The former slaves desired to control their own productive energies; they resisted orders from white men, and they concentrated their efforts on subsistence activities and not on cultivating staple crops such as cotton. DuPont acknowledged the blacks' "great dislike to do the work they have been accustomed to—that seems to make their condition the same as before. They will sit up all night and fish and catch crabs and go and catch horses and wild cattle and cross to the mainland on sculls and go and get corn and so on"; but they sought to free themselves of the enforced pace of fieldwork. This impulse—toward self-direction and away from slavery—foreshadowed the development of freedpeople's settlements along the coast after the war.[22]

In November 1862, General Rufus Saxton began forming the 1st South Carolina Volunteers under the command of Captain Charles T. Trowbridge. The 1st South Carolina was made up primarily of fugitive slaves from the coastal regions of South Carolina, Georgia, and Florida. Attached to the regiment was Colonel Thomas Wentworth Higginson, a Unitarian minister and prominent New England abolitionist. The famous Massachusetts 54th arrived in Beaufort in June 1863 commanded by Robert Gould Shaw, scion of a distinguished Boston family. Colonel James Montgomery, who had joined with the abolitionist John Brown in vigilante attacks on Kansas slaveowners before the war, also raised troops in the South Carolina and Georgia lowcountry and Sea Islands. By

---

[21]Taylor, *Reminiscences of My Life in Camp*, 11; Mansfield quoted in Mohr, *On the Threshold of Freedom*, 82–83.

[22]*DuPont Letters*, 2:71; *ORN*, ser. 1, 13:145.

June, the US Department of the South consisted of the 1st South
Carolina, which included remnants of General Hunter's regiment
assembled the year before; the 2nd South Carolina Volunteers under
Montgomery; and the 54th Massachusetts under Shaw.[23]

The arming of black troops held deep symbolic value for all parties.
Northern and Southern white men believed that soldiering was an affair
of honor and that the discipline and composure necessary under fire were
traits shared only by men who were free. Casting off the rags of slavery
and donning the blue uniforms of US soldiers, black men embraced the
opportunity to fight for freedom, their own and that of their families.
Writing in February 1863, Higginson acknowledged that the deployment
of troops familiar with the landscape and committed to the war effort in
deeply personal terms carried with it significant tactical advantages:
"Their superiority lies simply in the fact that they know the country,
while white troops do not, and moreover, that they have peculiarities of
temperament, position, and motive which belong to them alone. Instead
of leaving their homes and families to fight they are fighting for their
homes and families, and they show the resolution and the sagacity which
a personal purpose gives." Along the coast, white Southerners, military
and civilian, reacted with a mixture of fear and indignation to the news
that Union forces were now recruiting black troops in earnest. Official
Confederate policy held that black men in uniform should receive no
recognition as formal combatants, and that black soldiers captured in
battle be executed summarily and not taken as prisoners of war.[24]

Throughout spring and summer 1863, black troops made numerous
forays up the St. Marys and other coastal rivers in a concerted effort to
break up rebel pickets and harass their batteries; to capture corn, rice,

---

[23]Keith Wilson, "In the Shadow of John Brown: The Military Service of Colonels
Thomas Higginson, James Montgomery, and Robert Shaw in the Department in the
South," in *Black Soldiers in Blue: African American Troops in the Civil War Era*, ed.
John David Smith (Chapel Hill: University of North Carolina Press, 2002) 306–35; Ira
Berlin, Joseph P. Reidy, and Leslie Rowland, eds., *Freedom: A Documentary History of
Emancipation, 1861–1867*, ser. 2, *The Black Military Experience* (Cambridge:
Cambridge University Press, 1990) 40, 55, 57–60, 86, 366, 403, 406, 495, 518–19, 522–
27, 535–37.
[24]*OR*, ser. 1, 14: 198.

sheep cattle, rosin, turpentine, cotton, bricks, railroad iron, lumber, circular saws and belting from sawmills; and to destroy saltworks and "other things that might be of use to the enemy." The soldiers relished capturing ill-gotten gain from slaveowners and showed courage under fire that amazed their white officers. One officer wrote after a foraging mission up the Sapelo river, "The colored men fought with astonishing coolness and bravery.... They behaved bravely, gloriously, and deserve all praise." According to Higginson, "It would have been madness to attempt, with the bravest white troops what I have successfully accomplished, with black ones."[25]

For all the death and mayhem wrought by the war, Confederate and Union military officers (many of whom had attended West Point together) generally agreed on the rules of engagement: that soldiers should meet each other on the battlefield and refrain from attacking civilians or destroying private property. As we have seen, General Mercer was reluctant to authorize the wholesale execution of fugitive slaves; such a move would no doubt have incurred the wrath of lowcountry planters for whom bondage was a source of both wealth and principle. Throughout the early part of the conflict the Lincoln administration held out hope that slaveowners loyal to the Union would deny their support to the Confederacy; that strategic goal, combined with the Republicans' veneration of private property, led some US military officials to return runaways to their masters, and others to inquire politely about the loyalty of owners before "confiscating" their property, including human "contraband of war." Flag-Officer DuPont initially at least forbade his troops from seizing the furniture and other valuables of lowcountry elites, laying "great stress on the proper treatment of the people on shore and to express my abhorrence of plundering and depredations of all kinds, how they sullied all victories, etc." He condemned the robbing of planters and also the robbing of black people who had accumulated livestock and modest household stores; but he also favored respecting all kinds of possessions (including human) of loyal slaveowners. DuPont associated a disrespect for private property with a lack of military discipline generally; of the white seamen who used a fine

---

[25]OR, ser. 1, 14: 191, 192, 198.

piano for target practice, he wrote: "I can't tell you the disgust I feel for our soldiers—there is a moral degradation about them that haunts me." In any case, it was not unusual at different points in the war for naval officers to inform the peaceable white citizens of the lowcountry that they would remain safe in their persons and their property.[26]

And so it was with horror that Robert Gould Shaw witnessed the burning of Darien by his own troops in June 1863. The order to torch the city came from James Montgomery. Shaw condemned "this barbarous sort of warfare" on Montgomery's part and feared that such wanton destruction would reflect poorly on black troops, now being tested on the field of battle for the first time. In contrast, Montgomery refused to play by the conventional rules mandating respect for the property of civilians. As a young fighter he had completed a formative, if vicious, apprenticeship under the violent abolitionist John Brown, who paid his protégé the ultimate compliment: "He [Montgomery] understands my system of warfare exactly. He is a natural chieftain, and knows how to lead." Montgomery explained his decision to destroy most of the small town of Darien, by then deserted, by remarking cooly, "Southerners must be made to feel that this was a real war, and that they were to be swept away by the hand of God, like the Jews of old." Both Higginson and Shaw were alternately fascinated and repelled by their seemingly wanton colleague; Shaw in particular admired his self-discipline—he neither smoke nor drank—but remarked that "he burns & destroys wherever he goes with great gusto, & looks as if he had quite a taste for hanging people & throat-cutting whenever a suitable subject offers." Higginson expressed the situation a bit more euphemistically, juxtaposing Montgomery's stint in Bleeding Kansas before the war with his embrace of a somewhat Spartan existence at the front: "His conceptions of foraging [during these up-river raids] were rather more Western and

---

[26]DuPont, *Civil War Letters*, 1:247, 248; *ORN*, ser. 1, 12:585; Jones, *Saving Savannah*, 180–81; Berlin, et al., *The Destruction of Slavery*, 1–56, 101–56. See also Mark Grimsley, *The Hard Hand of War: Union Military Policy Toward Southern Civilians, 1861–1865* (Cambridge: Cambridge University Press, 1995).

liberal than mine, and on these excursions he fully indemnified himself for any undue abstinence demanded of him when in camp."[27]

The evidence suggests that many blacks were more sympathetic to the bushwhacker Montgomery's mode of warfare than the more re-strained approach represented by Higginson, Shaw, DuPont, and others. In recalling the burning of Darien, Corporal James Henry Gooding of the 54th expressed satisfaction with a raid in which dwellings belonging to "notorious rebels were burned to the ground." Other black soldiers saw the Darien attack primarily as a means to enhance their regiment's larder of sheep, cattle, and hogs; for them, the slaveowners' disregard for the humanity of their workers more than justified the soldiers' destruction of slaveowners' dwellings, and appropriation of their furniture, food, and livestock.[28]

White military officers did not fully comprehend the pent-up rage among African Americans after generations of exploitation at the hands of whites. United States Acting Rear Admiral William Radford remarked on "the bitter feeling known to exist between the white and black race at present, especially in the neighborhood of the seacoast," as if this "bitter feeling" were somehow strange and inexplicable. Other officials condemned blacks' destruction of white property, from houses to gravestones, as "great outrages." One officer, Captain Percival Drayton of the *Pawnee*, acknowledged the divergent combat tactics of blacks by suggesting that the true "guerillas" in the war "were our [the Union's] friends, the slaves," because "they had the knowledge of locality, of the forests, of the waters." His assessment was echoed, albeit in different terms, by a Confederate who hid in the brush for several days and managed to elude black forces on St. Simons Island in August 1862; the white man de-scribed his ordeal as "hell before your time [is being] hunted ten days by niggers." Naval officers interpreted the raid on Robert

---

[27]*Blue-Eyed Child of Fortune*, 343, 346, 339; Higginson, *Army Life in a Black Regiment*, 120.

[28]Virginia Matzke Adams, *On the Altar of Freedom: A Black Soldier's Civil War Letters from the Front* (Amherst: University of Massachusetts Press, 1991) 30. See also David Demus (Co. K, 54th Massachusetts) to Mary Jane Demus, Demus and Christie Family Letters, "The Valley of the Shadow Project," http://valley.vcdh.virginia.edu/personalpapers/collections/franklin/demus.html.

Stafford's Cumberland Island plantation as evidence of "mutiny" among soldiers and not vengeance among former slaves.[29]

Many black men felt betrayed by Union military policies on multiple levels. Some white officers treated black soldiers as fatigue workers only, a policy that that contrasted with traditional demands made upon white soldiers, who were considered fighting men but also within the normal course of combat diggers of trenches and hewers of water. On the Georgia and South Carolina Sea Islands, whites saw black men in general as menials who could free white soldiers of the routine drudgery associated with setting up encampments and building fortifications: "Contrabands will be attached to the regiment whenever they can be had, so as to cook for the men, pitch and stake tents, and perform all duties that can relieve the marines and leave them free for marching, fighting, etc." Even more egregious than the discriminatory division of labor was the discriminatory pay scale formalized by the War Department in summer 1863. Black men were to be paid $7 a month ($10 in total, but $3 deducted for uniforms and food), while their white counterparts received $13, with no deductions. Corporal James Gooding, who had served under Shaw at Darien and lived through the disastrous attack on Battery Wagner in Charleston Harbor in July 1863, linked the grievances of work assignments and pay in a letter to President Lincoln in September 1863. Gooding wrote, "Now the main question is, Are we *soldiers*, or are we LABORERS." Buoyed by the sacrifices of their families at home, "the patient Trusting Descendants of Africs Clim, have dyed the ground with blood, in defense of the Union, and Democracy." In their claim for equal treatment, "all we lack, is a paler hue, and a better Acquaintance with the Alphabet." Gooding asserted that the black men who joined the army should "be assured that their service will be fairly appreciated, by paying them as American SOLDIERS, not as menial hirelings." Nevertheless, when Sergeant William Walker of the 2nd South Carolina Volunteers led his men in a protest of Federal policies, he was arrested and in February 1864 executed by firing squad for what a court-martial court termed mutiny. Walker had served as a

---

[29]*ORN*, ser. 1, 16:356, 14:150; DuPont, *Civil War Letters*, 2:69; Heard, "St. Simons Colony," 263.

pilot under DuPont and joined the army only "on the promise solemnly made by some who are now officers in my regiment, that I should receive the same pay and allowances as were given to all soldiers in the U.S. Army."[30]

The latter part of the war brought striking accounts of new ways that black men and women advanced the Union cause, juxtaposed to the cynical determination of Union military officers to continue forcibly to appropriate the belongings and to exploit the labor of former slaves. In September 1864, Confederate authorities emptied the notorious Andersonville prisoner-of-war camp and sent several hundred malnourished, ragged, and diseased men to a makeshift stockade in Savannah. There, members of the black community risked arrest and worse by providing food for the desperate men. A free woman of color, Georgiana Guard Kelley, helped collect loaves of bread from other blacks and then dispatched youngsters to "ride past the stockade and throw them [the prisoners] bags of bread." The 60,000-person army of General William Tecumsah Sherman swept through Georgia in November and December of that year, marching from Atlanta to Savannah. Among the "pioneers" attached to the army were black men who labored to build corduroy roads, assemble pontoon boats, and construct fascine bridges from straw. Along the way, black men, women, and children emerged to greet the troops as liberators and to provide them with horses, mules, and a cornucopia of foodstuffs to speed them on their way to the coast. Yet black households, and especially those of rice hands in the lowcountry, were among the targets of Sherman's "bummers," men scouring the countryside for food and wreaking havoc on black and white civilians in the process. By this time, Union officials had abandoned whatever squeamishness they had initially felt about "plundering"—but not just from their enemies. Many black families watched as all their meager

---

[30]*ORN,* ser. 1, 14:429, 190; Berlin, et al., eds., *Black Military Experience,* 385–86, 393; Donald Yacovone, "The Fifty-Fourth Massachusetts Regiment, the Pay Crisis, and the 'Lincoln Despotism,'" in *Hope & Glory: Essays on the Legacy of the Fifty-Fourth Massachusetts Regiment,* ed. Martin Blatt, Thomas J. Brown, and Donald Yacovone (Amherst: University of Massachusetts Press, 2001) 35–51.

possessions and stores of food disappeared into Yankee saddlebags and stomachs.[31]

Sherman himself regarded black people as hands and not freedom fighters. In establishing guidelines for the occupation of Savannah, he approved the policy that decreed that "all able-bodied or other negroes" should enter, or be forced to enter, into the service of the US army to serve as teamsters, scavengers, or longshoremen. Even Sherman admitted that the high-handed tactics of so-called "recruiting agents" represented a "new species of slavery" of threats and coercion. Nevertheless, Sherman expressed a general disdain for black soldiers and remained sensitive to the sensibilities of former slaveholders, no matter how stubborn their commitment to the Confederate cause. Writing from Savannah, he noted of his reluctant white hosts, "the people are dreadfully alarmed lest we garrison the place with negroes. Now, no matter what the negro soldiers are, you know that people have prejudices which must be regarded." Yet after the cessation of hostilities, and long after the departure of Sherman and his men, Union officials decided to use black troops as an occupying force in the city, in order to allow enlisted white men to return to their homes in the North.[32]

The war's immediate impact on white racial ideologies was mixed and contradictory. In general, Northern and Southern whites began the war with the idea that only white men possessed the sense of personal honor necessary for military service. Despite some initial discussion about the use of slaves as soldiers, Confederate authorities decided that black people could best serve the Southern cause as field hands, factory operatives, and fatigue workers. Yet over the course of the conflict some whites began to abandon their antebellum rhetoric that blacks were childlike, servile, and dependent. The petition presented by Robert Q. Mallard and others to General Mercer acknowledged not only that slaves

---

[31]Georgiana Kelley, Chatham County claim no. 15586, Southern Claims Commission (hereinafter SCC), National Archives, Washington DC. See also Rachel Bromfield, Chatham County claim no. 13361 and Judy Rose, Chatham County claim no. 15867, SCC; *OR,* ser. 2, 7: 782, 874; *OR,* ser. 1, 44: 59; Anne J. Bailey, *War and Ruin: William T. Sherman and the Savannah Campaign* (Wilmington DE: Scholarly Resources, 2003).

[32]*OR,* ser. 1, 14: 847; *OR,* ser. 1, 47 (2): 37; *OR,* ser. 1, 44: 841.

were intelligent and resourceful, but also members of the "body politic"—in other words, political actors who must be held accountable for their actions. By late 1864, no less a Confederate leader than Robert E. Lee responded to his dwindling armies by proposing that black men would make efficient soldiers: "They possess the physical qualifications in an eminent degree. Long habits of obedience and subordination, coupled with the moral influence which in our country the white man possesses over the black, furnish an excellent foundation for that discipline which is the best guarantee of military efficiency." Where once Confederates had invoked the slaves' "long habits of obedience and subordination" to disqualify them from military service, now those same qualities were cited as critical for effective soldiering. Lee and others also suggested that for this proposal to work, the Confederate government must provide an incentive for black men to volunteer in the form of "a well-digested plan of gradual and general emancipation." Of course it can be argued that this new idea—the supposed eagerness of black men to serve as citizen-soldiers for the Confederacy—was just as self-delusory among whites as the old idea about black servility. Nevertheless, responding to the exigencies of war, some whites at least were altering their views of the black "race" in dramatic ways.[33]

Union officers also took note of the forceful actions of black men and women to gain their own freedom. Nevertheless, some of the officers stationed on or off the Georgia coast remained wedded to the prejudices they had developed during the war or before, regardless of evidence to the contrary. Thomas Wentworth Higginson saw his own role as that of a "philanthropist" transforming slaves into soldiers, with black people in general "representing a race affectionate, enthusiastic, grotesque, and dramatic beyond all others." Yet Higginson could also single out black men for praise, among them Corporal Robert Sutton, with his "meditative and systematic intellect," qualities that made Sutton, in Higginson's estimation, a natural leader of men. Likewise, though Robert Gould Shaw observed his own regiment's bravery and composure under fire, he nonetheless contended that blacks in general were "perfectly

---

[33]"General Lee's Views on Enlisting the Negroes," *Century Magazine* 36/n.s. 14 (August 1888): 599–601.

childlike, no more responsible for their actions than so many puppies." S. W. Godon saw firsthand the efforts of St. Simons colonists to provide for themselves in myriad ways, from growing crops to marketing their services to Federal gunboats; yet he remained wedded to the idea that the only legitimate labor for black people was staple-crop cultivation under the supervisions of whites. Accordingly, he condemned the "idleness, improvidence, theft, and a disposition to vagrancy [that] are the besting sins of the contraband race on the island."[34]

In the Georgia lowcountry, after the end of the war in spring 1865, the twin battles for black self-determination and civil rights continued, albeit in altered form. Black people sought to claim for themselves not only their own labor, but also the lands that their forbears had nourished with sweat and blood. Susie Baker, recently married to Sgt. Edward King, a young black veteran of lowcountry battles, later recalled the hopefulness that she and her husband shared with other former slaves: "A new life was before us now, all the old life left behind," she wrote of her return to Savannah in 1866. Yet in their effort to embrace a "new life," freedmen and women faced not only strenuous opposition from former Confederates; they also faced opposition from their purported friends, the Northern military officials, government agents, and even missionaries who feared that black self-assertion autonomy threatened the foundations of a reconstructed South. Responding to white hostility expressed through both violent and legal means, blacks embraced a wide variety of leaders, men and women who varied in their strategies for a just post-emancipation society. Presaging the turbulent history of lowcountry politics after 1865, the war itself had revealed in stark terms the pivotal role of black combatants, variously defined; for in the Union triumph over the Confederacy were inscribed the revolutionary struggles of black fugitives and colonists, no less than then the black scouts, spies,

---

[34]Higginson, *Army Life in a Black Regiment*, 29–30, 78–79; Russell Duncan, *Where Death and Glory Meet: Colonel Robert Gould Shaw and the 54th Massachusetts Infantry* (Athens: University of Georgia Press, 1999) 98–99; Heard, "St. Simons Island," 262.

pilots, and seamen and soldiers who rendered military service to the United States.[35]

---

[35]Taylor, *Reminiscences of My Life in Camp*, 54. See Paul A. Cimbala, *Under the Guardianship of the Nation: The Freedmen's Bureau and the Reconstruction of Georgia, 1865–1870* (Athens: University of Georgia Press, 2005); Jones, *Saving Savannah*.

"To the Youth of the Southern Confederacy": Georgia's Confederate Textbooks

by David B. Parker

In 1856, the Southern Commercial Convention convened in Savannah, Georgia. Meeting irregularly since 1837, the convention in its early years had served mainly as a forum for discussions on economic development. In the 1850s, however, more of its sessions were devoted to sectional issues. Delegates in 1856 heard a report from an ad hoc committee established to investigate textbooks used in Southern schools, especially those texts from Northern publishers: "The books rapidly coming into use in our schools and colleges at the South are not only polluted with opinions and arguments adverse to our institutions, and hostile to our constitutional views, but are inferior, in every respect, as books of instruction, to those which might be produced among ourselves, or procured from Europe."[1]

This was not the first time Southerners complained about Northern textbooks. Jedidiah Morse's *The American Universal Geography*, published in Boston, upset Southerners as early as 1793. Morse praised New England culture and education and criticized Southern indolence and excesses. "An aversion to labour is too predominant, owing in part to the relaxing heat of the climate, and partly to the want of the necessity to excite industry," he wrote in his section on Georgia, adding that "an open and friendly hospitality, particularly to strangers, is an ornamental characteristic of a great part of this people."[2]

But demands for Southern textbooks increased with the growing sectional tensions of the 1850s. In order "to relieve us from this growing and dangerous evil," delegates to the convention in Savannah in 1856

---

[1]"Future Revolution in Southern School Books," *DeBow's Review and Industrial Resources, Statistics, Etc.* 30/5 (May/June 1861): 607. See also Herbert Wender, "The Southern Commercial Convention at Savannah, 1856," *Georgia Historical Quarterly* 15/2 (June 1931): 186–87.

[2]Quoted in Edgar W. Knight, "An Early Case of Opposition in the South to Northern Textbooks," *Journal of Southern History* 13/2 (May 1947): 251.

suggested the establishment of a committee "to select or prepare such a series of books, in every department of study, from the earliest primer to the highest grade of literature and science, as shall seem to them best qualified to elevate and purify the education of the South." Once the books were prepared, "the Legislature of the Southern States [should] be requested to order their use in all the public schools."[3]

Nothing came of the convention's plan, but Georgians continued to grumble, especially as the Southern states began to secede. In January 1861, the *Educational Repository and Family Monthly*, published in Atlanta by the educational institute of the Methodist Episcopal Church, South, warned of "the infectious character of those plague-spots which are so often found in our school books of Northern production" and "the foul miasma that taints the Northern atmosphere." Later that spring, William A. Rogers, Methodist minister and president of Griffin Female College, complained that "Northern compilers, of reading books, seem studiously to ignore the *existence of Southern authorship* and *Literature*." The *Atlanta Daily Intelligencer* noted that the South had "talent sufficient…to supply every book that is needed, from the spelling book to the highest and purest style of literature." The editors of *Southern Field and Fireside*, published in Augusta, said that Georgians must "cease to supply our schools with text-books from a section so corrupt and inimical as the so-called United States."[4]

On 8 March 1861, a couple of weeks before it adjourned (and seven weeks after voting the state out of the Union), the Georgia Secession

---

[3]"Future Revolution in Southern School Books," *DeBow's Review and Industrial Resources, Statistics, Etc.* 30/5 (May/June 1861): 607–608.

[4]"Resignation of Our Late Editor, and the Future Management of the Repository and Monthly," *Educational Repository and Family Monthly* 2/1 (January 1861): 60, and "Book Notices," *Educational Repository and Family Monthly* 2/4 (April 1861): 241, both quoted in Michael Thomas Bernath, "Confederate Minds: The Struggle for Intellectual Independence in the Civil War South" (Ph.D. diss., Harvard University, 2005) 125, 128 respectively; William A. Rogers, "Review of Textbooks on Reading," *Educational Repository and Family Monthly* 2/1 (January 1861): 19, quoted in Bernath, "Confederate Minds," 126–27; *Daily Intelligencer*, 10 July 1861, quoted in Rachel Bryan Stillman, "Education in the Confederate States of America, 1861–1865" (Ph.D. diss., University of Illinois at Urbana-Champaign, 1972) 203; "Literary Independence," *Southern Field and Fireside* 2 (11 May 1861) 404, quoted in Bernath, "Confederate Minds," 125.

Convention heard a motion from Nathaniel M. Crawford, president of
Mercer College and a delegate from Greene county, that the governor
"be requested to offer a prize of five hundred dollars each" for textbooks
in various fields. (*DeBow's Review* reprinted the resolution and noted
that "we hope that [it] will be adopted in all the Southern States.") The
next day, Simpson Fouche, founder of Cherokee Female Institute (later
Rome Female College) and a delegate from Floyd County, suggested
that, because northern textbooks "are often made the vehicles for
imposing upon the unsuspecting and untrained minds of the young, their
absurd theories and dogmas upon the subject of African equality, and the
sinfulness of African slavery," the governor appoint a commission to
review and approve textbooks for Georgia students.[5]

Confederate textbooks were the biggest topic at the inaugural
meeting of the Teachers of the Confederate States, meeting in Columbia,
South Carolina, in April 1863. The Committee on Educational Interests
and Text-Books offered a resolution "to encourage our own citizens by
every means in our power, to prepare and publish suitable text-books for
our schools; and in all cases where such books are of equal merit with
foreign works, to give them the decided preference." Several states
offered progress reports. Georgia listed one book already completed
(Rice's *Geography*, discussed below, but the report missed several others
that had also been published) and five forthcoming: J. S. F. Lancaster of
Savannah, a Sunday school superintendent (and later librarian and
curator for the Georgia Historical Society), "has in course of preparation,
a Latin grammar"; Bernard Mallon, an Irish-born and New York-raised
educator from Savannah (and later the first superintendent of Atlanta's
public schools), was preparing "a common school speller"; James Ferris
Cann, a Delaware native who moved to Savannah in 1855 to superintend
the city's public schools, was working on "a juvenile speaker" (a book

[5]*Journal of the Public and Secret Proceedings of the Convention of the People of
Georgia, Held in Milledgeville and Savannah in 1861* (Milledgeville GA.: Boughton,
Nisbet & Barnes, 1861) 136–37, 142–43; *DeBow's Review and Industrial Resources,
Statistics, Etc.* 30/4 (April 1861): 506; Lucian Lamar Knight, *A Standard History of
Georgia and Georgians*, 6 vols. (Chicago: Lewis Publishing Company, 1917) 4:2110;
George Magruder Battey, Jr., *A History of Rome and Floyd County* (Atlanta: Webb and
Vary, 1922) 408.

containing pieces to be recited or read aloud) and another book "with recitations of choice selections of prose and poetry suitable for girls"; and J. J. Judge, a teacher at LaGrange Female College, was preparing another speaker.[6] As it turned out, none of the five "forthcoming" volumes ever appeared.

By the end of the war, North Carolina and Virginia led the field in number of textbooks published, each with more than twenty separate titles. Georgia's thirteen—eight spellers/primers, three arithmetics, one grammar, and one geography—put the state solidly in third place, in front of Tennessee, Alabama, Texas, South Carolina, and Louisiana.[7]

---

[6]*Proceedings of the Convention of Teachers of the Confederate States, Assembled at Columbia, South Carolina, April 28th, 1863* (Macon GA: Burke, Boykin & Co., 1863) 8, 14. The major long-range purpose of the Columbia meeting was to form the Educational Association of the Confederate States of America. See O. L. Davis, Jr., "The Educational Association of the C.S.A.," *Civil War History* 10/1 (March 1964): 67–79. F. D. Lee and J. L. Agnew, *Historical Record of the City of Savannah* (Savannah: J. H. Estill, 1869) 171, and "Officers of the Georgia Historical Society from Its Organization, June 4, 1839, to August 3, 1920," *Georgia Historical Quarterly* 4/2 (June/September 1920): 135–36 (for Lancaster, who is misidentified both by name and profession in the *Proceedings*); Charles W. Hubner, "Bernard Mallon," *Education: An International Magazine* 3/9 (May 1883): 476–82; Knight, *Standard History of Georgia and Georgians*, 6:3304 (for Cann); *Educational Repository and Family Monthly* 1/12 (December 1860): v (for Judge).

[7]For listings of Confederate textbooks, see T. Michael Parrish and Robert Marion Willingham, *Confederate Imprints: A Bibliography of Southern Publications from Secession to Surrender* (Austin TX: Jenkins Pub. Co., 1984) as well as the bibliography in Bernath. The Georgia-published Confederate textbooks not mentioned in this essay include *The Dixie Speller and Reader, Designed for the Use of Schools, by a Lady of Georgia* (Macon GA: John W. Burke, 1863); *Burke's Picture Primer, or, Spelling and Reading Taught in an Easy and Familiar Manner* (Macon GA: Burke, Boykin & Company, 1864); J. L. Dagg, *The Grammar of the English Language, Book First: Progressive Lessons in English Grammar* (Macon GA: Burke, Boykin & Company, 1864); George Y. Browne, *Browne's Arithmetical Tables, Combined with Easy Lessons in Mental Arithmetic for Beginners* (Atlanta: Franklin Printing House, J. J. Toon, 1865); M. P. Caldwell and W. W. Everett, *The Student's Arithmetic: A Collection of Concise Rules and Abridged Methods of Calculation, Adapted to the Use of Schools, Farmers, Mechanics, and Businessmen Generally* (Atlanta: J. H. Christy's Franklin Job Office Print., 1861); and Epes Sargent, *The Standard Speller, Containing Exercises for Oral Spelling: Also Sentences for Silent Spelling by Writing from Dictation* (Macon GA: J. W. Burke, 1861). John Leadley Dagg was a Baptist minister, president of Mercer College in the 1850s, and author of *A Manual of Theology* (1857), sometimes called the first systematic Baptist theology published in the United States. George Y. Browne, also a

This essay will examine some of Georgia's Confederate textbooks, emphasizing their Georgia connections and the lessons they might pass on "to the Youth of the Georgia Confederacy."[8]

John Holt Rice, author of *A System of Modern Geography*, was born in Virginia in 1824 but grew up in eastern Tennessee in a family of prominent Presbyterian clerics and educators; his uncle, also named John Holt Rice, was one of the founders of Union Theological Seminary at Hampden-Sidney College, and great-uncle David Rice was known as the father of Presbyterianism in Kentucky. In the mid-1840s, Rice moved to Cassville, Georgia, where he practiced law and was one of the founders of Cherokee Baptist College. (The school did not survive the war—it was burned, with the rest of Cassville, in November 1864—but two men associated with the college's decade-long existence ended up writing Confederate textbooks. In addition to Rice, there was Thomas Rambaut, a native of Ireland who came to Savannah as a young man, studied law, and entered the Baptist ministry. Rambaut accepted a position teaching ancient languages at Cherokee Baptist College in 1856 and was named president the following year. After the war, he became president of William Jewell College in Missouri. But while he was in Cassville, Rambaut wrote *The Child's Primer*, an introductory spelling and reading book. The textbook's preface is dated "Manassas, Georgia, Dec. 1st, 1862"; the state legislature had changed the name of Cassville to Manassas the year before, in honor of the first battle of the Civil War.)[9]

Baptist minister, headed Georgia Female College in Madison through the 1850s. Sargent was a Boston editor and poet; his *Standard Speller* and other textbooks had been published in Boston and Philadelphia for several years. The Atlanta edition was likely published without his permission. This essay does not cover the small number of books published for higher education (such as medical or chemistry textbooks).

[8]Quotation from Robert Fleming, *The Elementary Spelling Book, Revised and Adapted to the Youth of the Southern Confederacy, Interspersed with Bible Readings on Domestic Slavery* (Atlanta: J. J. Toon & Co., 1863). Similar essays for other states include O. L. Davis, Jr., "Textbooks for Young Texans during the Civil War," *Texas Outlook* 51/10 (August 1967): 19–21, 27; O. L. Davis, "Textbooks for Virginia School Children during the Civil War," *Virginia Journal of Education* 69/3 (November 1965): 16–19; and O. L. Davis and Serena Rankin Parks, "North Carolina's Textbooks," *North Carolina Education* 29/6 (January 1963): 14–15, 32–33.

[9]Thomas Rambaut, *The Child's Primer* (Atlanta: J. J. Toon, 1863). Biographical information from Norman Fox, *Preacher and Teacher: A Sketch of the Life of Thomas*

John Holt Rice also edited the *Cassville Standard*, a Democratic paper established in 1849 by John W. Burke. Burke sold the newspaper in the early 1850s and moved to Macon, where he set up a printing company that published, among other things, a half dozen Confederate textbooks. The *Standard* changed hands frequently; Rice owned it for just over a year before selling it in 1857 and moving to Atlanta, where he set up the Franklin Printing House, a book publishing firm.[10]

John Rice "was a Union man," he wrote several decades later, a supporter of Stephen Douglas who "wrote and spoke against [secession]."[11] But once secession was a fact, Rice used his business to help satsify the Confederacy's need for Southern textbooks. His *System of Modern Geography* was, he wrote in the preface,

> *the only work in existance* [sic] *that approximates doing justice to the country now composing the Confederate States of America*; its actual condition and resources have been studiously concealed by every *yankee* work, the only geographies in use in our schools. To avoid this evil, make us feel independent, and furnish the school of the Confederate States with a geography, compiled by a Southern man, published upon

---

Rambaut, D.D, LL.D. (New York: Fords, Howard & Hulbert, 1892). Aside from the preface, there is little obvious pro-Confederate bias in Rambaut's textbook. The same legislative act that created "Manassas" also changed the name of the county from Cass to Bartow. "Cass" was from Lewis Cass, who as President Andrew Jackson's secretary of war had supported Cherokee removal. Cass later became a Republican, though, and residents of the county were happy to have the name changed to Bartow, in honor of Savannah's Col. Francis Bartow, who fell at Manassas.

[10]General biographical information on Rice, here and below, is from William Gunn Calhoun, *The Rice Family, 1680 to 1973: Thomas Rice, David Rice, John Holt Rice* (Washington College TN: Pioneer Printers, 1973) and Oscar Rice, Comp., *A Memorial of John Holt Rice, Born Nov. 14, 1825, Died Oct. 5, 1904* (Fort Scott KS: n.p., 1905). [John W. Burke], *Autobiography: Chapters from the Life of a Preacher* (Macon GA: J. W. Burke & Co., 1884) is disappointing in his discussion of his Cassville years, covering the period in two sentences (12).

[11]Joel Moody, "The Marais des Cygnes Massacre," in *Collections of the Kansas State Historical Society, 1915–1918*, ed. William E. Connelley (Topeka: Kansas State Printing Plant, 1918) 210; "wrote and spoke" quotation from *Memorial of John Holt Rice*, 6.

our own soil—one that would approximate justice to ourselves, our institutions and our country[—]induced the attempt at this compilation.[12]

Rice also noted in the preface that his work was not original, but rather "a compilation, made up from the best authorities at hand, upon the plan in part of Mitchell's Intermediate Geography, a part of the work being a reprint of Mitchell's." Samuel Augustus Mitchell, of Philadelphia, was for several decades the nation's most popular geographer. Beginning in the 1830s, he turned out dozens of atlases, maps, travelers' guides, and other geographic reference works. His series of textbooks ("First Lessons," "Primary," and "Intermediate") were in print and widely used for years, even after his death in 1868. (A small number of revisions continued into the twentieth century.) As John Ezell noted, Mitchell's antebellum geography texts "[seem] harmless today," but they were "soundly condemned" at the time. "Most of the *geographies* used in our schools," wrote *DeBow's Review* in 1856, "are chiefly dedicated to the benevolent object of glorifying whatever is produced in the northern States, and especially in New England.... Any one, by examining 'Mitchell's Geography,'...may satisfy himself on this point." "A South Carolinian" later confirmed that "Mitchell the geography man" "ignore[s] the existence of any which might be supposed to reflect credit upon the literary or industrial enterprises of [the South]."[13]

Without a careful look, one could easily confuse Mitchell's original and Rice's version of the book—the formatting and physical appearance in general are that close. In a section entitled "Political Geography:

---

[12]John H. Rice, *A System of Modern Geography Compiled from Various Sources and Adapted to the Present Condition of the World; Expressly for the Use of Schools and Academies in the Confederate States of America, in which the Political and Physical Condition of the States Composing the Confederate States of America Are Fully Treated of, and Their Progress in Commerce, Education, Agriculture, Internal Improvements and Mechanic Arts, Prominently Set Forth* (Atlanta: Franklin Printing House, 1862) [iii]. The Mitchell edition used by Rice seems to have been *A System of Modern Geography, Designed for the Use of Schools and Academies* (Philadelphia: E. H. Butler & Co., 1859).

[13]Ibid.; John S. Ezell, "A Southern Education for Southrons," *Journal of Southern History* 17/3 (August 1951): 314; "Educational Reform at the South," *DeBow's Review and Industrial Resources, Statistics, Etc.* 20/1 (January 1856): 75; A South Carolinian, "Education at the South," *DeBow's Review and Industrial Resources, Statistics, Etc.* 21/6 (December 1856): 651.

Forms of Government," both books show the same portrait of George Washington (who Confederates were, of course, proud to call their own). But Rice's is definitely the Confederate textbook. To the question, "What is the best example of a republican government?" Mitchell answered, "The United States of America"; Rice replied, "The Confederate States of America." Rice adds a couple sentences in the chapter on "The United States of America" to point out that the number of states was reduced by the secession of Southern states ("caused by the gross injustice of the Northern States in repeated oppressive violations of the Constitution") and the creation of a new government, "the corner stone of which is African Slavery." (The "corner stone" phrase is a nod to Alexander Stephens, who, on 21 March 1861, a month after being named vice-president of the Confederacy, described the new government: "Its foundations are laid, its cornerstone rests upon the great truth, that the negro is not equal to the white man; that slavery—subordination to the superior race—is his natural and normal condition.") He also notes that "Yankees" are "money-loving and money-making, without much restraint as to means, *success* being the all absorbing object."[14]

A new division in Rice's volume, "The Confederate States of America," includes Kentucky and Missouri (each of which had a splinter group that voted to take the state out of the Union in late 1861) and Maryland: "Maryland cannot properly be placed in the list of the Confederate States; yet we have in this treatise placed it at the conclusion of the Confederate States, as we are satisfied she will ally herself with them so soon as free from the shackles of despotism with which she is now bound." In this section, Rice also notes that "Slavery is expressly recognized in the Constitution, *as it is in the Word of God*, and practiced in all the States, and universally approved of by the people."[15]

Under the heading "The Races of Man," Rice gives the following questions and answers. *"What is said of the Caucasian race?* The Caucasian race is found among the civilized nations of Europe and

---

[14]Rice, *A System of Modern Geography*, 12, 51. Stephens quotation in Thomas A. Scott, ed., *Cornerstones of Georgia History: Documents That Formed the State* (Athens: University of Georgia Press, 1995) 85.

[15]Rice, *A System of Modern Geography*, 20, 21.

America, and is superior to the rest in mind, courage, and activity." *"Of the Black race?* The African, or Black race, is found in all parts of Africa, except on the Northern coast; and in America, where they have been brought and humanly reduced to their proper normal condition of Slavery." One might read this as Southern racism, introduced here to justify slavery, but the words are identical to Mitchell's text except for the final words: Mitchell ends the last sentence with "where they have been brought and domesticated."[16]

Following the war, Rice served briefly as a purchasing agent for Federal forces in Georgia.[17] He then moved west, first to Missouri, then to Kansas, where he spent the remainder of his life (he died in 1904) in the newspaper business. The papers he owned or published during the Kansas years were inevitably Republican, and he was active in Republican Party politics. In 1889, the *New York Times* reported that his political opponents used his pro-Confederate statements in the textbook to keep him from getting a federal appointment as collector of internal revenue.[18] But "That 'Rebel' Geography," as the headline of the *Times* article called Rice's book, was actually fairly mild. Rice briefly justified secession and the existence of the Confederacy, and, of course, his book described one more country than did Northern textbooks.

Spelling books and readers made up the biggest category of Confederate textbooks, both across the South and in Georgia. In 1863, a Georgia publisher issued an exact (and presumably unauthorized) reprint of Noah Webster's *Elementary Spelling Book. Southern Field and Fireside*, a Georgia-based weekly that had just moved its publication to North Carolina, noted that "many would have preferred an original work,

[16]Rice, *A System of Modern Geography*, 7, 8; Mitchell, *A System of Modern Geography* 8. Susan Schulten discusses Mitchell's text, especially the racial aspects, showing how it drew on accepted anthropological ideas, in *The Geographical Imagination in America, 1880–1950* (Chicago: University of Chicago Press, 2001) 94–99. Ironically, several decades earlier, Rice's great-uncle had written about slaves "groaning under the galling yoke of bondage," "deprived of every privilege of humanity"; slavery, he said, was a "wretched situation," a "national crime" that "tends to destroy all sense of justice and equity." David Rice, *Slavery Inconsistent with Justice and Good Policy* (New York: Samuel Wood, 1812) 3, 4, 6, 7, 13.
[17]"From Georgia," *New York Times*, 20 August 1865, 2.
[18]"That 'Rebel' Geography," *New York Times*, 8 December 1889, 12.

to this reprint, but we may not sectionalize the English language.... In developing a native literature, it is not necessary or desirable that we discard everything that originates in the North."[19] Robert Fleming, headmaster of the Newnan (Georgia) Female Academy and pastor of the Newnan Baptist Church, agreed that "no better Spelling-book than Dr. Webster's has ever been presented to the American people," but he thought that the book might be better presented if it were "Revised and Adapted to the Youth of the Southern Confederacy." One change that Fleming introduced was the rejection of several of Webster's pronunciations: "The flat, or Italian sound of *a*, as heard in the word *father*, should not be heard in the word grass, mass, glass, bass, &c. In those words I have given to the letter *a* its short sound, as in *mat*. This is undoubtedly the usage among us.... The flat sound of the letter *a* in these instances is a New England provincialism." Fleming also revised several of Webster's definitions. For example, where Webster defined "despotism" as "a tyranny or oppressive government," Fleming added an example: "Despotism is a tyrannical, oppressive government. The administration of Abraham Lincoln is a despotism." Fleming introduced a few new features into his version of Webster's speller, such as a list of Confederate states. (Like Rice, Fleming added Missouri and Kentucky to the list; "Maryland ought to belong to the Confederate States, but does not, as yet." He also added a three-page story of the life of Stonewall Jackson, "one of the most eminent Generals who drew his sword in the cause of Southern independence." Jackson was "generous and unselfish," a "brilliant" military commander, but "his crowning excellence was his piety.... Let every Southern youth remember his great and good qualities and endeavor to imitate them."[20]

---

[19]*Southern Field and Fireside*, n.s. 1 (14 March 1863) n.p., quoted in Lawrence F. London, "Confederate Literature and Its Publishers," in *Studies in Southern History*, James Sprunt Studies in History and Political Science, vol. 39, ed. J. Carlyle Sitterson (Chapel Hill: University of North Carolina Press, 1957) 90. The book under review was Webster's *The Elementary Spelling Book, Being an Improvement on "The American Spelling Book"* (Macon GA: Burke, Boykin & Company, 1863).

[20]Fleming, *Elementary Spelling Book*, 3, 97, 128, 166–68. Fleming also wrote an English grammar that was never published. Mary Gibson Jones and Lily Elizabeth Reynolds, *Coweta County Chronicles for One Hundred Years* (Atlanta: Stein Printing Co., 1928) 82, 101.

The biggest change, though, is the introduction of Bible verses that explain and defend or justify slavery. (The book is dedicated in part "to all the lovers of learning and Bible truth in the Confederate States of America"). One is the first few verses of Ephesians 6, where Paul tells children to obey their parents; fathers to rear their children "in the nurture and admonition of the Lord"; slaves to "be obedient to them that are your masters, ...as unto Christ"; and masters to treat their slaves fairly, remembering that God is the master of all. Another interspersion, from 1 Peter 2: 15–20, again reminds servants to "be subject to your masters with all fear." After quoting the Ten Commandments (Exodus 20: 3–17), ending with the one about coveting thy neighbor's wife, ox, and so forth, Fleming reminded readers that "slaves are our neighbor's property, as much so as his house." The first few verses of 1 Timothy 6 tell slaves (yet again) to honor their masters, especially those who are Christians, "because they are brethren," and "if any man teach otherwise, ...from such withdraw thyself." Fleming added a Confederate twist to this last bit: "Southern Christians have withdrawn from Northern Abolitionists on this very ground." The book had several other biblical interpositions on slavery, from both Old and New Testaments.[21]

John Neely's *The Confederate States Speller & Reader* used conversational sentences (with words of more than one syllable divided) rather than scripture to teach reading. Some of the sentences did no more than implicitly acknowledge the existence of slavery: "It is hot. Ju-ba, run for fans to fan us"; "Make the ne-gro kill the spi-der"; "That stu-pid ne-gro girl fell in the dirt with the child." But one selection was more vigorous in defending the Confederacy's peculiar institution: "In Sep-tem-ber you may see the ne-groes pick-ing cot-ton. Hark! how mer-ri-ly they sing as they pick the white cot-ton from the pods, and throw it in-to the bas-ket. Those ne-groes are well fed, and well clad, and well cared for when they are sick. When their task is done, there is noth-ing to trou-ble them. Which of us who lives to an-y pur-pose, has not his task to do, as well as the ne-gro?"[22] Published as the war came to an end, Neely's

---

[21]Fleming, *Elementary Spelling Book*, [2], 57–58. 64, 72, 94–95.
[22]John Neely, *The Confederate States Speller & Reader: Containing the Principles and Practice of English Orthography and Orthöepy Systematically Developed, Designed*

textbook was popular, with its last printing being identified as "Fortieth thousand." It was one of the few Confederate textbooks from Georgia to survive the war. In 1872, the book was published in Philadelphia as *Neely's Elementary Speller and Reader*. Juba, presumably a slave in the first edition, is still there, though one imagines now free. "The stupid negro girl" is now simply a race-ambiguous "stupid girl," and the negro killing the spider and the happy slaves in the cotton field have disappeared altogether.[23]

Washington Baird's *Confederate Spelling Book* emphasizes another aspect of Confederate textbooks, what Christopher Clausen called the South's "predilection for moral or even moralistic kinds of education."[24] Baird was a Presbyterian minister who moved from Pennsylvania to Georgia in the early 1830s to head the Scottsboro (Baldwin County) Male Academy. He later edited the *Southern Presbyterian* and accepted pastorates in Arkansas and South Carolina. He was back in Milledgeville during the Civil War, and there he wrote his moralistic *Confederate Spelling Book*.[25] Baird pointed out in his introduction that the spelling book usually "elicits no thought, and affords but little mental culture. Obviously, then, every lesson in spelling should have connected with it an exercise in *Reading* which is at once *pleasing* and *instructive*, affording food for thought, exercise for the several faculties of the mind, and calculated to produce a good *moral impression*." Baird noted that "Rhyme and Poetry are eminently pleasing to children...and they assist greatly the memory in treasuring up and retaining knowledge. And yet,

---

to Accord with the "Present Usage of Literary and Well-Bred Society" (Augusta GA: A. Bleakley, 1865) 17, 36, 42, 100.

[23]Parrish and Willingham, *Confederate Imprints*, 636–37; John Neely, *Neely's Elementary Speller and Reader: Containing the Principles and Practice of English Orthography and Orthöepy Systematically Developed, Designed to Accord with the "Present Usage of Literary and Well-bred Society,"* 4th ed., carefully rev. and stereotyped (Philadelphia: J. B. Lippincott & Co., 1872) 17, 44. Of the ten "testimonials" (referring to the original 1856 publication) at the back of the 1872 edition, six are from GA and two from SC. After the war, Neely was a high school principal in Augusta and Americus and superintendent in Americus.

[24]Christopher Clausen, "Some Confederate Ideas about Education," *Mississippi Quarterly* 30/2 (Spring 1977): 241.

[25]James C. Bonner, *Milledgeville: Georgia's Antebellum Capital* (Athens: University of Georgia Press, 1978) 99.

strange to say, there is not a line of poetry in Webster's Spelling Book—
the one in which most of the present generation have been instructed!"[26]
An example of Baird's spelling-book poetry in the service of moral
instruction:

> I'll never use tobacco, no!
> It is a filthy weed;
> It never in my mouth shall go,
> Said little Robert Reed.[27]

The book's final paragraphs, a conclusion titled "Defective Education,"
are worth reprinting at some length:

> The preceding lessons on this subject present numerous examples of
> the ludicrous lights, and the utterly prostrated positions, in which certain
> persons have been placed—not from any mental or moral defects, but
> solely from the want of education.
>
> They know no better; and, therefore, they were to be pitied. But even
> pity, in such case, is no relief. It is but the testimony of the heart to the
> lamented fact of their ignorance, and the deep mortification it gives to
> their friends....
>
> Ignorance on the part of most children and youth in our day and
> country, is a sin—a grievous sin against God and man—against the
> highest interests also of themselves and their country.
>
> Even now, such examples are the rare exception, not the rule. Better
> days for our Confederacy are at hand. The ignorant, from this period
> onward, will be a small and an obscure minority. *Be not ye found among
> them.*
>
> Nor is it a vain boast to say, what, from personal acquaintance I know
> to be the fact, that the Confederate states abound in highly educated,
> refined and nobler-minded citizens.

---

[26]Washington Baird, *The Confederate Spelling Book, Interspersed with Choice
Reading Lessons in Poetry and in Prose, at Once to Please and Instruct, Many of Them
Conveying Valuable Information and Well Calculated to Make a Fine Moral Impression*
(Macon GA: Burke, Boykin & Company, 1864) 3, 4.
[27]Ibid., 23.

Our Orators, Statesmen, Judges, Generals, and other professional men, would do honor to any country. Our enemies themselves also being judges, it is an admitted fact, that in matronly dignity, elevated sentiments and refined taste, the ladies of this Confederacy are "chief among the highest."

Emulate, then, these notable examples; and avoid the solitary wrecks to which I have pointed. Be men *that are men*; women *that are women*— not *pretenders* to the name. Be worthy of your country and your expected destiny. Let your unremitting effort also be, to make your country—your *own "sunny South,"*—the model country of the world—"The land of all the lands the best."[28]

That last paragraph closely parallels what would become the Lost Cause.

Charles E. Leverett's *Southern Confederacy Arithmetic* was Georgia's best contribution to mathematics textbooks. Leverett, a Boston native and Episcopalian priest, presided over South Carolina's Beaufort College in the early 1830s and later served as rector at churches on Edisto Island and in McPhersonville, South Carolina. Shortly before the Civil War began, he moved his family to a farm near Columbia, where he wrote his arithmetic. His children—daughters at home, sons at war— were proud of his forthcoming book and frequently wrote or asked about it in letters, most of which have survived. Just before the textbook was released (late 1863), Leverett wrote to his son Milton that the book's chances of success would be hampered by its high price, necessitated by the cost of paper.[29]

Like those who wrote the Confederate spellers, Leverett wanted to make sure people understood how his book was different. "In the preparation of this volume," he wrote in the preface, "the author has been guided by what he understood had long been needed—a simple and comprehensive work.... The books, and the most popular ones, which

---

[28]Ibid., 184–85.

[29]"Charles Edward Leverett," *Memorial Biographies of the New England Historic Genealogical Society*, 9 vols. (Boston: New England Historic Genealogical Society, 1908) 6:303–304; Charles Edward Leverett to Milton Leverett, 30 November 1863, in *The Leverett Letters: Correspondence of a South Carolina Family, 1851–1868*, ed. Frances Wallace Taylor, Catherine Taylor Matthews, and J. Tracy Power (Columbia: University of South Carolina Press, 2000) 261–62.

the Northern market has in immense numbers exported to the South, have very glaring defects, especially in the attempt to teach too little, and again too much. The consequence has been embarrassment to the common order of minds, and a tendency to make a most pleasing science an occult study, and a useful and necessary branch of science a distasteful task." Writing of himself in the third person, Leverett noted that "it will be a source of deepest gratification to him, if, through his humble agency, any textbook of the section, which has developed the most malignant principles and exhibited the cruelest practice, should be forever excluded from a Southern school."[30] It is not obvious how successful Leverett was in creating a different sort of arithmetic; to the untrained eye, his appears as occult and distasteful as Northern math textbooks.

Leverett's arithmetic does not offer anything as dramatic as the Confederacy's most famous word problem—"If one Confederate soldier can whip 7 yankees, how many soldiers can whip 49 yankees?"—but it does show a sectional perspective. Word problems often involve "a merchant in Charleston," "a company in Savannah," "a company trading in Mississippi," or "a banker in Charleston." "South Carolina passed the ordinance of secession, December, 1860," began one problem; "how many years is that era from the discovery of America in 1492?"[31]

Georgia's Confederate textbooks became part of what James Marten called "a Confederate tradition in pedagogical literature."[32] They justified secession and defended slavery; conferred legitimacy and promoted patriotic feelings for the new nation; and insisted on a standard of morality that would make the Confederacy manifestly different than the Union. In addition to teaching math, geography, reading, and the like,

---

[30]Charles E. Leverett, *The Southern Confederacy Arithmetic, for Common Schools and Academies, with a Practical System of Book-keeping by Single Entry* (Augusta GA: J. T. Paterson & Co., 1864) v-vi.

[31]L[emuel] Johnson, *An Elementary Arithmetic, Designed for Beginners: The First Principles of the Science* (Raleigh: Branson and Farrar, 1864) 44; Leverett, *The Southern Confederacy Arithmetic*, 20, 155.

[32]James Marten, *The Children's Civil War*, Civil War America, ed. Gary W. Gallagher (Chapel Hill: University of North Carolina Press, 1998) 54.

Georgia's Civil War textbooks passed on ideological, social, and moral lessons "To the Youth of the Southern Confederacy."

Wars and Rumors of Wars
Hearsay as Information on Georgia's Civil War Home Front

by Chad Morgan

You will hear of wars and rumors of wars. —Matthew 24:6 (NIV)

Reliable information was a scarce commodity in Confederate Georgia. This is the natural state of a society at war. Wartime governments must withhold information about troop numbers and movement, for example, as a purely strategic matter. In this situation, rumor assumed a new importance as an information source. Rumor could be a stabilizing force; until 1864, white Georgians often seized on unsubstantiated reports of Confederate good fortune to assuage anxiety over the consequences of defeat. But as Sherman's men initiated their deadly progress through the state, the trickle of reliable information that Georgians had received from newspapers and other sources was shut off. Hearsay became Georgians' primary source of news with mostly dire consequences for the Confederate cause. White Georgians fled their homes and misallocated precious resources. Black Georgians flocked toward Union lines. In both cases, ironically, as rumor began to substitute almost completely for more conventional—and, one might assume, more "solid"—information sources, the information they received became in some ways more accurate. On the Georgia home front at least, whites tended not to cling to improbable tales of Confederate victory or the death of Lincoln. And blacks began to grasp that the hour of their freedom was at hand. The one commonality of most of the actions taken based on rumor was they severely destabilized Georgia's home front, ultimately hindering Georgia's and the South's capacity to make war.

Although historians have long made note of the role of rumor on the Confederate armies and home front in passing, the systematic study of the phenomena has gained momentum in recent years. This trend undoubtedly owes something to contemporary recognition of living in an "information age" and an increased interest in how past societies created, distributed, processed, and understood information. The examination of rumor and hearsay has, however, long been central to the new labor history tradition, which stresses the agency of subaltern groups. In his study of slavery in Confederate Georgia, Clarence Mohr demonstrated that rumor kept slaves reliably abreast of military events during the war. More recently, scholars have turned their attention to the effects of Civil War rumors on combatants and free noncombatants. Historian George C. Rable advanced the idea that positive rumors allowed Confederate citizens to hold out hope for victory well after the rational basis for such hope had been extinguished. Historian Jason Phillips amplified this insight, applying it to morale in the Confederate army. "As Confederate fortunes declined in 1864 and 1865, remarkably positive rumors swirled through rebel armies, spreading false hopes and postponing reality," Phillips wrote. "During the nadir of Confederate morale, diehards intoxicated each other with gossip of improbable victories, northern catastrophes, and foreign invasion." Thus fortified by rumor, Southern armies stayed in the field until Northern ones erased the last shreds of plausible deniability. Recently, scholar Yael R. Sternhell examined the information culture of Confederate Richmond and found that there, too, gossip played a vital role in informing and misinforming the populace. In the case of Richmond, the prevalence of rumor resulted not in redoubled dedication to the Confederacy but "in more confusion than certainty, more imagination than reality."[1]

On the Georgia home front, the case was much the same but, if anything, more pronounced as the state descended into chaos with the

---

[1]Clarence L. Mohr, *On the Threshold of Freedom: Masters and Slaves in Civil War Georgia* (Athens: University of Georgia Press, 1986) 86–209. Steven Hahn explored the ways in which rumors raised the hopes of former slaves in the immediate postwar period in "'Extravagent Expectations' of Freedom: Rumor, Political Struggle, and the Christmas Insurrection Scare of 1865 in the American South," *Past and Present* 157/1 (November 1997): 122–58. George C. Rable, "Despair, Hope, and Delusion: The Collapse of Confederate Morale Reexamined," in *The Collapse of the Confederacy*, ed. Mark Grimsley and Brooks D. Simpson (Lincoln: University of Nebraska Press, 2001) 130–31; Jason Phillips, "The Grape Vine Telegraph: Rumors and Confederate Persistence," *Journal of Southern History* 72/4 (November 2006): 754, 756. Phillips has since spelled his argument out at greater length in *Diehard Rebels: The Confederate Culture of Invincibility* (Athens: University of Georgia Press, 2007). Yael A. Sternhell, "Communicating War: The Culture of Information in Richmond during the American Civil War," *Past and Present* 202/1 (February 2009): 176.

arrival of Sherman's Bummers. That rumor became the primary source of information for Georgians late in the war ought not to obscure the fact that gossip had been rife in Georgia before the conflict even began. John Brown's raid on Harpers Ferry in 1859 had stimulated the fears of servile insurrection that always lay just beneath the surface of antebellum South life. "In the spring of 1860, mysterious fires broke out in Macon and six other Georgia towns," African-American historian Donald L. Grant has written. "All were blamed on slave conspiracy, with white abolitionists supposedly directing the operations. 'Confessions' of insurrection were whipped out of blacks all over Georgia in late 1860. Rumors of slave revolts were especially rife in Northeast Georgia, though no part of the state was immune." Nor, naturally, did this fear subside with the coming of war. In 1861, one Liberty County woman expressed concern about area men leaving to serve in the Confederate army since, in her words, "the Negroes in Tatnall have got beside themselves and were planning what they would do when the gentlemen went to fight and said they would take possession of plantations and would not kill the young ladies but take them for wives."[2]

Though rumors of servile insurrection kept Southern paranoia on simmer, a certain fuzziness on—or, at any rate, an unwillingness to explore—the details of previous slave revolts may have prevented full-on hysteria. Sallie Clayton of Kingston recalled that in late 1860 "there were rumors of an insurrection (among the slaves) which caused excitement and alarm throughout the entire neighborhood. All men were called upon to do patrol duty; while women and children, sometimes several families in one house, were huddled together, more for sympathy than pro-tection." After claiming that such rumors were generally baseless and played up by poor whites "to bring trouble between blacks and whites," Clayton added that, despite a general knowledge of Nat Turner's rebellion having occurred, there was "a great effort at that time to keep everything in connection with it as quiet as possible[;] few details were

---

[2]Donald L. Grant, *The Way It Was in the South: The Black Experience in Georgia* (Athens: University of Georgia Press, 2001) 79; Mrs. E. A. Fleming quoted in Randall C. Jimerson, *The Private Civil War: Popular Thought during the Sectional Conflict* (Baton Rouge: Louisiana State University Press, 1994) 58.

known beyond the scene of its enacting. Consequently, it was not until of
late years a full account was given to the public in this part of the
country." Unfortunately, Clayton did not go into what this "great effort"
entailed.[3]

Apprehension of a slave revolution never completely disappeared
from Confederate Georgia, of course, but from 1861 to 1863, the
incidence of such rumors was less frequent than it had been in the period
after Harpers Ferry, or would become after the arrival of Sherman.
During this hopeful interval, civilians on the Georgia home front became
increasingly susceptible to the kinds of wishful thinking and positive
rumors that sustained the Confederate army in the war's last days. One
Savannah clergyman attributed this tendency to a wish for the war to
end. "There has been for some time past a deep and widespread yearning
for peace," Stephen Elliott, Episcopalian Bishop of the Diocese of
Georgia, sermonized in March 1863. "It has exhibited itself in the
greediness with which the people of the Confederate States have listened
to every rumor of intervention that has floated across the Atlantic, and in
the credulity with which they have believed that the recent political
movements in the United States meant anything more than the customary
struggle for power." According to Elliott, this willingness to entertain
fantastical gossip so long as it was good news for the home team was "a
natural yearning," particularly for "a people unaccustomed as we have
been to a state of warfare, for the human mind abhors anxiety and doubt-
fulness, and shrinks from a condition of things which forces it to live
entirely in the present and for the present." In the same way that rumors
of Grant's death made it possible for Johnny Reb to keep marching into
battle in 1865, white Georgians needed to believe the good news in order
simply to carry on with everyday life. Without it, they could "form no
plans of life, nor look with reasonable probability upon the results of any
undertaking.... Our households are kept in perpetual agitation—our
pursuits are irregular and anomalous—our feelings oscillate between

---

[3]Sallie Clayton's account is found in *Requiem for a Lost City: Sallie Clayton's
Memoirs of Civil War Georgia*, ed. Robert S. Davis (Macon GA: Mercer University
Press, 1999) 32–33.

excitement and depression—our affections are ever on the rack of cruel suspense."[4]

Georgia whites seized on positive rumors for at least one other reason. They dared not imagine a future in which the Confederacy was defeated. Elliott again: "With a war pressing upon us which is continually changing its features and enlarging its proportions—to-day a war for the Union, and to-morrow a war for emancipation—now waged with the power of an ordinary government, and then with forces almost unprecedented in modern history—there is for us not even a conjectural future." As Northern war aims expanded in scope, who could say what horrors defeat would bring? It was best not to think about it.[5]

Not everyone with something to lose found solace in rumors of Confederate victories and the imminent intervention of European powers. In 1940, James Jackson Butler of Oglethorpe County told a WPA interviewer that his father cashed out on two plantations, at a time when precious few souls were looking to get into that particular market, lest they fell into the hands of the Federals. "All during the Civil War rumors were rife that all land was to be confiscated by the government," Butler recollected. "Trying to evade such a calamity my father sold his property for Confederate money. Of course, when the war closed he was flat broke and had a large family to support. Those were indeed hard days."[6]

Rumors can be accurate, of course, but by and large they tend not to be, at least in their details. Even the most accurate will distort the real picture quite a bit. It may therefore be time to modify a prevailing view of slaves that depicts them keeping easily and well informed of wartime events through the "grapevine telegraph." It has been fashionable since at

---

[4]The Rt. Rev. Stephen Elliott, *"Samson's Riddle": A Sermon Preached in Christ Church, Savannah, On Friday, March 27th, 1863. Being the Day of Humiliation, Fasting and Prayer, Appointed by the President of the Confederate States* (Macon GA: Burke, Boykin & Co., 1863) 5–6, available at *Documenting the American South*, http://docsouth.unc.edu/imls/samson/samson.html.

[5]Ibid., 5–6.

[6]James Jackson Butler, interview, 23 February 1940, *American Life Histories: Manuscripts from the Federal Writers' Project, 1936–1940*, American Memory, Library of Congress, available at http://memory.loc.gov/ammem/wpaintro/wpahome.html.

least the 1970s to ascribe more and more agency to oppressed minorities. Understandably, this correction was a reaction to a historical tradition that depicted slaves, women, American Indians, and others primarily as helpless victims, less historical actors in their own right than acted upon. Thus, where black Georgians are concerned, the principal experts emphasized slaves' ability to understand more accurately what was transpiring on the warfront than Georgia's white population and act rationally. This assessment would account, on the one hand, for the thousands of "contraband" slaves who thronged to Union lines. It is also true that, unlike whites, African Americans had less reason as the war went on to delude themselves with wishful thinking. It thus makes a certain amount of intuitive sense that slaves were better able to reckon reality than their masters.[7]

Even so, it defies common sense to suppose that slaves mostly saw through the thick fog of gossip and inferred the truth. It was one thing to seek out Union lines once the Federals had entered the district and the owners had fled, another thing again to see what was happening at any greater remove. An example: "About the first of June [1862] we were told that there was going to be a settlement of the war," wrote Susie Taylor King decades after the war. King had been born into slavery in Liberty County in 1848 and had escaped to St. Simons Island after Union forces occupied it in spring 1862. There, it emerged that "those who were on the Union side would remain free, and those in bondage were to work three days for their masters and three for themselves." Further, "It was a gloomy time for us all, and," she was apprised, "we were to be sent to Liberia. Chaplain French asked me would I rather go back to Savannah or go to Liberia. I told him the latter place by all means. We did not know when this would be, but we were prepared in case this settlement should be reached. However, the Confederates would not agree to the arrangement, or else it was one of the many rumors flying about at the time, as we heard nothing further of the matter." Clearly, King—who

---

[7]See especially Mohr, *On the Threshold of Freedom.*

was in a better condition to know than most Georgia blacks in 1862—did not exactly have a firm grasp on the truth in this case.[8]

Granted, then, that rumor constituted an important element of Georgia's information apparatus since before the beginning of the war, it is nonetheless important to note it was far from the only or predominant part. It is worth exploring briefly the whole of what was a fairly rich information environment before 1864. In the first place, there were the newspapers. All the state's major urban areas—Atlanta, Augusta, Columbus, Macon, and Savannah—boasted daily newspapers. Some boasted two. In addition, the second tier of Georgia cities, including Albany, Athens, and Rome, had their own regularly published papers. All, of course, exhibited a generally pro-Southern stance (although they were not at all loath to criticize state and national leadership). To do otherwise may have been to invite the government to intervene or, what was more likely, their own readership to throw their presses into the river. And in any case, the ideal of journalistic objectivity as practiced in the twentieth century was not known to the Civil-War South. Even so, these organs drew on newspaper exchanges, eyewitness reports, and, for the first time during the Civil War, a news service. They were, in short, fairly reliable information sources for their audience. They were, moreover, subject to few of the restrictions that the US government placed on the Northern press. Although Richmond was quite as diligent as Washington in centralizing national power, it was noticeably less active in trying to bring the press to heel. Dissident papers were not shut down; their editors were not jailed.[9]

---

[8]Susie King Taylor, *Reminiscences of My Life in Camp: An African American Woman's Civil War Memoir With the 33d United States Colored Troops, Late 1st SC Volunteers* (Boston: The author, 1902) 11–12. For a brief biography of King, who became "the first African American to teach openly in a school for former slaves in Georgia," see Ronald Butchart's 2006 entry in the *New Georgia Encyclopedia*, http://www.georgiaencyclopedia.org/nge/Article.jsp?id=h–1097.

[9]Debra Reddin Van Tuyll, "Two Men, Two Minds: An Examination of the Editorial Commentary of Two Georgia Editors during Sherman's March to the Sea," in *The Civil War and the Press*, ed. David B. Sachsman, S. Kittrell Rushing, and Debra Reddin Van Tuyll (Piscataway NJ: Transaction Press, 2000) 275–76. Differing Northern and Southern approaches to censorship are explored by Richard Franklin Bensel in *Yankee Leviathan:*

Then, too, letters kept Georgians informed of what transpired on the front and elsewhere in the Confederacy. The Confederate postal service was headed by an able administrator, John H. Reagan, which ensured that it functioned as well as could be expected. But the evolution of a bureaucracy to handle all the nation's mail was bound not to be an overnight process, and service was frequently interrupted. Matters were not helped by regular personnel cuts or paper and postal stamp shortages. Still, Georgia's letters and parcels were delivered with something approaching regularity prior to 1864.

Once Sherman and his men entered the state in spring 1864, the rumor machine, already humming along at a fairly rapid clip, kicked into higher gear. Even that metaphor puts the matter too mildly as the difference was not one of degree but of kind. During the conflict's first three years, rumors spread, but they were not the only or even the primary source of information for most Georgians. Instead, rumor tended to supplement what could be known about the conflict from newspaper accounts or letters from the front—sources that were not free of gossip themselves, to be certain, but which tended to have a closer relationship to reality than simple hearsay. And, it has to be said, the nature of the rumors changed. Before Sherman, rumors in general tended to cast a hopeful light on affairs; the whites in Stephen Elliot's congregation chose to comfort themselves with tales of smashing, improbable military victories, and the prospect of European alliances while blacks like Susie Taylor King entertained the possibility of a clean break with the past and a fresh start in Africa. But as traditional information sources dried up or were otherwise disrupted, Georgians of both races came to rely increasingly on hearsay. In this circumstance, an exceedingly curious phenomenon occurred: White Georgia began to understand its situation more accurately for what it was. As more and more refugees flooded past with their tales of woe, whites began to see that the tide of war had well and truly turned against them. This perhaps accounts for the bitterness with which they denounced Sherman and his purported atrocities. There was no similar change on the part of Georgia's African-American

---

The Origins of Central State Authority in America, 1859–1877 (New York: Cambridge University Press, 1990) 141–43.

population for the reason that there was no need to bring their hopeful assessments into tighter alignment with reality. Sherman was fuel for their hopes.

Bill Arp of Rome could count himself among the first wave of Georgians to be displaced by Sherman. "With our families and a little clothing, we crossed the Etowah bridge about the break of day on Wednesday, the 17th of May, 1864, exactly a year and two weeks [from] the time when General Forrest marched in triumph through our streets," he recalled. A newspaper humorist by trade, Arp painted a vivid picture of life on the run. "By and by the bright rays of the morning sun dispersed the heavy fog, which like a pall of death had overspread all nature. Then were exhibited to our afflicted gaze a highway crowded with wagons and teams, cattle and hogs, niggers and dogs, women and children, all moving in disheveled haste to parts unknown. Mules were braying, cattle were lowing, hogs were squealing, sheep were bleating, children were crying, wagoners were cursing, whips were popping, and horses stalling, but still the grand caravan moved on." A Confederate soldier retreating before the Yankee hosts in North Georgia, J. P. Austin, recorded that "thousands of [the South's] inhabitants were wandering all over the county like so many gypsies.... Refugees were to be found everywhere." As a group, women were particularly stricken. "Many refined and cultured ladies had attached themselves to the army for protection, and served in any capacity where they could be of advantage to the cause." Good information was virtually nonexistent in such an atmosphere, and rumor reigned supreme. "Everybody was continually looking behind, and driving before—everybody wanted to know everything, and nobody knew anything," wrote Arp. "Ten thousand wild rumors filled the circumambient air. The everlasting cavalry was there, and as they dashed to and fro gave false alarms of the enemy being in hot pursuit."[10]

---

[10]Bill Arp, *From the Uncivil War to Date* (Atlanta: Hudgins Publishing Company, 1903) 73; J. P. Austin, *The Blue and the Gray: Sketches of a Portion of the Unwritten History of the Great American Civil War* (Atlanta: Franklin Printing and Publishing Co., 1899) 119.

As Arp's case illustrates, refugees on the run were particularly at the mercy of rumors. But word of impending Yankee despoliation touched all parts of the state, even where actual invasion was unlikely. A native of Wilkes County but a refugee in Southwestern Georgia in the war's final year—albeit one living in the comfortably appointed house of a relative—Eliza Frances Andrews reported on New Year's Day, 1865, that she and her companions were "aggravated by perpetual alarms of Yankee raiders. For the last week we have lived in a state of incessant fear. All sorts of rumors come up the road and down it, and we never know what to believe." Andrews's "dread of the Yankees" was such that it caused her to become physically ill. Whatever anxiety she might have normally felt at such gossip was exacerbated by two factors. As a refugee she had witnessed the destruction wrought by Sherman's men. Having furthermore heard of the horrors at nearby Andersonville, she feared the retribution the Yankees would visit on her temporary home should Northern armies arrive at that appalling scene. "I used to feel very brave about Yankees, but since I have passed over Sherman's track and seen what devastation they make, I am so afraid of them that I believe I should drop down dead if one of the wretches should come into my presence," Andrews wrote. "I would rather face them anywhere than here in South-West Georgia," because "the horrors of the stockade" would mean the Union soldiers would show "no mercy on this country."[11]

During the March to the Sea, rumor had thousands of events transpiring simultaneously. Mostly useless at the time for their actual content, such rumors are immensely useful to historians seeking insight into Confederate psychology. Some intimated division over Confederate leadership if not the Confederate cause. One of the most frequently heard items as Sherman made his way from Atlanta to the Atlantic was that Jefferson Davis was soon to face impeachment proceedings. In a similar vein were the incessant reports of corruption on the part of quartermaster and commissary agents. Rumored negotiations between Sherman and either the Army of Tennessee commander Joseph Johnston or Georgia governor Joseph Brown revealed a desperate few hoping against hope for

---

[11]Eliza Frances Andrews, *The War-Time Journal of a Georgia Girl, 1864–65* (New York: D. Appleton and Co., 1908) 63–64.

a separate peace between the Union and Georgia. Gossip of the special treatment received by planters or, alternatively, of slaveholders who resisted government impressments of their slaves suggested something of the class divisions that beset the fledgling Southern nation. Finally, numberless accounts of Yankees raping white Southern women (which occasionally did occur) spoke volumes about the anxiety of the white South as a whole on the topics of threatened Southern ladyhood and the failure of Southern men to protect it. One faux-rumor even demonstrated a rare-for-the-nineteenth-century sense of absurdity. The Columbus *Times* lampooned the pervasiveness of gossip when it asserted that "the report that [Governor] Joe Brown is about to assume command of the Army of Tennessee, with Bill Arp as Chief of Staff, is unfounded."[12]

Even on the home front, most rumors were about the war itself: battles lost and won, the movement of armies, the major war personalities. But if rumor sustained soldiers on the front, it often had the opposite effect back home. Because of its distance from Confederate authorities or any active front, the pine barrens of South Georgia became a particular haven of refugees. "About the close of the Confederate war the woods in South Georgia were filled with...deserters, details, runaway negroes, tramps, and rogues of all sorts," recalled South Georgia resident Warren Ward. "The country was inhabited mostly by women and children and they were always in some fear that...harm would come to them." One South Georgia refugee, Loula Kendall Rogers, originally of Barnesville, despaired of rumors that "general Hood was killed, and

[12]Davis rumor reported in Carl Sandburg, *Abraham Lincoln: The Prairie Years and the War Years* (New York: Houghton Mifflin Harcourt, 2002) 622. On the rumors of malfeasance on the part of government agents, see Chad Morgan, *Planters' Progress: Modernizing Confederate Georgia* (Gainesville: University Press of Florida, 2005) 40–69. Reports of separate peace negotiations can be found in Richard Nelson Current, ed., *Encyclopedia of the Confederacy* (New York: Simon and Schuster, 1993) 854. George C. Rable makes reference to gripes over planters' special treatment and anxiety about rape in *Civil Wars: Women and the Crisis of Southern Nationalism* (Champaign-Urbana: University of Illinois Press, 1991) 108, 161. Peter Wallenstein writes of yeomen-spread rumors of planters withholding their slaves from government service in *From Slave South to New South: Public Policy in Nineteenth Century Georgia* (Chapel Hill: University of North Carolina Press, 1987) 120. Columbus *Times* quoted in Thomas Conn Bryan, *Confederate Georgia* (Athens: University of Georgia Press, 1953) 159.

President Davis is dead!" Such hearsay pushed Rogers to the edge of hopelessness. "If it is true, I shall feel as if we *are really forsaken* by Heaven and given up to be lost." Elsewhere in South Georgia, Eliza Frances Andrews took cold comfort in the fact that "rumors about Yankee raiders" in the area had to be false because "swamps of the Altamaha are so flooded that it would take an army of Tritons to get over them now." The reason the swamps and pine barrens of South Georgia attracted refugees in such great numbers, after all, was that its challenging terrain, combined with its remoteness and strategic inconsequentiality, meant that Union forces were unlikely to tread its ground.[13]

Rumor served soldiers equally well in the field. In his exhaustive study of desertion among Georgia's Civil War soldiers, Mark A. Weitz cited rumors of Sherman's actions in their home state as one of the prime reasons Georgians started deserting in far greater numbers in 1864. Understandably worried about what fate may have befallen their loved ones—from whom they more likely than not had heard nothing due to disruption of the mail—many an otherwise dedicated Southern soldier chose family over country, thus further compromising the Confederacy's diminishing ability to wage war.[14]

By the time Sherman reached Savannah in December 1864, he had rendered the entire state unable to function on virtually any level, a condition caused by more than the bloody swath he had cut in the state from Atlanta to Savannah. The mere rumor of imminent arrival of Union forces threw all parts of the state into disarray. To some extent, this confusion was by design. Historian Anne J. Bailey has argued that Sherman deployed the language of total war more than the practice. Sherman's aim was not to inflict damage so much as it was to break the South's will to fight. To this end, he waged a form of psychological warfare on the Georgia home front by utilizing provocative and

---

[13]Ward quoted in John G. Crowley, *Primitive Baptists of the Wiregrass South: 1815 to the Present* (Gainesville: University Press of Florida, 1999) 94; Rogers quoted in Sarah E. Gardner, *Blood and Irony: Southern White Women's Narratives of the Civil War* (Chapel Hill: University of North Carolina Press, 2006) 17; Andrews, *The War-Time Journal of a Georgia Girl*, 66.

[14]Mark A. Weitz, *A Higher Duty: Desertion among Georgia Soldiers during the Civil War* (Lincoln: University of Nebraska Press, 2006) 136.

extremely confrontational language. This approach was so effective that Bailey considers the "war of words" Sherman carried out "was far more devastating to the Southern nation than the actual events along his route."[15]

If Sherman did less actual damage than hysterical Southerners supposed, his actions served to amplify his "War is hell" rhetoric by giving the impression that he was coming to every major city in Georgia. Leaving Atlanta, Sherman feinted toward Augusta and Macon. "To divide and scatter their force is our main purpose," Union officer George Ward Nichols noted at the time. "Let them keep a large army in Augusta until we reach the sea, and then they can go where they please!" Leaving Savannah, Sherman employed the same strategy. He had, he said, "left Augusta untouched on purpose, because the enemy will be in doubt as to my objective point, after crossing the Savannah River, whether it be Augusta or Charleston, and will naturally divide his forces."[16]

Feints were not the only tactic Sherman used to confuse. Sherman also guarded his true plans from most of his own officers. Intentionally or not, this stratagem fostered rumors, which only confused the situation on the Georgia home front more. According to another Union officer, Charles Fessenden Morse, as the Northern columns left Atlanta, the mystery of their destination fostered rumors within the Army of the Tennessee. "The proposed movement is the most perfectly concealed I have ever known one to be; scarcely an officer on the staff or anywhere else knows our destination or intention," wrote Morse in a letter home to Massachusetts. "There are all kinds of rumors which are told as facts, but they only more effectually conceal the real campaign." Sherman's secrecy worked brilliantly as the hopelessly overmatched militia who stood between Sherman and the sea arrayed itself in long, attenuated lines in front of him. If the propagation of rumor through secrecy was not

---

[15]Anne J. Bailey, *War and Ruin: William T. Sherman and the Savannah Campaign* (Wilmington DE: Scholarly Resources, 2003) xiv.

[16]George Ward Nichols, *The Story of the Great March: From the Diary of a Staff Officer* (New York: Harper and Brothers, 1865) 82; Charles Royster, *The Destructive War: William Tecumseh Sherman, Stonewall Jackson, and the Americans* (New York: Vintage, 1993) 329.

a conscious strategy on the part of the Union brass, clearly it ought to have been.[17]

To make matters more difficult, what conventional sources of information still existed found reliable information quite beyond their reach. In Albany, the *Patriot* was one of the few papers that continued to operate as the Federals closed in on Savannah in fall 1864, but at this late stage, its editors had little to offer its readers except what it could glean from the grapevine. "By November, telegraphic news from the state had been lost and many of the newspapers north of Albany had shut down or moved out of state," journalism historian Ford Risley has written in his account of the wartime *Patriot*. Under the circumstances, the *Patriot* could do no more than sift through the great volume of hearsay then circulating, printing the most realistic-seeming items. But thanks to the Union brass's obfuscation, "even the rumor mill could not be sure of General Sherman's next target after Union forces captured Milledgeville." What was more, "the paper could report little news from nearby Macon because the city's daily newspapers had packed up and fled." In other words, the *Patriot*'s news gathering capacity extended no further than the city in which it was published, which helped its readers not at all.[18]

Eventually, gossip grew so prevalent as to bring total paralysis. Not knowing which rumors to trust, some bided their time preparing to evacuate quickly should it come to that. "We hear so many rumors of the movements of the Yankees and of our own troops, but they are not worth noting," wrote Emma LeConte of Columbia, South Carolina, in January 1865. "Mother has packed up the clothing and bed-linen that we may save those at least. All the books are packed too. I have not been in the library since they were taken down. It would make me too sad to look at the empty shelves." South Carolina's Susan Ravenel Jervey lay in Sherman's path and put the matter most succinctly. "Our news now is all rumor; no papers; no letters," she wrote in February 1865 as refugees and

---

[17]Charles Fessenden Morse, *Letters Written during the Civil War, 1861–65* ([Boston]: n.p., 1898) 196.

[18]Ford Risley, "The Albany Patriot, 1861–1865: Struggling to Publish and Struggling to Remain Optimistic," in *The Civil War and the Press*, 353–54.

retreating Confederate soldiers regaled her with all manner of wild tale. In a situation where all information was suspect, people on what may be called the "Sherman home front" had the choice of sitting tight or acting on spurious intelligence. What they could not do was make informed decisions. Ironically, refugee women sought more control over their information environment in many cases than those women who stayed in their homes. In order to reduce the level of uncertainty and hearsay, some refugees consciously settled near communication centers such as telegraph or post offices to ensure they received the most dependable information available.[19]

Given that positive rumors sustained many of those serving under the Confederate banner right down to Appomattox, the obvious question arises: Why did rumors appear to have the opposite effect on the Sherman home front? Why did hearsay multiply hope in one instance, despair in the other? The answer to this question awaits further research, but one factor that may have played a role was the perceived ability of the respective groups to shape their destiny. Soldiers continued to believe—had to believe—that they could still change the outcome of the war with a signal victory over the other side. (They were likely abetted in this fantasy by the fact that those of their number who did not share a faith in ultimate victory tended also to be among the thousands who deserted; Confederate bitter-enders, like all bitter-enders, were a self-selecting group.) People on the Sherman home front, by contrast, could not comfort themselves with the possibility, however notional, that they could do something to better their own lot. They were at the mercy of Sherman. And frankly, it could not have brightened their spirits much to have all those refugees and deserters amongst them, two groups known to be downers in any context.

---

[19]Emma Florence LeConte, diary, 23 January 1865, from transcript prepared by the Historical Records Survey of the Works Progress Administration, May 1938, available at *Documenting the American South*, http://docsouth.unc.edu/fpn/leconteemma/leconte. html; Susan R. Jervey and Charlotte St. J. Ravenel, *Two Diaries: From Middle St. John's, Berkeley, South Carolina, February-May 1865* ([Pinopolis SC]: St. John's Hunting Club, 1921) 4; Drew Gilpin Faust, *Mothers of Invention: Women of the Slaveholding South in the Civil War* (Chapel Hill: University of North Carolina Press, 1996) 116.

The inordinate, near total dependence on gossip did not end with the war. For many of Georgia's former slaves and slaveowners, word of how emancipation was to be accomplished leaked out only gradually. On her plantation near Covington, Dollie Sumner Lunt reported in May 1865 having "had a long conversation with my man Elbert to-day about freedom, and told him I was perfectly willing, but wanted direction. He says the Yankees told Major Lee's servants they were all free, but they had better remain where they were until it was all settled, as it would be in a month's time." All during this period, though, Lunt confessed to hearing "so many conflicting rumors we know not what to do, but are willing to carry out the orders when we know them."[20]

One of those rumors, bruited about by blacks and whites alike, held that a Federally mandated redistribution of property was imminent. "Rumors were rife throughout the South that the federal government would make a general land distribution to blacks on Christmas Day, 1865," according to Donald L. Grant. "One Georgia black was so certain he would receive land that he offered to sell part of it back to his former master." Among whites, another rumor circulated that a freedmen's revolt was in the offing should redistribution not come off, on the basis of which white citizens' patrols took to arms throughout the state.[21]

In conclusion, one is struck by what historians do not know concerning the critical role of hearsay. This essay demonstrates that greater systematic research into the wide-ranging impact of gossip on the Southern home front and war effort is sufficiently inchoate as to warrant some considerable caution. Clearly, hearsay helped buoy spirits in good times and bad, but, just as clearly, gossip prevented Georgians in particular and the South in general from making the best use of scarce resources. At this stage of the endeavor, any argument that posits even a predominantly positive or negative impact for gossip is necessarily reductionist. This essay suggests potential new directions for future research into the information culture of the Confederacy. Some of the

---

[20]Dolly Sumner Lunt, *A Woman's Wartime Journal: An Account of the Passage over a Georgia Plantation of Sherman's Army on the March to the Sea* (New York: Century Company, 1918) 50–51.
[21]Grant, *The Way It Was in the South,* 94; Hahn, "'Extravagent Expectations' of Freedom," 140–53.

possibilities include the following: the extent to which gossip kept slaves reliably informed of wartime events; strategies used by landowners to preserve what they could of their estate in extremely information-poor environments; what conditions correlate with the emergence of favorable and unfavorable rumors respectively; as a subset of the last, the relationship between historical actors' circumstances—whether slave or free, black or white, wealthy or not—and the rumors they elected to believe; what individual rumors or types of rumors tell us about the Confederate *mentalité*; and what kinds of situations led to the substitution of rumor for more traditional sources of information and why.

"The Bottomless Pit of Hell": The Confederate Home Front in Bartow County, Georgia, 1864–1865

by Keith S. Hébert

The Atlanta Campaign has received a lot of attention from scholars of the American Civil War. Historians, however, have paid considerably less attention to the lives of civilians caught in the wake of that pivotal campaign.[1] Between May 1864 and May 1865, the inhabitants of Bartow County, Georgia, halfway between Chattanooga and Atlanta, suffered from the effects of a massive Federal invasion followed by a prolonged occupation and then a quick withdrawal. Prior to the start of the Atlanta Campaign, hundreds of Bartow County residents fled southward to safety in anticipation of an impending Union Army invasion. Those who remained stayed in spite of serious doubts concerning the Army of Tennessee's ability to repel the enemy and uncertainties about the Confederacy's future. The events of the campaign confirmed those fears as General Joseph E. Johnston abandoned the county without a fight. Civilians responded to the start of the Union occupation in mixed fashion. Some fostered mutually beneficial relationships with Federal forces as a means of survival. Others welcomed the men in blue as liberators. A small faction of citizens actively provided bands of partisans with supplies and information and sometimes joined in guerrilla-style attacks upon "Yankee" stragglers, foraging parties, teamsters, and area Unionists. Union soldiers struggled to differentiate between noncombatants and partisans. Confusion, fear, and a desire for

---

[1]James Lee McDonough and James Pickett Jones, *War So Terrible: Sherman and Atlanta* (New York: Norton, 1987); Albert Castel, *Decision in the West: The Atlanta Campaign of 1864* (Lawrence: University Press of Kansas, 1992); Richard M. McMurry, *Atlanta 1864: Last Chance for the Confederacy* (Lincoln: University of Nebraska Press, 2000); Lee Kennett, *Marching through Georgia: The Story of Soldiers and Civilians during Sherman's Campaign* (New York: HarperCollins, 1995); Stephen V. Ash, *When the Yankees Came: Conflict & Chaos in the Occupied South, 1861–1865* (Chapel Hill: University of North Carolina Press, 1995).

retribution led Federal commanders to harden their treatment of civilians. Following the Atlanta Campaign, the assaults in the county escalated when the bulk of General William T. Sherman's forces returned in pursuit of General John B. Hood's Army of Tennessee. As Hood prepared for the disastrous Tennessee Campaign, Sherman received permission to "March to the Sea" and withdrew from the county. Before leaving the area in November Federal commanders, in retaliation for local support for guerrillas, ordered the destruction of the county seat of Cassville. The county descended into the "bottomless pits of hell" following the end of the occupation as armed bands of deserters, thieves, Unionists, and partisans fought one another and preyed upon civilians. The removal of Union troops left civilians and partisans without a common enemy, which in turn led to the escalation of violence locally as former bonds of allegiance became irrelevant and the county fell into a state of anarchy. Bartow County civilians' pro-Confederate sentiment disappeared during spring 1864 in the wake of the Union withdrawal.[2]

Most white residents of Cass County reacted to the firing on Fort Sumter with an exuberant outpouring of support for the Confederacy. Hundreds of local men such as William A. Chunn volunteered for military service "determined to forgo the pleasures of home & friends for a while to benefit the interest of [their] country." Major John F. Milhollin explained to his family that he joined the army "with a bold heart strong in opinion of the success of our cause, believing that we will with our cause succeed it being a holy one." Following the Battle of First Manassas, the county displayed its nationalism by changing its name to Bartow County in honor of slain 8th Georgia Infantry commander Colonel Francis S. Bartow of Savannah. Meanwhile, Cassville, the

---

[2]The Georgia General Assembly created Cass County on 3 December 1832, naming it in honor of Democratic Secretary of War Lewis Cass of Michigan. The legislature formed ten counties, including Cass, from Cherokee lands in the state's northwestern region. Surveyors laid out the county seat of Cassville in 1833. By 1840, the town had grown in size and prominence and emerged as Northwest Georgia's leading commercial and judicial center. Keith S. Hébert, "Civil War and Reconstruction Era Cass/Bartow County, Georgia" (Ph.D. diss., Auburn University, 2007) chap. 1; Alexa Ilene Claremont, "Creators of Community: Cassville, Georgia, 1850–1880" (MA thesis: University of Georgia, 2005) 11–25.

county seat, changed its name to Manassas. Local support for the Confederate government remained firm from 1861 until winter 1863 despite the usual bouts of war weariness.[3]

Local expectations of a Confederate victory, however, diminished following Union General Ulysses S. Grant's rout of the Confederate Army of Tennessee at Chattanooga in late November 1863. "Our poor country," wrote a Bartow County resident, "seems in such a deplorable condition, and men so wicked that we dare not expect the Almighty to help us." While the Army of Tennessee remained at Dalton, Cartersville in Bartow County emerged as a major transportation center in the region. Commissary agents combed the countryside in search of food to feed the nearby army. When locals appeared to be uneager to sell their goods, the agents resorted to impressing the necessary supplies. Such actions evoked the wrath of many residents who resented the Confederacy's abusive policies.[4]

While the large Confederate presence in Bartow County alarmed some residents, most viewed the nearby Army of Tennessee as their principal protectors. Locals remained uncertain about the army's chances of repelling any Federal invasion. William A. Chunn, a resident of Cassville serving in the 40th Georgia Infantry Regiment at Dalton, warned family members that the winter of 1863–1864 was "but the lull

---

[3]"Editorial Written by Charles W. Howard," *Southern Cultivator* (August 1859), Special Collections, Atlanta Public Library; William A. Chunn to Delila Land Chunn, 8 September 1861, Chunn-Land Papers, box 1:5, Georgia Archives, Morrow; A. J. McWhirter to Captain T. F. Jones, 2 May 1863, Confederate Miscellany Collection, 1860–1865, box 5:13, Robert W. Woodruff Library, Manuscript, Archives, and Rare Book Library, Emory University, Atlanta.

[4]Warren Akin to Joseph E. Brown, 29 January 1864, Executive Department, Governor's Letter Books, 1861–1865 [microfilm], drawer 61:79, p. 588, Georgia Archives, Morrow; J. P. Baltzelle to Col. E. J. Harris, 27 March 1864, Barnsley Papers, [microfilm], 204, Tennessee State Archives, Nashville. J. J. Howard to Jared L. Whitaker, 19 January 1864, Defense Department, Adjutant General Records, Commissary General Records, Incoming Correspondence, 1861–1865, RG 22: ser. 8, loc. 3337-04, Georgia Archives; Department of Defense, Adjutant General, Commissary General Records, Returns of Subsistence Stores, RG 22: ser. 8, loc. 3340-15, Georgia Archives; Letter to Commissary General, 22 January 1864, Defense Department, Adjutant General Records, Commissary General Records, Letters Received, 12 November 1861–12 May 1864, RG 22: ser. 8, loc. 3340-15, Georgia Archives.

of a gathering storm that pauses before it snaps the earth with all its fury.... This part of the country will not long be blessed with quiet." Yet Chunn remained optimistic. "I have of late," he wrote, "had an instinctive impression that the time for the beginning of our success is at hand. God grant that it may be." In spite of Chunn's declaration that the Army of Tennessee would not "yield another inch of territory," his family joined hundreds of others who fled southward. Rumors that the Army of Tennessee would abandon Bartow County in the spring and occupy defenses south of the Etowah River convinced locals that Federal soldiers would soon overrun them.[5]

Those fears were realized on the evening of 17 May 1864, as three Federal armies under the command of General William T. Sherman entered the county. Advance units of Union soldiers skirmished with the Confederate rear guard that night as well as during most of the following day. By the late afternoon of 19 May, three Federal Corps had been deployed in front of the Confederate's prepared defenses at Cassville. General Joseph E. Johnston, commander of the outnumbered Army of Tennessee, promised to engage the enemy there. The Battle of Cassville never happened. What could have been one of the largest collisions in the Western theater turned into yet another retreat. Johnston abandoned the county less than twenty-four hours after his proclamation.[6]

As the Federal army continued to pursue the Army of Tennessee, Sherman created the District of the Etowah on 23 May to protect his army's supply lines. The district was placed under the command of

---

[5]William Chunn to Judge Nathan Land, March 1864, Chunn-Land Papers, box 1:5, Georgia Archives, Morrow; A. J. Neal to "Ma," 3 February 1864, Bartow County vertical file, Georgia Archives; E. W. Marcum to "Cousin," 24 January 1864, Confederate Miscellany Collection, 1860–1865, box 1:57, Robert W. Woodruff Library, Manuscript, Archives, and Rare Book Library, Emory University, Atlanta; *Tri-Weekly Courier* (Rome GA), January 1864.

[6]US War Department, comp., *The War of the Rebellion: A Compilation of the Official Records of the Union and Confederate Armies*, 128 vols. (Washington, DC: Government Printing Office, 1880–1901) ser. 1, 38 (1): 102–103, 191, 222, 465–71; "Kingston, GA.," *Frank Leslie's Illustrated Newspaper*, 25 June 1864; research notes, Wilbur Kurtz Collection, MS-130, Kenan Research Library and Archives, Atlanta History Center, Atlanta; Timothy F. Weiss, "'I Lead You to Battle': Joseph E. Johnston and the Controversy at Cassville," *Georgia Historical Quarterly* 91/4 (Winter 2007): 424–52; Castel, *Decision in the West*, 200–204.

General James B. Steedman and staffed with several thousand soldiers. The district spanned a large territory from Bridgeport, Alabama, to Allatoona, Georgia (Bartow County). Steedman placed three small garrisons in Bartow County along the Western & Atlantic Railroad (W&A) at Cartersville, Cass Station, and Kingston. On 28 June, Brigadier General John E. Smith, commander of the Third Division, XIV Army Corps, was placed in charge of those garrisons. Smith's principal responsibility would be to guard the railroad from an array of potential saboteurs ranging from Confederate scouts to hostile civilians.[7]

The start of the Federal occupation reinvigorated the county's pro-Confederate sympathies. While the Army of Tennessee's retreat failed to restore confidence in the Confederate government, the prolonged close proximity of Union soldiers reaffirmed local disgust for the enemy. Civilians chose ways to oppose the occupation that were within the limits of their abilities. Confederate deserters and stragglers, who remained in the area following the Army of Tennessee's retreat, aided the resistance. Many citizens resisted by providing Confederate partisans with supplies and shelter. Others worked as spies who gave guerrillas knowledge about troop movements and train schedules. Some civilians joined the fray and helped sabotage the railroad or attack isolated Federal pickets and foragers.[8]

---

[7]O. P. Hargis, "Thrilling Experiences of a First Georgia Cavalryman in the Civil War: Three Months Inside the Federal Lines in Rear of Sherman," Confederate Miscellany Collection, 1860–1865, box 8:32, Robert W. Woodruff Library, Manuscript, Archives, and Rare Book Library, Emory University, Atlanta; *OR*, ser. 1, 38 (4): 492; 38 (5): 245; 38 (2): 494–97; Lizzie Gaines, "'We Begged to Hearts of Stone': The Wartime Journal of Cassville's Lizzie Gaines," ed. Frances Josephine Black, *Northwest Georgia Historical and Genealogical Quarterly* 20 (Winter 1988): 6; Karen R. Hamilton, "The Union Occupation of Bartow County, Georgia, May–November 1864" (MA Thesis, State University of West Georgia, 1998) 17; Lucy J. Cunyus, *History of Bartow County, Georgia, Formerly Cass* (1933; rpt., Greenville SC: Southern Historical Press, 2001) 125.

[8]William King, diary, July 1864, call no. 2985-Z, Southern Historical Collection, University of North Carolina, Chapel Hill; James H. Spears to Mrs. Hiram H. Thornton, September 1864, Confederate Miscellany Collection, 1860–1865, box 6:53, Robert W. Woodruff Library, Manuscript, Archives, and Rare Book Library, Emory University, Atlanta; Rebecca Rainey Hood Papers, 1862–1865, "Memories of the Civil War and Echoes from the Heart of Rebecca Hood," Mss 325, Emory University, Atlanta; "The Front," *Confederate Union* (Milledgeville GA) 7 June 1864.

The W&A was the artery that supplied Sherman's army during the Atlanta Campaign. Nearly forty miles of its track was located in Bartow County. The railroad became the focus of attacks launched by Confederate partisans that were intended to disrupt Sherman's supplies and frustrate the Federal occupation force. Steedman issued General Order 2 on 28 June in response to "the barbarities practiced by placing torpedoes under the track to blow up trains containing sick and wounded soldiers." The order threatened to arrest and prosecute civilians before a military commission as spies who were "found lurking" within three miles of the railroad in areas outside of Federal lines.[9]

Bartow County civilians protested; on 23 July, a group of women traveled to Kingston to petition the post commander, Colonel Jabez Banbury, to rescind the order. Banbury, a veteran of the 5th Iowa Infantry, told the women that he would not enforce the order, but he warned them that he was being mustered out of service in August. A week later, two Union lieutenants arrived in Cassville with orders to relocate the populace. Many citizens balked, while others passively gathered their remaining belongings into the wagons furnished by the army for the removal. Much to the civilians' dismay, soldiers plundered the wagons, robbing them of many of their valuables. When several women complained about the soldiers' behavior, the commanding officer strongly reprimanded the guilty parties and supervised the return of the stolen items.[10]

Many civilians who remained in Bartow County during the occupation were married women whose husbands were serving in the Confederate army. Women endured the stressful demands of preserving their family and home while continuing their support for the Confederate government. During the war, women had assumed new roles within the household, often becoming its principal provider and protector. They treated occupying soldiers as both friend and foe, depending upon the circumstance. Soldiers complained about the "secesh women" of

---

[9]*OR,* ser. 1, 38 (4): 492; 38 (5): 245; 38 (2): 494–97; *Daily Chronicle and Sentinel* (Macon GA), 13 September 1864.

[10]Benjamin F. Gue, *History of Iowa: From the Earliest Times to the Beginning of the Twentieth Century,* 4 vols. (New York: Century History Company, 1903) 4:13; Gaines, "We Begged to Hearts of Stone," 6.

Cassville who cursed and spat at passing troops. Those same men also cherished the motherly affection shown by others who provided momentary comforts such as biscuits and milk. Women frequently dealt with their situation by soliciting the patronage and paternalism of "Yankee" soldiers. Trusted Federal officers provided local women with a masculine safety net that, when needed, could address concerns that their husbands and fathers had once resolved. These relationships reflect the void that some soldiers filled within the lives of many female civilians struggling to preserve their homes and families amidst arduous and unfamiliar circumstances.[11]

Civilians often acted toward Federal soldiers so as to best protect a civilian's individual interests. Berry Houk, who had never expressed any Unionist sympathies prior to 1864, led a party of sixty people who traveled to Calhoun to take the amnesty oath. Soldiers rewarded Houk's efforts by posting an armed guard to protect his home from looting stragglers. In Cassville, two old men who remained during the occupation but had previously maintained their neutrality suddenly proclaimed their allegiance to the United States in an effort to prevent their relocation by Union soldiers. Some former secessionists hoped to receive special privileges from the occupying army in return for taking the oath. Women whose property had been stolen by soldiers frequently took the oath in order to curry favor with the local provost marshal. The provost marshal demanded that women who were seeking the return of property provide documentation that the women had taken the oath. Lizzie Gaines observed the "air of exultation" as women waved the required document, excited that they would retrieve their stole property. When Gaines asked the officer to return her stolen cow, he requested to see her papers. She replied, "I am a Southerner by birth and principle and would not take the oath for all the cows in the United States." Much to her surprise, another woman scolded her, saying that her insolent

---

[11]Petition of Rebecca R. Hood, Southern Claims Commission, (disallowed) claim 2845, National Archives and Records Administration-Southeast Division, Morrow; Gaines, "We Begged to Hearts of Stone," 5; Ash, *When the Yankees Came*, 6, 61–62.

behavior was putting everyone at risk of not having their cattle returned.[12]

Unlike pro-Confederates such as Lizzie Gaines, Unionists embraced Federal soldiers as liberators. During the initial occupation of Cassville, emboldened Unionists burned the homes of three "secesh" leaders. Concerned that Confederates might exact retribution, Unionist Oliver Vaughan organized a company of Union men to serve as a home guard during the occupation. The home guard unit helped the Union Army capture Confederate stragglers and deserters. After capturing two deserters visiting their families, Vaughan led the men to the Cartersville garrison where they were placed in shackles and transported northward to a military prison.[13]

Bands of guerillas targeted both Federal troops and home guard units. These attacks frustrated an occupation force that struggled to differentiate between hostile partisans and noncombatants. Following an attack, Union soldiers interrogated suspected saboteurs, typically threatening to burn their homes or towns if they did not reveal the culprit's identity. The Cartersville garrison temporarily jailed dozens of citizens accused of aiding and abetting guerrillas. Most returned home after a brief period of confinement, but military officials banished several dozen civilians to north of the Ohio River for the duration of the war.[14]

The Federals correctly suspected that a lot of women were Confederate spies. In July, soldiers garrisoned at Kingston arrested Julia and Jane Murchison. They had enjoyed a great deal of freedom during

---

[12]Testimony of Berry Houk, SCC, (disallowed) claim 802, Georgia Archives, Morrow; Godfrey Barnsley to Alfred A. Marsh, 3 March 1865, Godfrey Barnsley Papers, MS 1737, box 14:3, Hargrett Rare Book and Manuscript Library, University of Georgia, Athens; "Wife" to J. D. Bowdoin, 23 June 1864, GA14, Kennesaw Mountain National Battlefield Park Library, Marietta; Gaines, "We Begged to Hearts of Stone," 4.

[13]Testimony of Grandison Vaughan, SCC, (allowed) claim 520, NARA-SE, Morrow; Testimony of Nancy Russell, SCC, (allowed) claim 6058, NARA-SE; Testimony of Willis McDow, SCC, (allowed) claim 14920, NARA-SE; Testimony of Sarah Crow, SCC, (allowed) claim 71941, NARA-SE.

[14]Petition of Rebecca R. Hood, SCC, (disallowed) claim 2845, NARA-SE, Morrow; Testimony of Berry Houk, SCC, (disallowed) claim 802, Georgia Archives, Morrow GA; Mrs. William A. Chunn to Mrs. E. W. Chunn, 14 November 1864, Chunn-Land Papers, M 44-101, box 4:2, Georgia Archives, Morrow GA; Testimony of Richard Chitwood, Southern Claims Commission, (disallowed) claim 121, NARA-SE, Morrow GA.

the early months of the occupation. They regularly received passes from the Kingston provost marshal allowing them to visit families who lived along the W&A. On the morning of 19 July, the sisters walked into the Kingston train depot to request another pass. Lieutenant Colonel Ezekial Sampson, 5th Iowa Infantry, rejected the women's request, in part because of Julia's chosen attire; a gray Confederate jacket adorned with a captain's insignia. The sight of the uniform annoyed Sampson, who ordered the young woman to remove the coat. He believed it was part of the uniform that belonged to a suspected guerrilla. A few days earlier, while in pursuit of this renegade, Union cavalry found a pair of gloves that had been dropped by the fleeing guerrilla. Grabbing the woman's jacket, Sampson placed it on his desk and promptly removed the gloves from a nearby drawer and presented them to the women as evidence of their deceptions. Julia picked up the gloves and kissed them.[15]

After leaving Sampson's office, the sisters visited without a pass a family who lived along the W&A. Upon their return, Federal pickets arrested the women and charged them with aiding and abetting guerillas and violating General Order 2. The District of the Etowah's commanding officer sentenced the women to serve time in a military prison located in Louisville, Kentucky.[16]

Federal concerns about civilians relaying information to Confederates increased in August when General Joseph Wheeler dispatched Company I of the 1st Georgia Cavalry to strike the W&A for three months. The general handpicked the company, meaning that a majority

---

[15]Howard, *In and Out of the Lines*, 158–64.

[16]While imprisoned, the Murchison sisters endured harsh conditions that weakened their physical health. During the first six weeks, the women stayed at barracks 1, which lacked any proper sanitary facilities as well as adequate bedding. By the time the sisters were transferred to the Female Military Prison, Julia had developed pneumonia. Jane begged her to take the amnesty oath rather than risk death by remaining in prison. As her condition worsened, Julia consented, took the oath, and was released to remain north of the Ohio River for the remainder of the war. After living in Ohio for several weeks, she decided to return to Bartow County anyway. The journey required slipping through numerous Federal checkpoints while avoiding detection since her parole banned her return. While moving through a picket line in Tennessee, soldiers mortally wounded Julia. Jane remained in prison for the remainder of the war, unwilling to take the oath. She returned to Bartow County in May 1865.

of soldiers hailed from Bartow County and therefore knew the terrain well. His unit grew in size while operating in the county since many deserters were willing to ride with a cavalry detachment to avoid persecution. Othinel Pope Hargis's brothers, William Henry and Richard Reuben, deserted the Army of Northern Virginia to join the 1st Georgia Cavalry. Their orders included tearing up the railroad, cutting telegraph wires, derailing trains, and disrupting supplies traveling between Calhoun and Cartersville. Wheeler instructed the soldiers to avoid engaging the enemy whenever possible. The Federal Army immediately felt their presence. In August, Sherman ordered the revival of the old visual signal system since enemy scouts continued to cut their telegraph wires.[17]

Many civilians provided the cavalrymen and guerillas with intelligence and supplies that benefited their operations. Othinel Hargis, a scout serving in the 1st Georgia Cavalry, recalled that "the people would find out where we were camped and cook a basket full of rations and bring them to us, and we would get feed for our horses from them.... We had a good time out there." Warren Akin believed that most locals would have gladly surrendered their "last mouthful of bread" to feed a "rebel" scout. The county contained loyal Confederates who were "as full of rebel blood as a tick." A network of support developed, designed to foil Federal attempts to track the movements of suspected supporters. Federals were especially suspicious of women whose husbands and sons served in the Confederate Army. They knew that numerous deserters had returned to the county and had joined guerrilla bands or else were hiding out in the countryside near their homes. Any woman who traveled into the woods to visit their family members risked compromising both herself and their loved ones because Union soldiers and Unionists commonly watched their every move. Women therefore gave food and supplies to other local women who were not under enemy surveillance who in turn carried the items to the men.[18]

---

[17]Hargis, *Thrilling Experiences,* 24; Cunyus, *History of Bartow County*, 63.

[18]Hargis, *Thrilling Experiences,* 24; Joseph Wheeler to Joseph E. Brown, 12 January 1865, Joseph Emerson Brown Papers, 1859–1889, manuscripts department, William R. Perkins Library, Duke University, Durham NC.

Federal scouts routinely searched homes in search of Confederate soldiers. A Union officer once questioned Jane Howard if she had harbored Confederates. She responded that "we, like all true Southern women, will aid our soldiers whenever and wherever we can." Cassville, in particular, sheltered Confederate scouts, guerrillas, and deserters who attracted the nearby garrison's attention. After soldiers ransacked Lizzie Gaines's home looking for a suspected guerrilla, she told the intruders that "if they did not want the Rebels to visit the place, they must be more vigilant themselves, that we would not make it our business to keep them away."[19]

If captured, guerrillas expected to receive no quarter from Federal soldiers. While on a mission to destroy a bridge over the Etowah, a partisan known only as Hutchison detoured from his objective to make an unannounced visit with his mother. Federal scouts tracked his movements. While re-crossing the Etowah River, the Federals attacked Hutchison, who fled on foot into some nearby woods with the enemy in close pursuit. One week later, Federal soldiers knocked on Hutchison's mother's door. They told her that her son had drowned in the river while attempting to reach Confederate lines. Upon recovering his body, the mother was shocked to discover that his hands were bound together. He still had his hat, which would have been unlikely had he drowned. The mother claimed that Union soldiers caught and interrogated him hoping to learn the identity and location of his companions. The soldiers beat Hutchison to death after he refused to cooperate with their demands.[20]

The proximity of large numbers of scouts and guerrillas instilled a sense of paranoia among Federal soldiers. They feared that attackers lurked around every corner. During the summer, for example, a small band of foragers impressed several cows from the residents of Cassville. While herding the cattle toward Kingston, the soldiers noticed that they were being followed by two girls. Initially the soldiers ignored the girls, but upon reaching an isolated stretch of road their insecurities overwhelmed their emotions. The girls had stopped fewer than a hundred yards from the soldiers when they began clapping their hands while

---

[19]Howard, *In and Out of the Lines*, 158-64.
[20]Ibid.

shouting "here they are, catch them, catch them." Surrounded by a dense thicket, the soldiers panicked and "skedaddled," believing that the girls were signaling nearby guerrillas. Later that evening, the stolen cows wandered back into Cassville.[21]

Federals lived in constant fear of such ambushes. On 8 July, Jenkin Jones's commanding officer ordered him to graze their artillery unit's horses. Ordinarily, this duty would have been considered light, but Jones knew that grazing the horses would isolate him from the rest of his unit. After traveling as short of a distance as possible, he located an area suitable for grazing. A few minutes later, he was startled by a passing Unionist who warned him that a band of guerrillas was lurking in some nearby woods waiting to capture his horses. Jones appreciated the warning and returned to his post as soon as possible. Two weeks later, he recorded in his diary that a squad of about 150 guerrillas overran a picket post and then vanished into thin air. A month later, he reported "troublesome" rebels between Allatoona and Acworth. At this time, he suspected two missing comrades had been murdered, but he learned a few days later that these men had been taken prisoner and were in "humane hands." On 1 September, bushwhackers killed a Union soldier, whom they "stripped of all valuables, boots, and hat, leaving his corpse in the road, taking two others prisoners."[22]

The city of Atlanta surrendered on 2 September. The fall of Atlanta signaled the beginning of the end for the Confederacy, yet the fledgling nation managed to sustain itself for another eight months. Some Bartow Countians such as William Chunn believed that the Army of Tennessee would never surrender Atlanta. While serving in that city's trenches, Chunn told his wife that the army's morale had never been better and that he expected them to regain all of the valuable farmland they had abandoned during the spring. Several poorly executed Confederate

---

[21]*Letters of Warren Aiken, Confederate Congressman*, ed. Bell Irvin Wiley (Athens: University of Georgia Press, 1964) 28; Reuben S. Norton, diary, 27 June 1864 [microfilm], Special Collections Room, Sara Hightower Regional Library, Rome GA.

[22]Margaret M. Storey, *Loyalty and Loss: Alabama's Unionists in the Civil War and Reconstruction* (Baton Rouge: Louisiana State University Press, 2004) 109; Jenkin Lloyd Jones, *An Artilleryman's Diary* (Madison: Wisconsin History Commission, 1914) 228, 234, 243–44, 253. Jones was a member of the 6th Wisconsin Artillery Battery.

assaults combined with the enemy's superior numbers, firepower, and well-timed flanking maneuvers dashed his hopes. Writing from Palmetto a month after abandoning the city, Chunn, for the first time, stated that defeat was imminent and unavoidable.[23]

The strategy employed by General John B. Hood after the fall of Atlanta directly impacted Bartow County. His plan involved marching the Army of Tennessee into Northwest Georgia to strike Sherman's supply lines. If successful, Hood would force the Federals to abandon Atlanta and pursue him into Northern Alabama. If Sherman did not take the bait, the Army of Tennessee could then attack his rear.[24]

Sherman fell back to secure his lines. Hood's movements pulled additional Federal troops into Bartow County. Sherman moved his entire army, minus the XX Army Corps, into Northwest Georgia, reinforcing garrisons scattered along the W&A. Guerrilla attacks upon Federal soldiers increased in Bartow County as the Army of Tennessee returned. On 5 October, Union and Confederate armies battled to control a W&A railroad cut at Allatoona Pass. The defeated Confederates moved into Alabama following the battle.[25]

On 6 October, Sherman established his headquarters in Kingston at the Hargis house, located near the train depot. As during the previous May, tens of thousands of Federal soldiers poured through the county, looting civilian homes wherever they passed. From 10 to 13 October, the bulk of the Union Army marched through Cassville, stripping the town bare of all livestock, feed, and horses. On 12 October, soldiers pushed aside the Federal guard that had been ordered to protect Godfrey Barnsley's home and proceeded to ransack the lavish estate, causing more damage than the Army of the Cumberland had done six months earlier. The depressed owner lamented the fact that the wealth that he

---

[23]William A. Chunn to Elizabeth Word Chunn, 2 August 1864, Chunn-Land Papers, MS 44-101, box 1:2, Georgia Archives, Morrow.

[24]Joseph E. Brown to John B. Hood, 10 September 1864, Executive Department, governor's letter books, 1861–1865 [microfilm], drawer 61:79, p. 694, Georgia Archives, Morrow.

[25]William R. Scaife, *Allatoona Pass: A Needless Effusion of Blood* (Cartersville GA: Etowah Valley Historical Society, 1995) 5–10.

had worked a lifetime to build had vanished over the course of a single afternoon.[26]

Guerrilla activity in the county swelled as the size of the Federal occupation force increased. Bushwhackers attacked a detachment of the 100th Indiana on 9 October sent into the countryside to gather firewood. The partisans surrounded the men, forcing them to surrender. As the attackers began executing the soldiers, Private Charles Ellis, Company B, dropped his rifle to the ground and pleaded with the guerrillas to spare his life. They shot him at point-blank range despite his pleas. The following morning, Theodore Upson of the same regiment discovered the bodies of several civilians hanged for the attacks. Their executioners pinned a placard on each corpse warning bushwhackers to either halt their activities or watch as the occupiers destroyed all buildings within a ten-mile area.[27]

The warnings failed to thwart the guerrilla attacks. On 12 October, a Federal ambulance passing through Cassville broke down. Unable to repair the wagon, the driver set up camp for the night. As the evening progressed, nine Union stragglers joined the driver, drawn toward his camp by its warm fire. That night, an unidentified band of guerrillas killed the ten men while they slept. The following morning, the advanced guard of the XVII Corps found the driver with a bayonet protruding from his chest. Federal personnel stationed near the site discovered the bodies of the other nine soldiers.[28]

The way the ten soldiers died deeply angered Federal commanders. Members of the Brigadier General Kenner Garrard's Second Division Cavalry burned two colleges and the homes of Nathan Land and Dr.

---

[26]Rebecca Minis to Godfrey Barnsley, 27 July 1865, Godfrey Barnsley Papers, 1822-11890, MS 13, box 2.2, Manuscripts, Archives, and Rare Books Library, Emory University, Decatur GA, Clent Coker, *Barnsley Gardens at Woodlands: The Illustrious Dream* (Atlanta GA: Julia Company, 2000) 131–32.

[27]Theodore Frelinghuysen Upson, *With Sherman to the Sea: The Civil War Letters, Diaries, and Reminiscences of Theodore F. Upson* (Bloomington: Indiana University Press, 1958) 132.

[28]David Williams, *Rich Man's War: Class, Caste, and Confederate Defeat in the Lower Chattahoochee Valley* (Athens: University of Georgia Press, 2002) 74–75; Mahan, *Cassville*, 104–105; *Letters of Warren Akin*, 30; Gaines, "We Begged to Hearts of Stone," 6.

Thomas Rambaut, all in Cassville, in retaliation for these murders.[29] On 29 October, Federal soldiers informed the residents of Cassville that they would have to relocate. The following morning, Colonel Thomas Tinsley Heath and the 5th Ohio Cavalry arrived with wagons to help three families move their belongings. The 5th Ohio's orders demanded that they "permit the citizens to remove what they desire, and burn the town."[30]

On the afternoon of 5 November, the 5th Ohio ordered the remaining civilians to leave town immediately and then proceeded to burn Cassville. The soldiers watched as towering flames spewed black smoke skyward. Frightened residents pleaded with soldiers to put out the blaze before it reached their home, but the cavalrymen followed their orders and refrained from aiding civilians. Fire claimed the property of every Cassville resident, regardless of their political beliefs, except three. Indeed, some of the first homes destroyed belonged to Unionists William Sylar, Jesse James, and Hiram Holmes.[31]

As the sun set upon a blackened sky, rain and sleet began to fall upon the smoldering town. A local girl watched as "dark threatening clouds, which hung suspended for a while over the doomed spot, and then seemed to melt away in tears of grief. It appeared as if nature were weeping over the sad fate of Cassville." Most of the town's women and children endured the rain and sleet while remaining outside of their charred homes, guarding their few remaining possessions. A few stables and churches survived the fire, but many locals feared that the soldiers might return and set fire to them while the civilians slept. A few other families sought refuge from the storm in the town cemetery. Six months before, the center of the Confederate line stretched across this ground;

---

[29]Mrs. William A. Chunn to Mrs. E. W. Chunn, 14 November 1864, Chunn-Land Papers, MS 44-101, box 4:2, Georgia Archives, Morrow; Gaines, "We Begged to Hearts of Stone," 6.

[30]*OR,* ser. 1, 39 (3) 513; Thomas Tinsley Heath, *Straws: A Paper Read before the Ohio Commandery of the Loyal Legion, April 7, 1909* (Cincinnati OH: np, 1909).

[31]Bartow County, Inferior Court Minutes 1865–1868 [microfilm], drawer 166:54, Georgia Archives, Morrow; Claremont, "Creators of Community," 27; Deposition of Jesse James, 8 December 1877, and Deposition of Thomas Nance, 27 February 1878, claim of Nancy Russell, Records of the Southern Claims Commission (Allowed Claims) Bartow County GA, National Archives, Washington DC.

now, desperate civilians occupied the abandoned entrenchments that marked the site.[32]

In spring 1861, Cassville resident John F. Milhollin had enlisted in the Confederate Army, confident that God had ordained secession. He died in combat while serving in the Army of Northern Virginia. On 5 November 1864, his wife and their six children watched as Union soldiers torched their home. That night, the family huddled together in the cemetery using planks from their father's fresh gravesite and several heavy quilts to construct a makeshift shelter against a wrought iron fence. As the family endured the cold and rain, they could see the glowing embers of the decimated home glittering a few hundred yards away. The soldier's fourteen-year-old son spent the next morning searching the countryside for a suitable dwelling. Four miles outside of town, the young man of the house located an abandoned slave cabin on the Saxon plantation that would function as the family's home for months.[33]

Sherman watched the smoke rise above Cassville from his Kingston headquarters. He had not personally ordered the town's destruction; Brigadier General John E. Smith wrote the order. Indeed, four days later, Sherman demanded that guerrillas return Union prisoners, or else Kingston, Cassville, and Cartersville would be burned. Cassville already lay in ruins. The commander included the town to provide "post facto" validity to Smith's order of 30 October.[34]

The Federal Army ultimately destroyed Cassville because the town actively aided and abetted guerrillas. A majority of people in town supported the Confederacy. Union soldiers regarded Cassville as "a hot bed of saboteurs." Since the town lacked a garrison and was located

[32]"The News from Georgia," *Daily Richmond Enquirer* (Richmond VA), 1 December 1864; Gaines, "We Begged to Hearts of Stone," 6; Hamilton, "Union Occupation of Bartow County," 75.

[33]Hamilton, "Union Occupation of Bartow County," 76–77; Mahan, *Cassville*, 109; Cunyus, *History of Bartow County*, 83; Mary Dodgen Few, *The Dodgen Story: An Account of a Truly American Family* (Greenville SC: Southern Historical Press, 1985) 123; Sean Michael O'Brien, *Mountain Partisans: Guerrilla Warfare in the Southern Appalachians, 1861–1865* (Westport CT: Praeger Publishers, 1999) 168.

[34]O'Brien, *Mountain Partisans*, 168.

along several critical roads, partisans and Confederate scouts moved in and out of the area with little resistance. A member of the 1st Georgia Cavalry reported that locals regularly fed, hid, and provided information to both scouts and irregulars.[35]

As the 5th Ohio Cavalry burned Cassville, the entire Union Army made preparations for the upcoming March to the Sea. The beginning movements of this campaign marked the end of the Federal occupation of Bartow County. Ten days later, Sherman abandoned his Kingston headquarters. As the last train passed through the county, Union soldiers destroyed the railroad and telegraph lines. The following morning, Federals burned Kingston and several homes in Cartersville. A soldier ordered to spread the blaze commented that "most of the families have either gone north or south, but a few, from some cause, have failed to get away and now they are weeping over their burning homes. The sight is grand but almost heartrending."[36]

The end of the Federal occupation removed the sole source of local authority, creating a power vacuum as the county spiraled dangerously toward anarchy. In the wake of the occupation, a lawless consortium of thieves and deserters descended upon the populace like locusts upon a wheat field. They preyed upon vulnerable female-headed households and unarmed travelers. Hiding in nearby wooded areas, caves, and swamps during the day, they used the cover of darkness to conceal their actions. A scheme commonly employed involved donning Confederate uniforms and presenting themselves to women as malnourished soldiers in desperate need of a Good Samaritan. Many of the women had husbands, sons, and brothers serving in the Confederate Army. From their letters, they read horrifying depictions of the poor conditions that existed within camps or defensive lines such as those surrounding Petersburg. Eager to help a soldier in need and hopeful that women elsewhere were doing the same for their loved ones, women opened their homes to these deceptive wolves in sheep's clothing. Once inside, the outlaws held the women and

---

[35]*Letters of Warren Akin*, 30.

[36]*Styles Porter Diary* (Columbus OH: Ohio Historical Society, 1865); Kennett, *Marching through Georgia*, 228–33; Castel, *Atlanta Campaign,* 554.

children at gunpoint, demanding money, jewelry, and food in exchange for not burning the home or physically assaulting its inhabitants.[37]

Captain Charles W. Howard returned home in January 1865 after recovering from a wound received during the Battle of Atlanta. Shortly after his arrival, a small group of men dressed in Confederate uniforms stormed into his home after his wife offered them some food. The men claimed to be cavalry scouts but probably belonged either to John Gatewood's or Jack Colquitt's partisans, who had been active in the area. Unaware of Howard's presence, the thieves began emptying drawers in the family's parlor, searching for valuables. When the veteran entered the room still wearing his captain's uniform from the 63rd Georgia, the robbers fled into the night. Their flight was short-lived, however, as they stumbled upon a tenant home located on Howard's property. The miller who worked at Howard's mill lived in the house with his family. The irregulars broke into the home at gunpoint, startling the residents. Panicked, the miller's wife offered to do anything for the men in exchange for the safety of her family. The partisans calmly sat at their dinner table and ordered the woman to cook them dinner. That night, the supposed scouts slept on the family's beds while the miller and his wife spent a restless night on the floor.[38]

Jack Colquitt's partisans preyed upon Northwest Georgia residents. Colquitt had connections to the region. Prior to the war, he had married the daughter of an area merchant, Jerry Isbell, but nothing else about Colquitt's early life is known. His tactics frequently included mock executions designed to force their targets to reveal hidden valuables. When Rome's Judge Lewis D. Burwell refused to reveal the location of a stash of gold he had hidden for a local Jewish merchant, Colquitt tied a

---

[37]Joseph E. Brown to Col. A. Hansell, 7 December 1864, Executive Department, governor's letter books, 1861–1865 [microfilm], drawer 61:79, Georgia Archives, Morrow; Joseph E. Brown to Col. William Phillips, 19 December 1864, Executive Department, governor's letter books, 1861–1865 [microfilm], drawer 61:79, Georgia Archives; Joseph Wheeler to Joseph E. Brown, 12 January 1865, Joseph Emerson Brown Papers, 1859–1889, manuscripts department, William R. Perkins Library, Duke University, Durham, North Carolina.

[38]Howard, *In and Out of the Lines*, 153; Hamilton, "Union Occupation of Bartow County," 85.

noose around the jurist's neck and hanged the man until he finally disclosed its whereabouts.[39]

Colquitt's reign of terror eventually cost him his life. Shortly after the incident with Judge Burwell, his company murdered H. M. Pryor of Cedartown. Pryor's three sons swore revenge. After several weeks spent tracking Colquitt across portions of Northwest Georgia, they ambushed the scouts, killing the leader and seven others. Had the Pryor boys not caught up with the guerrilla leader, he would likely have been killed by members of J. Woodville Baker's scouts, whose leader he killed "over the ownership of a mule" weeks earlier.[40]

Partisans regularly targeted Unionists. Cartersville resident Richard Chitwood initially supported secession. Four of his brothers enlisted in the Confederate Army. Sometime during the war, he became disenchanted with the Confederacy and developed a reputation for being a Union man. During the last weeks of the Federal occupation, Benjamin McCullom's band raided Chitwood's farm, stealing two horses. Through the use of a courier, the guerrillas notified him that if he traveled to their camp located near Canton that he could recover his property. Desperately in need of those horses, Chitwood made the twenty-plus-mile journey only to be detained by the scouts who tried to persuade him to join their ranks. He refused but negotiated his release in exchange for a suit of clothes.[41]

Unionists who had served as guides, scouts, informants, and foragers for the occupation army lived in constant fear of pro-Confederate guerrillas. McCullom's partisans routinely executed their victims. Jim Pitts served as a guide for Federal cavalry during the occupation. When the irregulars captured him, they transported him several dozen miles to

---

[39]George Magruder Battey, Jr., *A History of Rome and Floyd County, State of Georgia, United States of America: Including Numerous Incidents of More Than Local Interest, 1540–1922* (Atlanta: Webb and Vary, 1922) 206.

[40]Battey, *History of Rome and Floyd County*, 206–208; Gordon D. Sargent, "Bloody Legacy in Polk: A Frontier Family and Some Prior Commitments," in *A North Georgia Journal of History*, 4 vols., ed. Olin Jackson (Alpharetta GA: Legacy Communications, 1989) 1:36–43; Cunyus, *History of Bartow County*, 248–49; Hamilton, "Union Occupation of Bartow County," 86.

[41]Testimony of Richard Chitwood, Southern Claims Commission, (disallowed) claim 121, NARA-SE, Morrow.

Pine Log where they lynched him while forcing a local minister to read Psalm 23. On several occasions, McCullom's men captured Unionists, carried them to their camp located along the Etowah River, and placed their hostages on horseback before shooting them off the horses, watching the dead bodies fall down the riverbank into the water.[42]

The situation in Bartow County remained bleak throughout fall 1864. The creation of the Confederate Department of North Georgia offered some relief for the area's beleaguered civilians. Confederate Brigadier General William T. Wofford and Congressmen Warren Akin, both Cassville residents, petitioned President Jefferson Davis and General Robert E. Lee to create an independent military command in North Georgia that would restore order to the region. Some members of the Confederate high command opposed the plan. They were worried that Wofford's command would increase the number of desertions among Georgia soldiers serving in the Army of Northern Virginia. The new command presented a significant number of Georgia soldiers serving in Virginia with an honorable alternative to their current service. The return of large numbers of military-aged males to their homes and families helped rescue Bartow County from being conquered by the "bitter dregs of war." Ultimately, Bartow County benefited from the Confederacy's loss.[43]

The formation of the Department of North Georgia and the return of numerous deserters to their homes combined to diminish the impact of lawless bands preying upon Bartow County civilians. Wofford divided his force into small units that effectively patrolled major roads in the area. Informants provided these soldiers with the intelligence necessary to track down guerrilla outposts and hideouts. Capturing guerillas and deserters proved to be an arduous undertaking. While his command arrested several hundred of these individuals, a much larger number

---

[42]Ibid.; *Southern Banner* (Athens GA), 15 February 1865, 3; Marlin, *The History of Cherokee County*, 73–77.

[43]Joseph E. Brown to John B. Hood, 17 August 1864, Executive Department, governor's letter books, 1861–1865 [microfilm], drawer 61:79, p. 684, Georgia Archives, Morrow.

remained beyond their reach. The force's presence, nevertheless, helped keep most of these outlaws running rather than attacking civilians.[44]

The department's efforts to restore order to North Georgia received substantial aid from an unexpected source. While Wofford scoured the countryside searching for deserters and criminals, he maintained amicable relations with Union Major General George H. Thomas, who commanded the closest enemy forces stationed in East Tennessee. After arresting a member of John Gatewood's partisans in Northeast Georgia, Wofford learned that this band planned to strike the railroad near Knoxville. The commander became concerned that if the raid took place, Thomas might retaliate by occupying North Georgia. Wofford informed Thomas of the impending raid. His decision helped form a bond of trust among the battle-hardened commanders that greatly reduced the unnecessary bloodshed in the area during the war's final months.[45]

The détente between the Department of North Georgia and General George Thomas's command brought a level of law and order to the region that had been absent since Sherman had ended its occupation during fall 1864. Relief came at a critical moment. According to official reports, 62 percent of the inhabitants of Bartow County lacked enough food and supplies to get through the spring. The state of Georgia had purchased $800,000 worth of corn during the previous fall specifically intended to be distributed to North Georgia civilians. Wofford appreciated the corn but worried that, during transport, it might be captured by lawless bands of thieves and deserters. The railroad between Cassville and Dalton was still inoperable, and the only way to distribute the corn was by horse-drawn wagons. Those caravans required armed guards in order to fend off potential attackers. Wofford wanted his forces to supervise the distribution of this much-needed corn, but to do so might have attracted the suspicions of the nearby Union Army. To avoid any confrontation, the general traveled to Dalton where he met with Brigadier General Benjamin M. Judah to gain the enemy's permission to

---

[44]Joseph E. Brown to Col. A. Hansell, 7 December 1864, Executive Department, governor's letter books, 1861–1865 [microfilm], drawer 61:79, p. 736, Georgia Archives, Morrow; *Letters of Warren Akin*, 148; Smith, *The Most Daring of Men*, 133; Hamilton, "Union Occupation of Bartow County," 89.

[45]*OR*, ser. 1, 49: (2): 396, 456, 469.

escort those wagons. At that meeting, Judah permitted Wofford to send wagons behind Federal lines to supply starving families. In exchange, the Confederate general agreed to keep his main forces south of the Etowah River.

Wofford and Judah's meeting in Dalton occurred three days after General Robert E. Lee surrendered the Army of Northern Virginia. The Department of North Georgia remained active for a time, receiving orders from the Army of Tennessee and the fleeing Confederate government. Judah wanted Wofford to surrender as soon as possible, but the general delayed that action since so many lawless groups still roamed the region and because Johnston's army remained in the field. On 21 April, the commander received word that Johnston had surrendered in North Carolina. Wofford surrendered the Department of North Georgia on 2 May.[46]

The Civil War had ended, much to the relief of many Bartow Countians, but the area still needed protection from lawless bands of outlaws. Wofford telegraphed Thomas requesting that Judah leave a portion of his army in the county to protect civilians from further attacks. The commander consented to the request and stationed regiments in Adairsville, Kingston, Cartersville, and Cassville. As Reconstruction began, civilians embarked upon a new era of struggle and deprivation as they rebuilt their tattered lives and communities.[47]

The events of 1864 and 1865 before, during, and after the Federal occupation in Bartow County eroded the populace's will to continue fighting the war. Federal soldiers between May and November of 1864 struggled to make a distinction between noncombatants and partisans. The actions of civilians irritated Union soldiers and commanders, forcing the latter to adopt harsher policies toward noncombatants suspected of aiding guerrillas. Following the withdrawal of Union forces, civilians found themselves in a similar situation as they too could no longer differentiate between friend and foe and appeared to be surrounded by an enemy who did not follow the same rules of conduct practiced by the

---

[46]Ibid., 488.

[47]Hébert, "The Bitter Trial of Defeat and Emancipation: Reconstruction in Bartow County, Georgia, 1865–1872," *Georgia Historical Quarterly* 92/1 (Spring 2008): 65–92.

Federals. The home front's collapse left a lingering bitterness among wartime survivors who grappled with the terms and conditions of the Confederacy's defeat.

From Gate City to Gotham:
Sam Richards Chronicles the Civil War in Atlanta

by Wendy Hamand Venet

In October 1861, six months after the start of the Civil War, Sam Richards, his wife Sallie, and their four children arrived in Atlanta and began a new life in what was then called "Gate City of the South." After months of indecision, Sam relocated his family from Macon to find wartime business opportunities. Richards's diary provides the best individual chronicle of civilian life in Atlanta.[1] Through the writings of Sam Richards, we learn about a city where residents were initially skeptical about Southern nationalism, but where citizens eventually embraced the cause with enthusiasm. We learn about a city troubled by wartime shortages and inflation, filled with sick and wounded soldiers, and decimated by Union invasion and occupation. Ultimately, Confederate civilians became refugees when they were expelled by order of General William T. Sherman. In Sam's case that meant traveling to New York City. Yet what crushed the city's Confederate civilians liberated its slaves. Atlanta was transformed by war.

Sam Richards was one of eight children born in England to a Baptist clergyman and his wife. At age six, Sam moved with his family to Hudson, New York, then to Penfield, Georgia, where Mercer Institute (later Mercer University) was located. After attending Mercer for a brief period, he entered into a business partnership with his older brother Jabez, called Jabe by the family. The brothers opened a book, stationery, and sheet music store in Macon, and earned extra cash by taking turns

---

[1] *Sam Richards's Civil War Diary. A Chronicle of the Atlanta Home Front*, ed. Wendy Hamand Venet (Athens: University of Georgia Press, 2009). This book covers the years 1860–1865. Richards kept a diary from 1842 to 1909. The fifteen volumes of his manuscript diary are located at the Atlanta History Center, Atlanta GA. In 1937, Russell Richards gave permission to Wilbur Kurtz, an Atlanta artist and amateur historian, to read his father's diary. Kurtz was a friend of the author Margaret Mitchell, shared the diary with her, and used it as a source when serving as technical advisor for the movie *Gone with the Wind*, based on Mitchell's novel. See scrapbooks 11 and 12, Wilbur G. Kurtz, Sr., Collection, Atlanta History Center.

peddling books in the Middle Georgia countryside. By 1855, sensing that Atlanta, not Macon, offered greater long-term business prospects, Jabez Richards opened a second branch of the store there. He wrote frequently to his brother, urging him to leave Macon for a brighter future in Atlanta. In 1861 Sam decided his brother was right. He closed the Macon store and made Atlanta his home for the rest of his life.[2]

Judging by the way its citizens voted in the election of 1860, Atlanta was not a city initially enthusiastic about Southern independence. Indeed, Atlanta's citizens seemed to care more about economic opportunity than politics before 1860, in part because Atlanta was a relatively young city dominated by its business class rather than a planter elite.[3] In the highly charged presidential contest of 1860, Republican Abraham Lincoln received no support in the state, but three candidates vied for Democratic votes. The party's official nominee, Stephen A. Douglas, running on a platform of avoiding secession and war, won the support of Northern Democrats and some Southerners, while two breakaway Democrats took most Southern votes. John Breckinridge represented the interests of those favoring Southern independence, while John Bell attracted the support of those who hoped to avoid separation from the North. The two Unionist Democrats, Douglas and Bell, won a total of 63 percent of Atlanta's votes.[4] Sam Richards did not reveal how or even whether he voted in 1860, but he opposed secession and hoped that war with the North might be avoided. Still living in Macon in November 1860, he went to hear the speech of Stephen A. Douglas, who campaigned in both Atlanta and Macon in the weeks before the national election, introduced on the platform by his friend, Alexander Stephens. Richards disparaged

[2] *Sam Richards's Civil War Diary*, 1–18, 33.

[3] Mary A. DeCredico, *Patriotism for Profit: Georgia's Urban Entrepreneurs and the Confederate War Effort* (Chapel Hill: University of North Carolina Press, 1990) 22.

[4] *Atlanta Daily Intelligencer*, 7 November 1860, reported these totals: Breckinridge 835, Douglas 335, Bell 1,070. The following day, the newspaper printed totals for Fulton County: Breckinridge 1,018, Douglas 347, and Bell 1,195. See also Thomas G. Dyer, *Secret Yankees: The Union Circle in Confederate Atlanta* (Baltimore MD: Johns Hopkins University Press, 1999) 42.

secessionists as "young *squirts*" and "*politicians* who aspire to office in a Southern Confederacy."[5]

Once the election ended in Lincoln's triumph, Confederate nationalism grew dramatically even among former Unionists such as Sam Richards. A moderately successful businessman who owned no slaves, Richards had been a political centrist throughout the 1840s and 1850s, voting for Whig candidates and later, following Whig demise nationally, for those seeking state office in Georgia who sought compromise with the North. A reader of newspapers both in Macon and Atlanta, he saw the press condemn the election of Lincoln. The *Macon Telegraph* intoned, "Our very worst prognostications are realized," while the *Atlanta Daily Intelligencer* announced, "We are destined to wear the yoke of Black Republican rule, unless we rise up in our defence." Like thousands of white people across the South, Samuel Richards concluded that Lincoln's election represented an effort to force an antislavery agenda on the Southern states. He wrote, "The Republican party—has succeeded in forcing upon the South Abraham Lincoln as president, with the expectation that we would submit...and all would go on calmly and quietly as ever." Then he added, "The whole country is in a ferment."[6]

Throughout the South, support for Confederate nationalism gained momentum. On 12 November, 400 to 500 Atlantans met at the courthouse to hear patriotic orations and pass resolutions, including one that stated, "The only adequate remedy for the State of Georgia is secession from the Union." Groups for home defense called Minute Men formed in the weeks following Lincoln's election. In Atlanta, anticipating the election's result, the city's Minute Men held a preliminary meeting a few days before the election. Additional military

---

[5]*Sam Richards's Civil War Diary*, 30-39 (8 December 1860). For the two speeches, see *Macon Telegraph*, 1 November 1860, and *Atlanta Daily Intelligencer*, 31 October 1860.

[6]*Macon Telegraph*, 8 November 1860; *Atlanta Daily Intelligencer*, 8 November 1860; *Sam Richards's Civil War Diary*, 36 (10 November 1860). Anne Sarah Rubin has written that "the speed with which white Southerners, many of them staunch Unionists through the election of 1860, shed their American identity and picked up a sense of themselves as Confederates was startling" (*A Shattered Nation: The Rise and Fall of the Confederacy 1861–1868* [Chapel Hill: University of North Carolina Press, 2005] 1).

units formed, including the Atlanta Grays and the Gate City Guards. Leading citizens in Atlanta lent their names, their financial support, and their sons to join these units.[7] Those promoting separation from the North actively sought women's participation. In the *Atlanta Daily Intelligencer*, an article appeared on 19 November 1860, by "A Georgia Woman" calling on all female patriots to oppose "submission to a Black Republican President." While reminding her readers that it was "unlady-like for women to interest themselves in political affairs," the writer asked women to encourage men's enlistment in local military units. Atlanta's Minute Men called upon the city's female population to match the efforts of "fairest daughters of Charleston, Augusta, Savannah, Columbia, and Macon" by wearing a blue cockade, the "insignia of Southern Rights," and by stitching them for others. Although "your arms cannot fight...your *fingers* can sew." Within a week, women made several formal presentations of their hand-stitched cockades to the Minute Men, their names printed in the *Daily Intelligencer*.[8]

Between the election of Lincoln and Georgia's secession, Sam Richards dropped his previous support for Unionism. Richards did not say exactly when he became a secessionist, but on 1 December 1860 he went to hear Eugenius Nisbet address the Macon Minute Men. A prewar Whig whose 1850 speech eulogizing Zachary Taylor had impressed Richards, Nisbet now played a leading role in Georgia secession. On 19 January 1861, Nisbet introduced the resolution that led Georgia to secede from the Union. Richards called the move "a stern necessity" forced upon the South by abolitionists, and he wrote that "a just God" would bring victory to the South. Although he claimed he would not celebrate Georgia's withdrawal from the Union, he did meet with friends to practice singing what he called "a Southern Marseilles Hymn" to serenade Macon's Minute Men. In Atlanta, secessionists staged a demonstration that included firing rockets and cannon and the illumination of houses, hotels, newspaper offices, and the railroad depot.

---

[7]*Atlanta Daily Intelligencer*, 2 November 1860, 10 November 1860, 12 November 1860, 13 November 1860.

[8]*Atlanta Daily Intelligencer*, 19 November 1860, 3 December 1860, 6 December 1860, 10 December 1860.

Members of Sam's extended family showed their patriotism as well. Two of his wife's brothers joined the Confederate army and one of his sisters wrote and published verses in support of the Confederacy.[9]

By moving to Atlanta, the Richards family became part of a vast in-migration. Founded as a rail center in the 1830s, Atlanta grew and prospered in the succeeding decades to a prewar population of nearly 10,000. With the war, Atlanta's importance increased. Its railroads transported agricultural products to feed the Confederate armies. Factories produced war materials to sustain the military. By 1862 Atlanta's population was estimated to be 17,000, and a city once known as the home of railroad employees, speculators, and rowdies seemed more affluent and polished. By the time the Union army captured the city in 1864, its population was nearly 22,000.[10]

As an industrial center, Atlanta grew in importance early in the war, especially after Nashville and New Orleans fell to the Union early in 1862. A variety of private factories produced materials for the Confederate military, including the Atlanta Rolling Mill, which made rails, plating, and machinery. Several factories relocated from elsewhere in the Confederacy, including the Atlanta Sword Factory of H. Marshall and Company, formerly of Nashville, which produced 170 cavalry and artillery swords per week. The Spiller and Burr pistol factory relocated from Richmond. Other private factories made whiskey, vinegar, clothing, even false teeth, for use by the military. Far and away Atlanta's most important enterprise was the Confederate Arsenal, which by 1862 had

---

[9]*Sam Richards's Civil War Diary*, 29, 36 (10 November 1860); 38 (1 December 1860); 41–42 (19 January 1861); *Macon Telegraph*, 30 November 1860; Michael P. Johnson, *Toward a Patriarchal Republic: The Secession of Georgia* (Baton Rouge: Louisiana State University Press, 1977) 114–17; *Atlanta Daily Intelligencer*, 12 December 1860, 23 January 1861. For Savannah's celebrations, see Jacqueline Jones, *Saving Savannah: The City and the Civil War* (New York: Knopf, 2008) 123. James Dunbar Van Valkenburg joined the 61st Georgia. George Van Valkenburg joined Georgia's 2nd Battalion. Mrs. C.W. DuBose [Katherine Richards DuBose] and Hermann Schreiner, "God Defendeth the Right" (Macon GA: Schreiner, 1861).

[10]James Michael Russell, *Atlanta 1847–1890: City Building in the Old South and the New* (Baton Rouge: Louisiana State University Press, 1988) 92; Charles C. Jones, Jr., to Reverend C. C. Jones, 25 July 1862, in *The Children of Pride: A True Story of Georgia and the Civil War*, ed. Robert Manson Myers, abridged ed. (New Haven CT: Yale University Press, 1984) 284.

thirteen shops that manufactured cannon, sabers, percussion caps, cartridges, saddles, knapsacks, and canteens. The arsenal employed nearly 5,500 men and women. The Confederate Quartermaster's Depot employed 3,000 seamstresses to make pants, shirts, jackets, hats, and undergarments. Private firms also produced clothing, including Lawshe and Purtell, which placed ads in local newspapers under the headline, "Work Plenty for the Ladies," seeking one hundred women to sew uniforms.[11]

When the Richards family relocated to Atlanta in October 1861, Sam observed a city growing so rapidly that housing was hard to find. Sam and his family boarded with Jabez, his wife Stella, and their two daughters. Their home on Washington Street was a few blocks from city hall and Second Baptist Church, where the extended Richards family worshiped. The home was also easily accessible to Atlanta's business district on Whitehall Street, making Sam's walk to work an easy one. But the living arrangement was far from ideal. Sam's family of six was sandwiched into two rooms in the Washington Street house. While both brothers regarded the arrangement as temporary, Sam and his family would spend most of the war in this house. The extended visits of Richards's siblings who lived in Middle and South Georgia and South Carolina made for a very full household. Moreover, Jabez and Stella periodically took in boarders, including an employee of the Spiller and Burr pistol factory.[12]

The same factors that made Atlanta attractive to industrialists—its railroads, location in the Confederacy's interior, and relatively mild climate—made it an ideal location for Confederate hospitals. With the surrender of Confederate garrisons at Forts Henry and Donelson in February 1862, wounded soldiers began arriving in the city in significant numbers. By the following month Sam estimated there were between 3000 and 4000 soldiers in area hospitals. More than a dozen facilities cared for Confederate wounded in 1862, including Atlanta Medical

---

[11]*Atlanta Daily Intelligencer*, 6 June 1862; *Atlanta Southern Confederacy*, 5 August 1862; Ralph Benjamin Singer, Jr., "Confederate Atlanta" (PhD diss., University of Georgia, 1973) 158–61; Russell, *Atlanta 1847–1890*, 102–104.

[12]*Sam Richards's Civil War Diary*, 75 (1 October 1861); 139 (15 November 1862).

College, the African Church, the City Hotel, and a private hospital run by
Dr. Daniel Heery. In June 1862, the Confederate government
commissioned a major hospital to be built near the Georgia Railroad on
land previously used for farm shows. Called Fairgrounds Hospitals
because there would eventually be multiple facilities within one
complex, they would care for thousands of soldiers, many from the Army
of Tennessee. Fairgrounds Hospitals received the largest groups of
wounded following the battles of Murfreesboro in January 1863 and
Chickamauga in September of that year.[13]

A combination of soldiers, paid staff, slaves, and volunteers cared
for Atlanta's wounded and sick soldiers. Fairgrounds Hospitals
employed surgeons, wardmasters, "Sanitary Officers," nurses, and
"Negro attendants," who were given their own "Negro quarters" and
served as cooks, laundry workers, and nurses. Medical personnel placed
ads in local newspapers in an attempt to hire slaves. They offered $15.00
per month to the owners of slaves, but apparently found insufficient
response. Slave owners could make better profits leasing their slaves
elsewhere. Women volunteers formed several organizations, including
the Ladies' Hospital Association, the Ladies' Soldiers' Relief Society,
and St. Philip's Hospital Aid Society, which was associated with the
Episcopal Church. Sallie Richards volunteered with the Ladies' Soldiers'
Relief Society. She and other women members of the Second Baptist
Church were assigned to "alleviate in some degree the sufferings and
wants of the sick" at Denny Hospital and to report to the society on a
weekly basis. In addition, she sewed "comforts," homemade coverlets
that women stitched, often using their own household linen. Although
she had four children under the age of eight, Sallie Richards was
expected to pitch in.[14]

---

[13]Ibid., 96 (5 March 1862); Jack D. Welsh, *Two Confederate Hospitals and Their Patients: Atlanta to Opelika* (Macon GA: Mercer University Press, 2005) 12–32.

[14]Welsh, *Two Confederate Hospitals*, 13; Singer, Jr., "Confederate Atlanta," 154; Clarence L. Mohr, *On the Threshold of Freedom: Masters and Slaves in Civil War Georgia* (Athens: University of Georgia Press, 1986) 132–35; *Sam Richards's Civil War Diary*, 96 (5 March 1862); *Atlanta Southern Confederacy*, 5 August 1862; *Atlanta Daily Intelligencer*, 10 July 1862. Other hospitals under the care of the Ladies' Soldiers' Relief Society included Empire Hospital, Henry Hospital, Gate City Hospital, City Hotel,

Sam Richards felt pity and sadness for the city's ailing and convalescent soldiers, but he also felt uneasy about the presence of so much sickness in his midst. Newspapers printed lists of the dead organized by hospital-by-hospital and filling several columns of newsprint. Often a soldier's cause of death was listed next to his name. In the pages of his diary, Richards expressed fear that his children might contract the diseases prevalent among convalescing soldiers, including typhoid fever, cholera, and tuberculosis. When scarlet fever swept through Atlanta in January 1863 and took the life of a neighbor's child, Richards and his wife resorted to a folk remedy. They tied "asafetida bags" around their children's necks, containing a gum-like substance in the carrot family believed to provide protection from disease. Two months earlier they had lost their baby, Alice, who died from what Sam called "cholera infantum."[15]

No disease brought more fear to Atlanta's civilians than smallpox, which the city tried and failed to contain. In this case, Sam did not depend upon folk remedies. When the disease struck wartime Atlanta for the first time in fall 1862, he saw to it that every member of his family was vaccinated. City officials took the precaution of quarantining patients with smallpox either in their homes (households of the afflicted were told to fly red flags to warn others) or in a special hospital designated to treat smallpox sufferers. By January 1863, with the disease still not contained, Mayor James M. Calhoun and the city council appointed a committeeman in each of the city's five wards whose responsibility it was to oversee vaccination locally. To obtain enough vaccine material, doctors visited those previously inoculated and collected fresh material. A physician came to the Richards home with this intent in February 1863. In 1864 the disease struck again. At the city council's request, army officials agreed to treat civilian patients at

---

Alexander Hospital, Concert Hall Hospital, Wilson's Hospital, Medical College Hospital, and Janes and Hayden Hospital.

[15]The *Atlanta Southern Confederacy* printed names of dead soldiers, including the diseases that took their lives. See, for example, 11 May 1862. *Sam Richards's Civil War Diary*, 137 (8 November 1862); 139–40 (26 November 1862); 161–62 (26 January 1863).

military hospitals if beds were not available in the city's smallpox facility.[16]

Despite the travails of living in a city filled with so many reminders of war, families like the Richardses managed to have fun. Sam and Sallie Richards enjoyed Atlanta's cultural amenities, including performances of the Queen Sisters and Palmetto Band, a traveling group of young women from Charleston, South Carolina. Their dancing, singing, and acting routines often explored wartime themes, with titles like "Young Widow" and "The Conscript." Appearing at the Athenaeum periodically during the war, the Queen Sisters charged admission of 75 cents for adults, half fare for children and slaves.[17] The young slave pianist "Blind Tom" Wiggins played to enthusiastic Atlanta audiences during the war. Owned by James Bethune of Columbus, Georgia, the sightless and possibly autistic Wiggins learned to play piano pieces after hearing them once and then played them thereafter from memory. He began performing around the state in 1857 at the age of seven. For white people, Wiggins seemed to be the ultimate curiosity. Richards described him as "truly one of the *seven wonders*.... [He] plays the most difficult operatic music correctly and composes pieces of his own and is yet for 12 years old and little better than an idiot."[18] The Richards family celebrated holidays with special meals. They enjoyed "a fine *rooster* for Christmas dinner" in 1862 and there were presents for the children. Sam and his brother Jabe entertained the household by singing and playing the flute. The brothers had fine singing voices and enjoyed sacred singing in church and light-

---

[16]*Sam Richards's Civil War Diary*, 125 (9 September 1862); 161 (25 January 1863); 163 (8 February 1863); *Atlanta Daily Intelligencer*, 25 January 1863, 13 February 1863, which identified the "Small Pox Hospital, Markham's Farm"; *Atlanta Southern Confederacy*, 5 September 1862, 24 January 1863. On 25 January 1863, F. D. Thurman placed an ad in the *Atlanta Southern Confederacy*: "I shall visit every house in the Third Ward." Welsh, *Two Confederate Hospitals*, 31; Dimgor, Ir "Confederate Atlanta," 202–203, 238.

[17]*Sam Richards's Civil War Diary*, 93 (27 February 1862); 118 (9 July 1862); 119 (18 July 1862); *Atlanta Daily Intelligencer*, 10 July 1862.

[18]*Sam Richards's Civil War Diary*, 85 (19 December 1861). Even after the end of slavery, members of the Bethune family controlled Tom's career. Wiggins may have been what is today called an autistic savant. Geneva Handy Southall, *Blind Tom, the Black Pianist-Composer* (Lanham MD: Scarecrow, 1999) 1–2, 148–54. *Atlanta Southern Confederacy*, 20 December 1861.

hearted singing at home. On one occasion they performed "Mr. and Mrs. Snibbs: A Comic Duet" for friends and family.[19]

The Richardses could afford theater tickets, rooster dinners, presents for their children, and leisure time to sing because they were among Atlanta's affluent residents. Their bookstore in the heart of the city's business district on Whitehall Street did well. In January 1862, Sam wrote: "Business is pretty good and the profits *splendid* on what we do sell." Richards did not reveal many details about how he kept his store stocked during the war, but one of his closest friends was the blockade-runner Sidney Root. Richards met Root shortly after he moved to Atlanta and joined Second Baptist Church, where Root was Sunday school superintendent and sang in the choir. Root and Richards became the principal male singers in the Baptist choir and Sallie Richards became a leader among the women vocalists.[20]

Sidney Root was already an established merchant in Atlanta when the war began, and like Richards he was a reluctant secessionist. Nonetheless, Root and his partner John Beach immediately set up a blockade-running operation out of Charleston, South Carolina, through which they smuggled cotton and brought back goods. According to an unpublished memoir he wrote for his children in 1893, Root owned, "if I remember correctly, from 19 to 21 ocean steamers." In July 1862, the *Atlanta Daily Intelligencer* announced a new shipment to Root's dry goods store. Calling Root and Beach's operation a "successful venture" of "importers," the *Intelligencer* noted, "Our True Southern women will, doubtless, be ambitious to secure a dress." Sallie Richards purchased a calico dress that month. Her husband wrote in his diary that it had been smuggled aboard Root's ship, the *Memphis*.[21]

---

[19]*Sam Richards's Civil War Diary*, 85 (17 December 1861); 145 (27 December 1862).

[20]Ibid., 88 (9 January 1862). The Richards brothers also operated a grocery store on Decatur Street, which they sold in July 1863. See p. 187 (2 July 1863). Sallie Conley lived in Atlanta during the war and heard the Second Baptist choir sing. She recalled: "its lovely choir was composed of Mr. and Mrs. [S.] P. Richards, Mr. and Mrs. West, and Mr. Sidney Root, the tenor." Robert Scott Davis, Jr., ed., *Requiem for a Lost City: A Memoir of Civil War Atlanta and the Old South* (Macon GA: Mercer University Press, 1999) 36.

[21]Sidney Root, "Memorandum of My Life," 14, 18–19, unpublished typescript, 1893, Atlanta History Center; *Atlanta Daily Intelligencer*, 13 July 1862. Additional Atlanta

By 1863, Sam Richards was earning profits that were unimaginable to him before the war. In February, for example, he reported cash sales for the previous month of $6,773.80, the brothers' best month to date. "*Some* of our profits are enormous truly," Sam confided to his diary, noting that they had sold pens for $28.00 that cost them 75 cents. In most cases, goods brought twice their prewar prices. The brothers began investing in city lots and country acreage, including the jointly purchased Pleasant Hill farm. In December 1862, Sam had bought his first slave, a teenager named Ellen, whom he estimated to be thirteen years old. For several years he had rented Ellen from her owner in Macon, and she helped Sallie Richards in caring for the couple's children. Far from having doubts about the morality of slavery, Sam was immensely proud of being a slaveowner, for Southern society bestowed special status on those able to afford human property. The following month Abraham Lincoln issued the Emancipation Proclamation, freeing Ellen in theory if not in fact. Sam scorned the measure, calling it a "dreadful ukase" and predicting ever higher values for slaves as world demand for cotton escalated. By the time the war ended, Sam would own half a dozen slaves, most of them working on his farm property.[22]

At the same time that Sam Richards's profits escalated, so did his expenses. Inflation gripped the city of Atlanta, exacerbated by the Confederate government's policy of printing unbacked paper money when it needed revenue, food shortages created by a weak harvest in 1862, and government impressments of crops. Unable to afford wheat

---

blockade-runners were Richard Peters and two associates and the Fulton County Export and Import Company. Russell, *Atlanta 1847–1890*, 96; *Sam Richards's Civil War Diary*, 121 (27 July 1862).

[22]*Sam Richards's Civil War Diary*, 145 (27 December 1862); 158 (1 January 1863); 165 (23 February 1863). The historian Walter Johnson wrote that when white Southerners went from renting to owning slaves, it was like "coming into their own in a society in which they were otherwise excluded from full participation." See *Soul by Soul: Life inside the Antebellum Slave Market* (Cambridge MA: Harvard University Press, 1999) 81–82. Edward L. Ayres, *In the Presence of Mine Enemies: The Civil War in the Heart of America, 1859–1863* (New York: Norton, 2003) 354–55, suggests that the Emancipation Proclamation, which freed slaves in areas of the South still in rebellion, rallied Southerners in the belief that slave profits would continue to expand. *Atlanta Southern Confederacy*, 9 January 1863, predicted that the proclamation would "show our people the real policy of that faithless, perverse and unprincipled nation of people."

flour, the family ate biscuits made from rice flour or corn meal. Sam paid $10 for five chickens so that his family might have eggs and $160 for an old cow so that the children could have milk. Jabez Richards, who moved to Pleasant Hill farm following the death of his wife, rode into town on what Sam described as his "$900 mule."[23]

While the Richardses were never without food or shelter, needy citizens suffered terribly in wartime Atlanta. Inflation and food shortages left some with little to eat. Because of the poor harvest during 1862, the Confederacy suffered some of its worst food shortages during spring 1863. Food riots ensued, including one in Atlanta. On 18 March 1863, a dozen women held up a butcher shop on Whitehall Street, stealing several hundred dollars worth of food. When the butcher refused their demand that he lower his price of bacon from $1.10 per pound, one woman brandished a gun, though the group dispersed after being confronted by the city marshal. Both city officials and the business community reacted humanely. City marshal J. N. Williford collected $500 for the benefit of these women. The Atlanta City Council allocated an increasing amount of money for "pauper relief." Local merchants helped out as well with donated food, perhaps because they feared citizen backlash against high profits being made at their expense. The *Southern Confederacy* newspaper appealed for civic unity by asking Atlantans to "pause and reflect. Whither are we drifting?"[24]

During the first half of the war, Atlanta's white population showed strong support for Confederate nationalism. In February 1861, Jefferson Davis spent the night in Atlanta on the way to his inauguration in Montgomery, Alabama. An estimated 5000 people—half the city's population—turned out to welcome the president-elect, who received a seven-gun salute and a reception at the city's premier hotel, the Trout

---

[23]*Sam Richards's Civil War Diary*, 179 (6 June 1863); 182 (27 June 1863); 201 (25 October 1863).

[24]Atlanta City Council minutes, vol. 4, 31 March 1863, 1 April 1863, Atlanta History Center; *Atlanta Daily Intelligencer*, 19 March 1863; *Atlanta Southern Confederacy*, 20 March 1863; Russell, *Atlanta 1847–1890*, 99–100; DeCredico, *Patriotism for Profit*, 43; James M. McPherson, *Ordeal by Fire: The Civil War and Reconstruction*, 3rd ed. (Boston: McGraw Hill, 2001) 410–11; George C. Rable, *Civil Wars: Women and the Crisis of Southern Nationalism* (Urbana: University of Illinois Press, 1989) 96–102.

House on Decatur Street. Davis addressed the assembled crowd from the hotel balcony, reminding Atlantans of the North's "abolition fanaticism" that "has driven us to this step." He was interrupted with "wild applause," according to the *Daily Intelligencer*. Confederate Vice President-elect Alexander Stephens also received a warm reception when he visited in March, according to the *Intelligencer*. Both this paper and the city's other major daily, the *Southern Confederacy*, were unwavering supporters of Southern independence. When a thousand men gathered in Atlanta for a military muster in March 1862, meeting the county's enlistment quota, the *Southern Confederacy* nonetheless concluded that the South must draft all able-bodied men to ensure victory in the field. Both newspapers printed detailed reports about women's volunteer efforts in area hospitals.[25]

In April 1862, Atlantans were startled to learn that in nearby Marietta a group of Union saboteurs led by James J. Andrews stole the locomotive *General*, its tender, and several boxcars while the crew dined in a local restaurant. A 90-mile chase ended with the conspirators abandoning the locomotive near the Tennessee border. While several men escaped, Andrews and seven others were tried and hanged in Atlanta on 7 June 1862. A crowd of Atlantans witnessed the execution, motivated by patriotism, curiosity, or voyeurism. Sam Richards did not attend the execution and suggested only that the "poor fellow...ought to have engaged in better business."[26]

Sam Richards showed his personal commitment to the Confederacy by participating in days of fasting, prayer, and humiliation called by Confederate President Jefferson Davis, Georgia Governor Joseph E. Brown, and occasionally by Atlanta's mayor, James M. Calhoun. Before the war, such days were usually practiced in New England, part of its Puritan legacy, but in the wartime South government officials used these occasions to unite the citizenry, bestow a sense of sacred purpose, and

---

[25]*Atlanta Daily Intelligencer*, 18 February 1861, 21 March 1861; *Atlanta Southern Confederacy*, 6 March 1862.

[26]*Atlanta Southern Confederacy*, 8 June 1862; *Sam Richards's Civil War Diary*, 114 (7 June 1862); Russell S. Bonds, *Stealing the General: The Great Locomotive Chase and the First Medal of Honor* (Yardley PA: Westholme, 2007) 89–260 (The execution is described on pp. 245–47.).

build a national identity through worship. A deeply religious man, Richards closed his bookstore, attended services, and fasted when told to do so. He also went to church several times a week, regularly at Second Baptist but also visiting Presbyterian, Episcopal, and Methodist congregations in the city. Like many Southerners, he saw God's hand behind early Confederate military victories, including the Battle of First Manassas, which he attributed to "the direct interference of god." Until the war's very end, he believed that a "righteous God" would never allow the "unjust and bloody programme of the North" to prevail. Richards's tendency to give a positive spin to military news came in part from his religious convictions and in part from reading the city's newspapers, which often disseminated early accounts of battles that proved false in the long run. For example, on 9 July 1863, the *Daily Intelligencer* reported that General Robert E. Lee won at Gettysburg and took 40,000 prisoners.[27]

Samuel Richards's support for the Confederacy did not lead him into military service. Indeed Richards spent much of the war trying to dodge conscription. Regarding himself as too old (he celebrated his fortieth birthday in 1864), too virtuous (he disdained the drunkenness that he associated with some military officers), and temperamentally unsuited for military life, he went to extraordinary lengths to avoid enlistment. In 1863 he paid $2,500 to hire a substitute. When the Confederate Congress raised the draft age to forty-five, Richards sought other avenues to escape conscription. Because compositors were exempt, he set type for a religious weekly called *Baptist Banner*. To shore up his ties to religious publishing, he and Jabez purchased *Soldier's Friend*, a publication that tried to raise the morale of soldiers in the field. Sam wrote articles in addition to setting type. When in December 1863 the Confederate Congress voted to end all exemptions, Richards called it "a grand Government Swindle." In May 1864 he finally received a formal exemption based upon his role with the *Soldier's Friend*. Although

---

[27]*Sam Richards's Civil War Diary*, 60 (27 July 1861); 188 (11 July 1863); 268 (3 April 1865); *Atlanta Daily Intelligencer*, 9 July 1863; Harry S. Stout, *Upon the Altar of the Nation: A Moral History of the American Civil War* (New York: Viking, 2006) 47–49.

Richards joined the Atlanta Press Volunteers along with other writers, editors, and typographers, he never saw military duty.[28]

Atlanta's Confederate civilians, including Sam Richards, greatly admired cavalrymen known as "partisan rangers," those who performed amazing feats in harassing the Union military during the war. In the pages of their newspapers, Atlantans eagerly followed the exploits of Nathan Bedford Forrest, but John Hunt Morgan they admired above all. A talented and handsome Kentuckian, Morgan tried to "liberate" his Union slave state for the Confederacy. Morgan visited Atlanta several times during war, recruiting volunteers and raising funds for his mission. In June 1862 women of the Atlanta Hospital Association presented Morgan with a ceremonial cane in recognition of his "deeds of daring." Morgan's formal message of thanks was printed in the *Daily Intelligencer*. Sam Richards was proud to write in his diary that one of his acquaintances served with Morgan.[29]

In February 1864, Morgan appeared in Atlanta one more time. After a series of successful raids in Kentucky and Ohio in 1862, Morgan was captured and held in a Federal penitentiary in Columbus, Ohio. In November 1863, fellow prisoners helped him escape by constructing a tunnel. Disguising his appearance and aided by sympathizers along the way, Morgan found his way to the Confederate capital of Richmond, where he was greeted by adoring crowds. Next he appeared in Atlanta, which with its railroads, factories, and hospitals had become so vital to the Confederacy that it was now second in importance only to the capital itself. Atlantans already knew the details of Morgan's capture and escape. In addition to newspaper coverage, pamphlets were sold recounting the remarkable story. For beleaguered Confederate civilians, increas-

---

[28]*Sam Richards's Civil War Diary*, 159 (14 January 1863); 166 (4 March 1863); 193 (21 August 1863); 208 (31 December 1863); Samuel P. Richards draft exemption, private collection, displayed at Atlanta History Center.

[29]*Atlanta Daily Intelligencer*, 11 June 1862; *Atlanta Southern Confederacy*, 6 March 1862, 24 July 1862, 2 August 1862, when the newspaper called one raid "the most brilliant, daring and successful warlike expedition that ever was undertaken in any age or country." This newspaper also advertised for sale at $3.50 a book entitled *Raids and Romance of Morgan and His Men*. See 27 June 1863. *Sam Richards's Civil War Diary*, 121 (2 August 1862).

ingly aware that the military tide was turning against their cause, Morgan's story offered hope for the future.[30]

On 6 February 1864, morning newspapers announced Morgan's impending arrival. A throng of citizens, including Sam and Sallie Richards, greeted the cavalry hero at the railroad depot, escorting him to the Trout House. From the hotel balcony, Mayor James Calhoun presented Morgan to the crowd, praising Morgan's "gallant" defense of his country. Morgan then offered his thanks to Atlantans for their welcome and "retired amid the enthusiastic cheers of the vast crowd in the street below." The city council entertained the general and his wife and staff with a reception, hailing Morgan for having "shed so much luster on the Military prowess of our Country." Morgan spent several days in the Gate City, raising money for his cavalry, visiting friends, and attending church services with his wife.[31]

Sam Richards did not know it at the time—no one did—but Morgan's visit would represent Atlanta's last major celebration of Confederate nationalism. One day before his visit, the *Daily Intelligencer* announced that Atlanta would be "very likely...the main object" of the Federal army in the spring campaign. "The importance of Atlanta, both to the Federal and Confederate government, cannot be over-estimated," the *Intelligencer* concluded. If Atlanta fell, the lower South would be lost, and Robert E. Lee's army could not be fed without Atlanta's rail lines carrying agricultural products to Virginia.[32]

By early 1864, Atlanta's civilians lived a perilous existence. Inflation and shortages affected every household. In 1861 Sam Richards had complained when coffee reached 50 cents per pound. By 1864 coffee could not be found for less than $15.00 a pound. Butter cost $8.00 a

---

[30]James A. Ramage, *Rebel Raider: The Life of General John Hunt Morgan* (Lexington: University Press of Kentucky, 1986) 170–98. Mary S. Mallard to Mary Jones, 8 February 1864, in *Children of Pride*, 437–39.

[31]*Sam Richards's Civil War Diary*, 218 (6 February 1864); 219 (21 February 1864); Atlanta City Council minutes, vol. 4, 19 July 1864, 30 March 1864, 8 April 1864, Atlanta History Center, reveal that the city appropriated $10,000 for the reception. *Atlanta Daily Intelligencer*, 7 February 1864. Another contemporary account of Morgan's visit is that of Sallie Conley. See Davis, Jr., ed., *Requiem for a Lost City*, 92–95.

[32]*Atlanta Daily Intelligencer*, 5 February 1864.

pound. Syrup was $20.00 per gallon. Even locally grown sweet potatoes cost $16.00 per bushel. The city's neediest citizens lived in the most dire straits. Emblematic of Atlanta's travails: its railroad passenger depot, constructed in 1854 and the city's great pride, was now ringed with homeless people and refugees living in tents and abandoned rail cars. Inside the depot wounded soldiers filled the space, lying on pallets and awaiting transfer to the city's already overcrowded hospitals. Passengers arriving and departing the Gate City now had to negotiate their way through a sea of despondent humanity.[33]

Everyone feared lawlessness. Problems with theft, counterfeiting, drunkenness, and lewd behavior filled the newspapers. One nurse who traveled with the western armies called Atlanta "the most wicked place in the world." Fed-up citizens tarred and feathered a suspected thief who preyed on guests at the Trout House. But white Atlantans especially feared slaves and were quick to blame them for both real and imagined lawlessness. Before the war, enslaved African Americans made up 20 percent of the city's population. During the war, slaves worked in private homes but also worked in factories and helped build the fortifications that were intended to protect the city from the invading Union army. Early in the war, slaves had exercised a certain amount of freedom, for example periodically circumventing their 9:00 P.M. curfew by holding "Negro Balls" ostensibly to raise money for Confederate soldiers. The *Southern Confederacy* editorialized against the practice and it stopped. Increasingly, the city cracked down on slaves. The Code of the City of Atlanta forbade slaves from hiring or delivering a horse or buggy to another African American, selling food or liquor, smoking in a street or alley, and carrying a cane, stick, or club. Nonetheless, real or perceived acts of insubordination continued. In January 1864, a group of sixty black men and boys joined by fifteen white men and boys were caught

[33]*Sam Richards's Civil War Diary*, 79 (3 November 1861); 221 (26 March 1864); *The Journal of Kate Cumming, a Confederate Nurse, 1862–1865*, ed. Richard Harwell (Savannah GA: Beehive, 1975) 128; Mary Mallard to Mary Jones, 24 March 1864, 19 May 1864, in *Children of Pride*, 449, 464; Franklin M. Garrett, *Atlanta and Environs: A Chronicle of Its People and Events*, 2 vols. (New York: Lewis, 1954) 1:487; Mary Elizabeth Massey, *Refugee Life in the Confederacy* (Baton Rouge: Louisiana State University Press, 1964) 105.

cockfighting near the Rolling Mill. Military guards broke up the gathering and in the resulting melee one African American died and one white boy injured his hand. Blacks were presumed to have caused the incident, and thirty-two were carted off to be jailed and whipped. Sam held the view that slave "impudence" must be dealt with a firm hand. His diary records several occasions when he whipped his teenaged slave Ellen for minor acts of stealing. He believed that Jabez was not strict enough with his own slaves and warned him of the need to crack down.[34]

As Atlanta's white civilians tried to cope with worsening economic and social conditions, they faced a new challenge, for reports reached them of military clashes between the armies of Generals Joseph E. Johnston and William T. Sherman. From March to June 1864 they remained hopeful, but their optimism faded when Sherman's army, slowed by a loss at Kennesaw Mountain, nonetheless made its way south toward the Gate City. On 6 July, Confederate authorities began evacuating the medical facilities, sending convalescing soldiers to Macon and other venues or home on furlough. And that point, metropolitan Atlanta began to implode. Thousands of civilians left the city. Sam Richards called it "a complete swarm." Newspapers closed shop and moved to Macon, the *Southern Confederacy* firing off one last editorial telling all citizens to "aid the cause in some way" because "Atlanta cannot be abandoned." The city council stopped holding meetings. The legal system no longer functioned. Saying only that he doubted that the Yankees "are as bad as they are said to be," Sam Richards stayed, part of an estimated 2,000 to 5,000 civilians who took their chances.[35]

Richards soon had reason to question his judgment. When Sherman's army began shelling the city, Richards and his wife and children

---

[34] *Journal of Kate Cumming*, 215; *Atlanta Daily Intelligencer*, 13 February 1863, 20 and 21 November 1863, 26 January 1864; *Atlanta Southern Confederacy*, 21 December 1861; Garrett, *Atlanta and its Environs*, 1:553; *Sam Richards's Civil War Diary*, 109 (5 May 1862); 166 (28 February 1863). See also p. 206 (13 December 1863).

[35] Lee Kennett, *Marching through Georgia: The Story of Soldiers and Civilians during Sherman's Campaign* (New York: HarperCollins, 1995) 120; Welsh, *Two Confederate Hospitals*, 35–36; Albert Castel, *Decision in the West: The Atlanta Campaign of 1864* (Lawrence: University of Kansas Press, 1992) 464; *Sam Richards's Civil War Diary*, 227 (10 July 1864); *Atlanta Southern Confederacy*, 5 July 1864. The city council held its last meeting on 18 July.

were in danger. After a Federal shell landed on their street, throwing a hail of gravel onto the windows, Sallie Richards pulled the children's mattresses onto the floor behind the chimney. To further protect the family, Sam dug a bomb shelter called a pit or gopher hole in the cellar. Nevertheless, the Richardses had some close calls. A shell weighing nearly 20 pounds struck the Richards bookstore. A shell fragment landed in their backyard. Another hit Second Baptist Church and lodged in the front wall after passing through a seat close to the one usually occupied by Sallie Richards. Some of their fellow Atlantans were not so fortunate. On 7 August 1864 Richards wrote that "A gentleman and his little girl, ten years of age were both killed in bed by the same shell last week," a reference to J. F. Warner and his daughter who lost their lives when a Union artillery shell hit them while they slept in their home near the Atlanta gasworks. Richards estimated that twenty civilians died in Union shelling of the city. A hundred or more were injured.[36]

When Sherman's army arrived in Atlanta on 2 September, Richards remarked that "the scene would have required the pencil of Hogarth to portray," a reference to the eighteenth-century English artist whose engravings often depicted scenes of urban upheaval. Soldiers, civilians, and African Americans looted the downtown business district, including the Richards store. The previous night Sam saw and heard the commotion caused by Confederate soldiers setting fire to an ammunition train. "It was terrific to listen to and know—the object," he wrote. By 4 September, order had been restored in the city, and Sam marveled as an "*Abolition* preacher from Indiana" took over the pulpit of Second Baptist Church. Yankee soldiers claimed city hall for their provost guard headquarters. Perhaps the most dramatic change of all came when African Americans, including slaves previously owned by Sam and Jabez Richards, celebrated their liberation. "Our negro property has all vanished into air," Sam wrote, complaining as well of the "impudent airs the negroes put on, and their indifference to the wants of their former

[36]*Sam Richards's Civil War Diary*, 228 (23 July 1864); 229 (1 August 1864); 230–31 (7 August 1864); 232 (21 August 1864); 233 (28 August 1864); Stephen Davis, "How Many Civilians Died in Sherman's Bombardment of Atlanta," *Atlanta History* 45/4 (Winter 2003): 5–23. Another account of the bombardment is *A Confederate Girl: The Diary of Carrie Berry, 1864*, ed. Christy Steele (Mankato MN: Blue Earth Books, 2000).

masters." Ellen, the slave whom Sam had rented and later owned, disappeared from the pages of his diary and presumably from his life.[37]

The Richards family left Atlanta along with other Confederate civilians on orders of General Sherman. Hoping to escape the war zone, they chose New York City, where they had family. Sam financed their trip by selling furniture to Union officers, and he also held a small amount of gold. On Christmas day, 1864, he wrote, "We little thought a year ago that we should spend this day in the Yankee Gotham!" Relieved to be away from the fighting, but unhappy to be away from Atlanta, he read New York newspapers in the hopes of learning news about his former home. He read an article in the *New York Herald* citing an eyewitness who reported only 675 residents living in Atlanta, approximately 600 of them women and children and fifteen to twenty of them African Americans. The article noted the destruction of "all the railroad depots...foundries, railroad shops, government works and mills" torched by Sherman's departing army and identified individual neighborhoods and homes that had burned in the process. Sam was relieved to learn that the home of Jabez Richards had not burned.[38]

Sam Richards returned to Atlanta and to the bookstore business in August 1865. Over the years, he prospered. In 1884 he and Jabez ended their partnership and Sam reorganized the company with his adult sons. Richards, who so carefully and effectively chronicled his city's tumultuous history during the Civil War years, became part of what made postwar Atlanta an economic success story.[39]

---

[37]*Sam Richards's Civil War Diary*, 233–36 (1, 2, 4, 9 September 1864). On 9 September, Richards recorded the death of John Hunt Morgan, killed in an ambush in East Tennessee. Ramage, *Rebel Raider*, 233–38.

[38]*Sam Richards's Civil War Diary*, 237 (21 September 1864); 255 (24 December 1864), 254 (11 December 1864); *New York Herald*, 8 December 1864, citing *Memphis Appeal*.

[39]The S. P. Richards Company, which remained in family hands well into the twentieth century, is today a subsidiary of Genuine Parts Corporation. It is Atlanta's oldest company in continuous operation. Richards continued writing in his diary until 1909. He died a few months later in 1910. *Sam Richards's Civil War Diary*, 293–96. Frank J. Byrne, "Revolution in Retail: A Tale of Two Merchants in Confederate Atlanta," *Georgia Historical Quarterly* 79/1 (Spring 1995): 30–56.

"I Cannot Give the History of This Campaign Language to Describe Its Suffering": The Confederate Struggle for Atlanta

by John D. Fowler

I am not discouraged, though there is some discontent in the army. Oh God, how long will this cruel war last? My heart yearns for the society of home. I count each day and ask when will the last come?… Through many dangers I have been led, have just escaped death time and again. It seems that I have led a charmed life. God be praised for his goodness. I see around me such distress my heart sickens at the destruction of life and property on every hand, in the army and out of it. I see grey hairs and helpless infancy driven from home, penniless and almost friendless. I see the strong man cut down without a moment's warning, or left a cripple for life. I see the poor soldier as he toils on, sustained by the hope of better days and by the love he bears for those far away. I saw but yesterday the Captain commanding this regiment barefoot. Such men will not be conquered. I cannot give the history of this campaign language to describe its suffering. It has been long and bloody, many of our noblest have fallen. "Requiescant in pace." They live in our hearts.

Chaplain Thomas H. Deavenport of the 3rd Tennessee Infantry Regiment wrote these disheartened words in his diary after witnessing the four-month-long struggle for Atlanta culminate in the city's fall and the subsequent expulsion of its civilian population by the victorious Federal invaders. He, like the other soldiers in the Army of Tennessee, had fought mightily against the well-equipped and -supplied Federal army group commanded by Major General William Tecumseh Sherman. On the shoulders of these men and their Yankee enemies rested the fate of two nations in the summer of 1864. The loss of Atlanta sent shock waves throughout the Confederacy and the United States. The South's last forlorn hope of independence was gone. Atlanta's fall inexorably led to Lincoln's reelection and doomed the Southern Republic to his unrelenting drive to reunify the nation. Although Deavenport's faith gave him resolve, elsewhere in the Confederacy the reality of the situation sapped the will of many to continue the struggle. The war's most famous diarist, South Carolina socialite Mary Boykin Chesnut, phrased it best: "Atlanta is gone. The agony is over. There is no hope, but we will try to have no fear."[1]

An examination of the historiography of the Atlanta Campaign reveals a complex and debatable series of mysterious events and conflicting interpretations. Six questions are crucial to understanding the Confederate view of the campaign: Was Joseph E. Johnston the best choice to head the Army of Tennessee in 1864? Why did Johnston fail to defeat or at least stall longer General William T. Sherman's advance? What really happened at Cassville? Should Johnston have been removed? Why did John B. Hood fail to defeat Sherman? Could the Confederates have won the Atlanta Campaign? This essay will compare and analyze historians' answers to these questions in order to develop a better understanding of what happened during what was arguably the single most important campaign of the entire war.[2]

Historians generally agree on the events leading up to the Atlanta campaign and on its importance to the outcome of the war. The last six months of 1863 were catastrophic for the Confederacy. The three disasters of Gettysburg, Vicksburg, and Missionary Ridge shook the young republic to its core. Yet despite the loss of men, material, and territory, the Rebels fought on with grim determination. By 1864, however, the Confederacy retained only one realistic hope of success— the collapse of Northern resolve. The United States faced great war

---

[1]Thomas H. Deavenport, diary, Civil War Collection, Confederate, box 6, item 5a, Tennessee State Library and Archive, Nashville TN; Mary Boykin Chesnut, *A Diary from Dixie,* ed. Isabella D. Martin and Myrta Lockett Avary (New York: D. Appleton and Company, 1905) 326.

[2]The most important works on the Atlanta Campaign include Albert Castel, *Decision in the West: The Atlanta Campaign of 1864* (Lawrence: University Press of Kansas, 1992); Richard M. McMurry, *Atlanta 1864: Last Chance for the Confederacy* (Lincoln: University of Nebraska Press, 2000); Stephen Davis, *Atlanta Will Fall: Sherman, Joe Johnston, and the Yankee Heavy Battalions* (Wilmington DE: Scholarly Resources, 2001); *The Campaign for Atlanta and Sherman's March to the Sea,* ed. Theodore P. Savas and David Woodbury, 2 vols. (Campbell CA: Savas Woodbury Publishers, 1992, 1994); Thomas Lawrence Connelly, *Autumn of Glory: The Army of Tennessee, 1862–1865* (Baton Rouge: Louisiana State University Press, 1971).

weariness by the fourth year of the conflict. Tens of thousands of men had been killed or maimed, and yet the war raged on despite the great victories of 1863. The presidential election of 1864 served as a referendum on the war and the resolve of the United States to see it through to the end. The Democratic Party advocated a suspension of hostilities and the negotiation of a voluntary restoration of the Union. Southerners knew that a Democratic victory at the polls would not lead to a restoration of the Union; too much blood had been shed for that. Rather, because it was doubtful that once the unpopular war stopped it could be restarted, the North would have to accept Southern independence. The Southern strategy, then, was to wear the North down. This meant that in the period leading up to the election, Southern armies had to hold on to as much territory as possible while inflicting as many casualties as possible. As the editor of the *Augusta Constitutionalist* succinctly put it, "Every bullet we can send against the Yankees is the best ballot that can be deposited against Lincoln's election. The battlefields of 1864 will hold the polls of this momentous decision. If the tyrant at Washington be defeated, his infamous policy will be defeated with him, and when his party sinks no other war party will rise in the United States."[3]

Lincoln knew of his precarious position prior to the November 1864 elections and sought to end the war or at least demonstrate that the North would win. To accomplish this, he gave the new Union general-in-chief, Ulysses S. Grant, a free hand to bring the Confederacy to its knees. Grant planned to overextend Confederate resources by executing simultaneous Federal advances across all fronts. The two major campaigns would be directed against Robert E. Lee's Army of Northern Virginia and Joseph E. Johnston's Army of Tennessee. To conduct the campaign against Johnston and Atlanta, Grant chose his friend, William Tecumseh Sherman. On 4 April 1864, Grant sent Sherman his instructions. He was to "move against Johnston's army, to break it up, and get into the interior of the enemy's country as far as you can, inflicting all the damage you can against their war resources." Sherman commanded an army group consisting of the Army of the Cumberland under Major General George

---

[3]Quoted in Castel, *Decision in the West*, 26.

H. Thomas, the Army of the Tennessee under Major General James B. McPherson, and the Army of the Ohio under John M. Schofield. In all, Sherman would have well over 100,000 men to invade the Confederate heartland. Facing Sherman would eventually be some 60,000 Rebels organized in the early stages of the campaign into three corps commanded by Lieutenant Generals William J. Hardee, Leonidas Polk, and John B. Hood.[4]

If the South had any hope to win this last attempt at victory, it had to hold out in Virginia and Georgia. Robert E. Lee and the Army of Northern Virginia would face Ulysses S. Grant traveling with Major General George G. Meade's Army of the Potomac. In Georgia, it would be Joseph E. Johnston. But why Johnston? Was he the best choice to command one of the Confederacy's principal armies on the eve of the republic's greatest challenge? After the near annihilation of the Army of Tennessee at Missionary Ridge in November 1863, Jefferson Davis had no choice but to replace General Braxton Bragg. Although Davis knew Bragg had to be relieved, he had no viable replacement. Once Hardee refused the position, Davis's choices were limited, and the position was crucial to Southern success at the most critical juncture of the war. Indeed, historian Richard McMurry believes this decision to be one of the most important made by Davis during the course of the war.[5]

Historians generally support Davis's decision to replace the unpopular and unsuccessful Bragg with Johnston for a variety of reasons. First, Davis needed to choose a general of appropriate rank or face a storm of protest from the Confederate Congress and the army's general officers. Johnston was the second-ranking field general in the Confederacy, behind Lee only. Second, Davis needed a general who had experience leading a large army. Reasoning that Lee needed to be left in Virginia, Davis felt he had only two choices: Joseph E. Johnston, commanding the Department of Mississippi and East Louisiana, or Pierre Gustave Toutant Beauregard, commanding Rebel forces along the east

---

[4]Ulysses S. Grant, *Personal Memoirs of U. S. Grant*, ed. E. B. Long (1885–1886; reprint, New York: Penguin Books, 1999) 366; McMurry, *Atlanta 1864*, 1–41.

[5]McMurry, "A Policy So Disastrous: Joseph E. Johnston's Atlanta Campaign," in *Campaign for Atlanta and Sherman's March to the Sea*, 2:223.

coast. After weeks of deliberation, Davis settled on Johnston. On the surface, this appears to be a wise decision. Johnston was the senior general available, he had experience leading a large army, he had administrative ability, and he was respected by the civilian population and army personnel.[6]

Nonetheless, serious problems plagued Johnston's appointment. First, the general's relationship to the president was strained. Since summer 1861, Davis and Johnston had been at odds over the general's rank. Johnston expected to be the ranking Confederate general based on his pre-Civil War rank. Moreover, in 1862, the two clashed over Johnston's defense of Richmond during the Peninsular campaign. Johnston's refusal to discuss his plans and his penchant for retreat exasperated and angered Davis. Again in 1862–1863, the two were at odds over Johnston's command of the Department of the West and his inability and unwillingness to direct both Braxton Bragg's army in Tennessee and Major General John C. Pemberton's forces in Mississippi. Davis and Johnston blamed each other for the fall of Vicksburg, which led to bitter recriminations. Davis's political enemies were quick to use Johnston's denunciations of the president's ability to skewer Davis, creating a poisonous atmosphere between the two men. While Davis viewed Johnston as vain, petty, uncooperative, and pessimistic, Johnston viewed Davis as arrogant, misinformed, and determined to injure Johnston's reputation. This meant that neither man could really trust or depend on the other and that cooperation and communication would be at a minimum.[7]

---

[6]McMurry, *Atlanta 1864*, 6–11; Castel, *Decision in the West*, 27–29; Connelly, *Autumn of Glory*, 281–83; Davis, *Atlanta Will Fall*, 18; Steven E. Woodworth, *Jefferson Davis and His Generals: The Failure of Confederate Command in the West* (Lawrence: University Press of Kansas, 1990) 256–58.

[7]McMurry, *Atlanta 1864*, 11; Castel, *Decision in the West*, 29; Richard M. McMurry, "'The *Enemy* at Richmond': Joseph E. Johnston and the Confederate Government," *Civil War History* 27/1 (March 1981): 5–31; "Ole Joe in Virginia: Joseph E. Johnston's 1861–1862 Period of Command in the East," in *Leadership and Command in the Civil War*, ed. Steven E. Woodworth (Campbell CA: Savas Woodbury, 1996) 1–27; and Joseph T. Glatthaar, "'I Cannot Direct Both Parts of My Command at Once': Davis, Johnston, and Confederate Failure in the West," in *Partners in Command: The Relationship Between Leaders in the Civil War* (New York: Free Press, 1994) 94–133. For greater background

The second problem with choosing Johnston was the general's command record. Based on his prior service, nothing indicated that Johnston would be the aggressive and resourceful general needed to defeat Sherman. Indeed, evidence suggested that Johnston would be a poor choice. Historians Stephen Davis, Richard McMurry, and Steven Woodworth find the same major fault with Johnston that Jefferson Davis and his advisors pointed out—Johnston's timidity and reluctance to move against the enemy. Despite his administrative and logistical skills, Johnston always hesitated to commit his forces to battle. Over the course of the conflict, he commanded every major Confederate army east of the Mississippi, yet he initiated only two major attacks, one at Seven Pines outside of Richmond on 31 May 1862 and another at Bentonville in North Carolina on 19 March 1865. Given the need for a bold commander for this last desperate opportunity to achieve independence, it is surprising that Davis chose to give command to Johnston. So why did he? McMurry speaks for the majority of historians when he says the choice represented "the triumph of hope over experience. It can be explained only on the grounds that no better alternative existed."[8]

Johnston's lack of aggression helps to answer the next question of why Johnston did not defeat or at least stall longer Sherman's advance. Historian Stephen Davis posits that it was Sherman's generalship, the greater Federal numbers, and Johnston's poor performance that prevented the Confederates from defeating the Union advance. Most historians agree to a point, but Johnston's ineptitude appears to be the critical factor. Sherman's generalship is often judged as merely adequate, and Federal numbers could have been offset by a skillful commander.[9]

Johnston's deficiencies include his lack of aggression, his failure to develop a sound strategy, his fear of defeat, his poor tactical skills, and his damage to Confederate morale. Since December 1863, President Davis had been urging Johnston to stage an offensive into Tennessee to

---

into the cantankerous Davis-Johnston relationship, see Connelly, *Autumn of Glory*, especially 30–43.

[8]Davis, *Atlanta Will Fall*, 7–18; Stephen Davis, "A Reappraisal of the Generalship of John Bell Hood in the Battles for Atlanta," in *Campaigns for Atlanta*, 1:44–46; Woodworth, *Jefferson Davis and His Generals*, 176–77; McMurry, *Atlanta 1864*, 11.

[9]Davis, *Atlanta Will Fall*, ix-x, 197–200.

regain territory and, more importantly, the initiative. Spurious reports from Hardee and others convinced Davis that the army at Dalton was capable of advancing. Historians support Johnston's refusal to mount such an offensive because the Army of Tennessee clearly was unable to do so through winter 1864. This, however, does not excuse Johnston for the rest of his blunders.[10]

Only at one point in Johnston's tenure as commander of the Army of Tennessee did he seriously propose an attack—at Cassville. Otherwise, he remained on the defensive, giving Sherman the initiative. He never struck at Sherman's flanking columns or attempted to impede the movement of the Federals, even at river crossings. He had given up the military principle of "concentration of mass" at a critical point of the battlefield. Even an outnumbered force can strike a numerically superior foe at isolated points with planning and aggressive movement. In short, Johnston would not risk battle unless his entire army was present and entrenched; he would fight only if the enemy attacked. Indeed, Johnston's strategy was to concentrate his forces behind massive earthworks and wait for his enemy to make a mistake. Given the larger Federal numbers, it is easy to see why Sherman opted simply to outflank Johnston time and time again and why Johnston opted to retreat time and time again. Worse still, Johnston's tactical incompetence nearly cost him the campaign at the outset. Johnston failed to guard Snake Creek Gap south of Dalton, which allowed Sherman to flank him and nearly cut the Confederates off from Atlanta. He made more tactical blunders by not destroying the Western and Atlantic Railroad as he retreated (allowing the Federals to use it for resupply), by not contesting river crossings, by not slowing the Federal flanking columns with rear guard attacks and ambushes, and by overpreparing defensive works to discourage the very frontal attacks he desired. Johnston's mistakes and his retreats destroyed the morale of his troops and fellow officers, and by the time of his

---

[10]Davis, "Generalship of John Bell Hood," 45; McMurry, *Atlanta 1864*, 21–25; Castel, *Decision in the West*, 30–38, 73–79, 99–104; Connelly, *Autumn of Glory*, 281–325, esp. 299–300; Thomas L. Connelly and Archer Jones, *The Politics of Command: Factions and Ideas in Confederate Strategy* (Baton Rouge: Louisiana State University Press, 1973) 41–42; Richard Goff, *Confederate Supply* (Durham: Duke University Press, 1969) 209. Goff argues that Johnston did not have the supply problems that he claimed.

removal, the Army of Tennessee had begun to lose faith in his ability to lead them.[11]

As alluded to earlier, Johnston's best moment as commander came near Cassville. After retreating out of the North Georgia Mountains above the Oostanaula River on 19 May 1864, Johnston announced to his army that the time had come to strike the invaders:

> Soldiers of the Army of Tennessee, you have displayed the highest quality of the soldier—firmness in combat, patience under toil. By your courage and skill you have repulsed every assault of the enemy…. You will now turn and march to meet the advancing columns. Fully confiding the conduct of the officers, the courage of the soldiers, I lead you to battle.[12]

While the words are inspiring, they proved hollow. There would be no battle. Exactly what happened and why has become an interesting and divisive story in the study of the Atlanta Campaign. The importance of the "Cassville controversy" cannot be overstated. McMurry correctly asserted that "for the men of the Army of Tennessee the day turned out to be one of the most frustrating and demoralizing of the war. For later historians it would prove one of the most confusing." Essentially, the normally cautious Johnston suddenly saw an ideal opportunity. The roads connecting the towns of Adairsville, Kingston, and Cassville form a triangle. As the Confederate forces retreated from Adairsville, they split their forces along the Kingston and Cassville roads to facilitate rapid movement. Anticipating that the pursuing Federals would do the same, Johnston proposed to ambush one of the Federal columns. The rough terrain between the two routes would prevent aid from coming from the other column in time, and the Rebels could achieve a stunning victory

[11]Davis, "Generalship of John Bell Hood," 45–51; McMurry, "A Policy So Disastrous," 243–48; Richard M. McMurry, "The Atlanta Campaign of 1864: A New Look," *Civil War History* 22/1 (March 1976): 5–15; Richard M. McMurry, "Confederate Morale in the Atlanta Campaign of 1864," *Georgia Historical Quarterly* 54/2 (Summer 1970): 226–43; Larry J. Daniel, *Soldiering in the Army of Tennessee: A Portrait of Life in a Confederate Army* (Chapel Hill: University of North Carolina Press, 1991) 140–46.
[12]US War Department, comp., *The War of the Rebellion: A Compilation of the Official Records of the Union and Confederate Armies*, 128 vols. (Washington, DC: Government Printing Office, 1880–1901) ser. 1, 38 (4): 728.

over an isolated portion of Sherman's army group. Stephen Davis noted that "such an attack would surely succeed in at least stopping, if not routing, part of Sherman's forces. It was a good plan." Albert Castel observed that a defeat such as this would "force Sherman to retreat or at the very least to halt and assume the defensive." Why did the battle not occur? The heart of the controversy stems from Hood's failure to attack. Spotting a small force of Federal cavalry and believing it to be a vanguard of a larger force, the normally aggressive Hood did not launch his attack and reported the enemy to Johnston. Johnston issued a retreat order based on Hood's idea that a Federal unit was on the flank of the Confederate army. Both Confederate commanders later argued whether Johnston had ever ordered an attack and blamed each other for the failure and the retreat that followed. It appears that Johnston did verbally issue an attack but quickly lost heart after Hood's report of Federal troops on his flank. The sad affair dampened morale among the rank and file and led to a growing rift among the high command.[13]

Following the retreat from Cassville, Johnston continued to follow the same strategy of placing his army in front of Sherman's forces and awaiting attack behind powerful entrenchments. Sherman continued to flank the Rebel lines. Johnston's long retreat from Dalton to the outskirts of Atlanta, however, caused great concern around the Confederacy, especially in Richmond where an exasperated Jefferson Davis waited in vain for Johnston to fight for North Georgia. The retreat threatened to undo all of the sacrifices made by Lee's men in holding Grant at bay around Richmond and Petersburg. Unless Johnston could find some way to force the Federals back or at least to stall further progress, it appeared he would lose Atlanta, giving the North and the Lincoln administration a much-needed morale boost in time for the 1864 presidential elections. If

---

[13]Timothy F. Weiss, "'I Lead You into Battle': Joseph E. Johnston and the Controversy at Cassville," *Georgia Historical Quarterly* 91/4 (Winter 2007): 424–52 (This is the best and most detailed analysis of the events at Cassville from the Confederate point of view.); McMurry, *Atlanta 1864*, 79–83; Davis, *Atlanta Will Fall*, 51–58 (quotations, 53, 58); Castel, *Decision in the West*, 194–202 (quotation, 195); Stanley F. Horn, *The Army of Tennessee* (1941; reprint, Norman: University of Oklahoma Press, 1993) 327–29.

this occurred and Lincoln was reelected, the fate of the Confederacy would be sealed.[14]

Johnston began to call for another force, especially Major General Nathan Bedford Forrest's cavalry, to strike at Sherman's railroad supply lines in Tennessee. Johnston rebuked repeated calls by Davis to use the Army of the Tennessee's own cavalry force to cut the lines. Historians generally argue that President Davis was wise in not leaving Mississippi defenseless in order to send Forrest to Johnston's aid when Johnston clearly had cavalry enough of his own. It was becoming obvious to Richmond that Johnston could not stop Sherman and showed no intention of trying.[15]

Concerned that Johnston would not fight, Davis sent numerous telegrams and even his military aide, Bragg, to Atlanta in July 1864 to try to sway Johnston. In dealing with the growing crisis, the Confederate president had two overarching concerns—whether he should replace Johnston and, if so, with whom. To Davis it was obvious that Atlanta had to be saved in order to force Lincoln from office. Yet, Johnston showed no sign that he would undertake a real campaign to defend the city. On 17 July, Davis made his decisions—he removed Johnston and replaced him with Hood. Several historians rank those two decisions among Davis's most critical and controversial of the entire war.[16]

Many early writers criticized the president for removing Johnston. Historians Thomas Robson Hay, Bruce Catton, and Joseph B. Mitchell all contend that Johnston should have been left in command and that he could have held Atlanta. Mitchell even went so far as to state that "of all the mistakes ever made by Jefferson Davis perhaps his most fatal was in relieving Joseph E. Johnston from command just as the battles for Atlanta began." Indeed, Johnston's reputation as a superb commander stretched for a century after the Civil War. It appears, however, that this reputation has more to do with perception than reality. Leading the counterattack of modern scholars, McMurry points out that Johnston had

---

[14]McMurry, *Atlanta 1864*, 121–28; Castel, *Decision in the West*, 344–47.

[15]McMurry, *Atlanta 1864*, 95–99; Woodworth, *Jefferson Davis and His Generals*, 277–79.

[16]McMurry, *Atlanta 1864*, 137–38; Connelly, *Autumn of Glory*, 391–426.

the good fortune of succeeding Bragg and preceding Hood. He never suffered humiliating defeats such as Missionary Ridge or Franklin, and Davis removed him before his failure at Atlanta could become obvious to all. Also, being wounded at Seven Pines had saved him from possible disaster at Richmond in 1862, and his removal from overall command of the West in 1863 allowed him to wash his hands of Bragg's defeat at Murfreesboro and Pemberton's defeat at Vicksburg in 1863. Luck and inaction kept Johnston's reputation intact well into 1864. His stature continued mainly due to unreliable and self-serving accounts of the war (including his own *Narrative of Military Operations*) and the neglect scholars gave the Western Theater until the 1970s.[17]

Modern scholars such as Davis, McMurry, Castel, Connelly, Daniel, and Woodworth have all but discredited Johnston as a competent commander. Woodworth maintains that in Virginia, in Mississippi, and now in Georgia, Johnston had "furnished ample evidence that he simply did not have the inner strength necessary to lead an army." Woodworth also advocates that Jefferson Davis should have found a better initial choice than Johnston given the general's propensity to retreat, and he admonishes Davis for waiting too long to remove the timid general. Stephen Davis asserts that "well before 1864, he [Johnston] had shown President Davis and uncounted other observers his several unhappy characteristics as army leader: passivity, over caution, fear of failure, uncommunicativeness." Johnston was simply a retreater. Indeed, Davis blames Johnston for Atlanta's fall in that his lack of ability placed Hood in an untenable position by the time Johnston had been removed from command. Thomas Connelly declares that "Johnston's standing was based more upon what he allegedly could have done if he had been given the opportunity than any real achievement." In reality, Johnston had passed over several opportunities to engage Sherman and gave no

---

[17]Thomas Robson Hay, "The Atlanta Campaign," pt. 1, *Georgia Historical Quarterly* 7/1 (March 1923):19–43; pt. 2, *Georgia Historical Quarterly* 7/2 (June 1923): 99–118; Bruce Catton, *Never Call Retreat*, vol. 3 of *The Centennial History of the Civil War* (Garden City NY: Doubleday & Company, 1965) 330; Joseph B. Mitchell, *Military Leaders of the Civil War* (New York: G. P. Putnam's Sons, 1972) 19; Greg Biggs, "Jefferson Davis' Greatest Mistake," *Blue & Gray* 8/3 (February 1991): 38; McMurry, "A Policy So Disastrous," 227–30.

indication he would fight to save Atlanta. McMurry is perhaps Johnston's harshest critic, pointing to his tactical blundering at Snake Creek Gap that should have resulted in his army's destruction, the loss of North Georgia without a fight, exposing the vital industrial and agricultural regions of Alabama to Federal assault, and, perhaps most importantly, his inability to grasp the strategic and political necessity of holding Atlanta until after the 1864 presidential election in the North. McMurry sums up his indictment by using the same words as Jefferson Davis to describe Johnston's conduct of the campaign—"a policy so disastrous."[18]

While Johnston is now being castigated by scholars, his replacement, John Bell Hood, is being rehabilitated. Hood's failure to hold Atlanta and his disastrous campaign into Tennessee have been used by historians reading backward to assess Hood's qualifications for command. Yet, if one examines the situation and personalities at the moment Davis made his decision, the selection of Hood appears logical. Hardee had declined command the previous December, and the president had been warned by Hood and Bragg that he favored Johnston's policy of retreat. He may have proved to be another Johnston and in any case was not particularly skillful. That left Hood or Beauregard. Davis believed that Hood was a bold fighter who understood the situation better than a new general, just arriving on the scene in the midst of a coming battle, could. Most historians support Davis's decision. Hood at least would fight and in the subsequent battles around Atlanta showed surprising tactical skill.[19]

---

[18]Davis, *Atlanta Will Fall*, 198 (quotation); Davis, "Generalship of John Bell Hood," 45–52; McMurry, *Atlanta 1864*, 183–86; McMurry, "A Policy So Disastrous," 242–48 (quotation, 248); Daniel, *Soldiering in the Army of Tennessee*, 140–46; Stephen E. Woodworth, "A Reassessment of Confederate Command Options During the Winter of 1863–1864," in *The Campaign for Atlanta & Sherman's March to the Sea*, 1:1–7; Woodworth, *Jefferson Davis and His Generals*, 277, 303 (quotation); Connelly, *Autumn of Glory*, 287.

[19]Connelly, *Autumn of Glory*, 429–69; Castel, *Decision in the West*, 562; Wiley Sword, *Embrace an Angry Wind: The Confederacy's Last Hurrah: Spring Hill, Franklin, and Nashville* (New York: Harper Collins, 1992) 34; McMurry, *Atlanta 1864*, 129–40. The greatest defense of John Bell Hood's generalship has come from Stephen Davis; see

So, if Johnston should have been removed and if Hood was indeed the right choice to replace him, at least at this point in the campaign, why did the Texan fail to stop the Federal advance? This question, like myriad others attached to the Atlanta Campaign, opens up another controversy. Rarely has any general assumed command of an army under more inauspicious circumstances than Hood. First, his army was too small to cover all weak points. The force, weakened by casualties, disease, and desertion, had to guard the city, protect the prisoner of war camp at Andersonville, and hold at least one rail line in order to remain supplied. Second, the high command lacked competence and experience. Hood was new to army command and had led a corps for only six months. With Johnston's departure and Hood's elevation in rank, a regalement had to be found. Also, the recent death of Lt. General Leonidas Polk meant that the army needed another corps commander. As a result, Major General Alexander Stewart and Major General Benjamin F. Cheatham were elevated to corps command, joining William J. Hardee, until a new corps level commander, Major General Stephen D. Lee, arrived.

None of these commanders were ready to exercise corps command. Stewart was inexperienced, and Hardee resented Hood being placed in command above him even though he had previously refused command. Finally, Cheatham's competence at the corps level was doubtful, as events proved. Command issues filtered down to the division and brigade level as officers were shifted to new responsibilities. Adding to the command problems, Hood had virtually no staff with which to help manage the day-to-day operations of the army. Worse still, his crippled condition meant that he had trouble adequately maintaining a presence in the field and had to rely on his corps commanders to take charge at key points. Despite all of the problems facing Hood as he took over the army, he would have no time to work out the kinks. In order to drive Sherman's forces back or hold them at bay, he would have to take the offensive.

---

especially Davis, "Generalship of John Bell Hood," 58–82, and Davis, *Atlanta Will Fall*, 127–200.

Being outnumbered, Hood would have to use maneuver, deception, and speed to his advantage if he were to defeat Sherman's horde.[20]

Hood has been harshly rebuked for his leadership of the Army of Tennessee, and historians at one time perceived him to be among the worst of Confederate leaders. Current scholarship, however, is more sympathetic and nuanced. While historians such as James Lee McDonough, Thomas Connelly, and McMurry agree that the Texan was far from brilliant, they assert that he does not deserve to be castigated for Atlanta's fall. Much of Hood's negative perception comes from his disastrous Tennessee campaign, especially the battles at Franklin and Nashville, where he all but destroyed his army. Yet, prior to the ill-fated offensive, Hood's military record was excellent. He had risen to become the best division commander in the Army of Northern Virginia before serious wounds and the amputation of a leg led to a long convalescence. Returning as a corps commander under Johnston, Hood outperformed his contemporaries and was Johnston's logical replacement. Given the task of preventing Atlanta's fall, he did the best job he or anyone else could have done. Three times in little more than a week (from 20–28 July) Hood struck at Sherman first at Peachtree Creek, then Bald Hill (Battle of Atlanta), and finally at Ezra Church. Despite the postwar criticism of Johnston and his supporters, these battles were well designed and failed mainly due to Hood's subordinates and not the general himself.[21]

Immediately on taking command, Hood saw the best opportunity since Cassville to defeat the Federals. Confederate scouts discovered that Sherman had allowed a massive gap to open in his lines. As the Yankees moved out from the Chattahoochee crossing, McPherson swung the Army of the Tennessee far to the east to cut the railroad beyond Decatur. Schofield followed with the Army of the Ohio to the northwest. The two armies were miles away from Thomas's Army of the Cumberland. This gap meant that the elements of Sherman's army group could not support

---

[20]McMurry, *Atlanta 1864*, 141–45.

[21]James Lee McDonough and Thomas Lawrence Connelly, *Five Tragic Hours: The Battle of Franklin* (Knoxville: University of Tennessee Press, 1983) 15; Richard M. McMurry, *John Bell Hood and the War for Southern Independence* (Lexington: University Press of Kentucky, 1982) 23; Davis, *Atlanta Will Fall*, 127–29; Davis, "Generalship of John Bell Hood," 61; Castel, *Decision in the West*, 431–32.

each other. Hood realized that he had a chance to deliver a stunning blow to part of the Federal army. He proposed to block McPherson and Schofield while the main body of the Confederate army struck Thomas after his men crossed Peachtree Creek but before they could entrench. By a mixture of boldness and luck, Hood had brought a superior force to the point of battle. The attack should have succeeded, but it never transpired. The bulk of the blame belongs to Hardee, whom Hood placed in command. Because the senior corps commander did not adequately reconnoiter the ground, the Rebels became confused in the rough terrain. Worse, the supposedly reliable Hardee sent in his forces piecemeal, allowing the Federals to absorb the attacks and hold their lines.[22]

Still hopeful he could exploit the gap between the Federal armies, Hood proposed a new and more daring plan for the next day. He ordered Hardee to make a night march with part of the Rebel army and strike the exposed rear and flank of McPherson's army moving from Decatur toward Atlanta. Once Hardee had shattered the flank, the rest of the Rebel force would hit the befuddled Yankees and shatter the Army of the Tennessee. Hood had in essence planned another Chancellorsville. Again the plan was brilliant but poorly executed. Hardee did not get his men into position in time, he again failed to reconnoiter the ground properly, and he again sent his men in piecemeal. Serendipity also smiled on the Federal forces, who just happened to be moving into position to protect McPherson's flank when the Confederate assault hit. The engagement (generally called Bald Hill or the Battle of Atlanta) was the largest of the campaign, yet the Confederates once more squandered an opportunity for a great victory.[23]

Having his eastward advance blocked by Confederate assaults, Sherman decided to shift his forces to the west around Atlanta's powerful entrenchments. Hood planned another flank attack. Stephen D. Lee (the newly arrived corps commander) would block the Federal

---

[22]The best secondary accounts of the Battle of Peachtree Creek are Castel, *Decision in the West*, 365–83; Connelly, *Autumn of Glory*, 440–44; McMurry, *Atlanta 1864*, 146–52, 187.

[23]The best secondary accounts of the Battle of Atlanta (Bald Hill) are Castel, *Decision in the West*, 383–414; Connelly, *Autumn of Glory*, 444–51; McMurry, *Atlanta 1864*, 152–55, 187–88.

advance while Stewart would assault the right flank. However, Hood's subordinates, as usual, failed him with premature and uncoordinated assaults. At the Battle of Ezra Church, Lee attacked entrenched Federals piecemeal before a flank attack could be launched. The result was a disaster.[24]

Hood had planned three attacks in succession, all of which should have worked. The fact that they did not is blamed largely on the condition of his army, the ineptitude of his officer corps, and his physical ailments, which kept him from the front lines. In the end, Hood needed extraordinary skill and luck to pull off his bold maneuvers. He had neither. Although he tried desperately to emulate what he had seen in Virginia with Robert E. Lee and Thomas "Stonewall" Jackson, he had neither the officers nor the army to make that a reality.[25]

Tired of pitched battles, Sherman sought to end the impasse by sending his cavalry on raids to the south of Atlanta. He planned for Brigadier General Edward McCook and some 3,500 troopers to ride to Lovejoy's Station on the Macon and Western about 26 miles below the city and cut Hood's last supply line, thereby forcing the Rebels to give up the city. Another simultaneous raid under Major General George Stoneman with about 5,500 men would ride to Macon and liberate the Federal officers camp and then continue 55 miles farther south to liberate the prisoner of war camp at Andersonville. Hood's cavalry under Major General Wheeler countered the raids, decimating McCook's column and inflicting even worse casualties on Stoneman. The raids had done no serious damage to the railroads and had wrecked two divisions of Sherman's cavalry.[26]

---

[24]The best secondary accounts of the Battle of Ezra Church are Castel, *Decision in the West*, 414–36; Connelly, *Autumn of Glory*, 453–55; McMurry, *Atlanta 1864*, 156–57, 187.
[25]Connelly, *Autumn of Glory*, 430–32, 443–44, 447, 449–51, 454–55; Davis, "Generalship of John Bell Hood," 61–73; McMurry, *Atlanta, 1864*, 158–59.
[26]Connelly, *Autumn of Glory*, 452–53; McMurry, *Atlanta, 1864*, 157–58; David Evans, *Sherman's Horsemen: Union Cavalry Operations in the Atlanta Campaign* (Bloomington: Indiana University Press, 1996) chaps. 12–19; Byron H. Matthews, *The McCook-Stoneman Raid* (Philadelphia: Dorrance, 1976).

For almost a month after the engagement at Ezra Church and the failure of the McCook-Stoneman Raid, the opposing armies remained in relatively stable positions around Atlanta. A frustrated Sherman instituted an ineffectual artillery bombardment of the city. By 13 August, he decided to shift his entire force westward and southward toward Hood's last remaining rail line. Although Hood detected elements of the shift, he did not ascertain the scope of the movement because most of his own cavalry had moved northward into the mountains and into East Tennessee in a vain attempt to cut Sherman's supply lines.[27]

Frustrated, Sherman again moved his forces in late August to cut the last link to Atlanta and force Hood to fight or abandon the city. Knowing that he must preserve his hold on the Macon and Western Railroad to retain Atlanta, Hood ordered Hardee south with his own corps and that of Stephen D. Lee. Early in the morning of the last day of August, the two corps were to attack the Federals at Jonesboro. The attack turned into a fiasco yet again due to a lack of reconnaissance and piecemeal assaults against an entrenched opponent. It was a needless attack. The railroad had already been cut to the north, and Atlanta was isolated and had to be abandoned. Sherman's 2 September telegram to Washington summed up the campaign: "Atlanta is ours and fairly won." The South's struggle to hold the Federals at bay until the November presidential elections in the North failed and with it the last desperate hope of Confederate independence.[28]

Hood failed. Despite his earnest efforts to emulate Rober E.Lee and the Army of Northern Virginia, Hood and his bedraggled army were inadequate substitutes for Lee and his well-oiled machine. Yet, as Castel, McMurry, and Davis postulate, Hood's situation was so impossible that Lee himself could not have salvaged it. Castel believes that Hood overstepped himself;

---

[27]Stephen Davis, "'A Very Barbarous Mode of Carrying on War': Sherman's Artillery Bombardment of Atlanta, July 20–August 24, 1864," *Georgia Historical Quarterly* 79/1 (Spring 1995): 57–90; Davis, *Atlanta Will Fall*, 167–73; Connelly, *Autumn of Glory*, 456–57.

[28]The best secondary accounts of the Battle of Jonesboro and the fall of Atlanta are Castel, *Decision in the West*, 480–547; Connelly, *Autumn of Glory*, 456–69; McMurry, *Atlanta 1864*, 160–76.

Hood did his best to fulfill the mission that his government gave him, which is more than Johnston did. The trouble is, Hood's best merely made worse what already was bad, as he constantly endeavored to do too much with too little and without sufficient allowance for the factors of time and distance, physical and emotional endurance, and chance. In sum, while possessing many of the attributes of a fine commander— notably, indomitable determination—he was lacking in realism about his own army, the enemy's army, and above all the nature of war itself as it had evolved in America in 1864.

Davis is more sympathetic, pointing out that Hood "was the only Confederate officer in July 1864 who believed he could drive the enemy away from Atlanta, and who aggressively pursued the only plan that had a possibility of success. For this he deserves a more favorable verdict in history than he has heretofore received."[29]

If Hood could not save Atlanta, could anyone? This is a key question to understanding the war and its outcome. By 1864, the South's only real hope of achieving its independence rested with the North's unwillingness to continue the war. Lincoln losing the presidential election to the Democrats who were running on a negotiated-peace platform would signal the North's reluctance to continue the struggle at any price. Lincoln himself expected to lose the election and looked to his lame duck period to convince the next president to continue the war. Given the huge casualty figures of Grant's campaign against Lee and the already tens of thousands of dead and wounded, if the South could have achieved an armistice, then it was unlikely the war would have been started again in the North regardless of failed peace negotiations. Jefferson Davis and most Confederates had no intention of returning to the United States after the sacrifices made thus far, and Northern morale was at its lowest point in summer 1864. Further, considering that it is highly unlikely that Lincoln would have ever considered Confederate independence during his presidency, it holds that his removal from office was the South's only real opportunity to achieve victory during the entire war. Therefore, the 1864 campaigns take on an even greater significance. Perhaps the Confederacy should have developed a strategy that looked to

---

[29]Castel, *Decision in the West*, 562; Davis, "Generalship of John Bell Hood," 82.

the Northern 1864 election as the key to victory instead of other factors such as European recognition. By 1864 the Rebels had gambled and lost so many resources that holding Richmond and Atlanta was nearly impossible.

The Atlanta campaign and the lack of adequate Confederate leadership reveal just how impressive and skilled Robert E. Lee and his army were. Clearly, without that force in the field, the Confederacy could not hope to win its independence. Finally, the performance of the Army of Tennessee at Atlanta demonstrates the weakness of the force and its officers. By 1864, the army was a shell and incapable of anything but defense and limited local attacks. The army had lost its offensive punch with Bragg.[30]

Regardless, if the Confederacy's only hope of independence in 1864 lay in disrupting Grant and Sherman, could the Rebels have won in Georgia? It seems unlikely that Atlanta could have been held unless a commander other than Joseph E. Johnston had been given the reins. He simply was not suited for army command, especially one that required him to be bold and resourceful. The task called for an aggressive commander who utilized terrain, entrenchments, and rapidly moving flanking columns to harass and slow the enemy. If this hypothetical "Lee-like" commander could have kept part of the Rebel army entrenched and used other elements to scout and block Federal flanking movements, he could possibly have achieved a numerical superiority against isolated elements of the Federal army group. Instead of looking for a climactic battle, he would have harassed, delayed, and struck portions of the Federals until frustration and fatigue led to mistakes.

Some scholars support the so-called "Railroad Strategy" as one possible option of victory. This idea calls for the use of cavalry to cut Sherman's railroad supply line from Tennessee. Jefferson Davis, Braxton Bragg, Robert E. Lee, Johnston, and Hood all believed that this offered the best chance to stop or at least impede Sherman's advance. Modern scholars, however, consider this a chimera. Based on the performance of

---

[30]The best study to date comparing the Army of North Virginia and the Army of Tennessee is Richard M. McMurry, *Two Great Rebel Armies: An Essay in Confederate Military History* (Chapel Hill: University of North Carolina Press, 1996).

cavalry in other railroad raids, the use of skilled repair crews, and Sherman's decision to keep large amounts of supply with his army, it is unlikely that Wheeler, Forrest, or anybody else would have been able to damage the railroad sufficiently to force Sherman to abandon his campaign in Georgia. Moreover, Davis would never allow Mississippi to be stripped bare of protection to send Forrest against Sherman's lines. At best, the Rebel horsemen could have harried the Federals, disrupted supply, and slowed the advance.[31]

McMurry has quipped that nothing less than a nuclear device could have saved Atlanta by the time Hood took command. In essence, what the Army of Tennessee needed was the leadership of Lee. Instead, it lacked an aggressive commander until the point that it did not matter and a command structure that could not respond to his wishes. The result: Atlanta fell and Lincoln was reelected.[32]

Interestingly, the Atlanta Campaign for all its importance is not properly analyzed in Civil War textbooks. Bruce Catton in his *Centennial History of the Civil War* viewed the campaign as key to Lincoln's reelection. Preeminent Civil War historian James McPherson in his classic *Battle Cry of Freedom: The Civil War Era* declares the campaign to be critical to the election. However, no detailed examination of the battle is included in the text. Much more space is given to other military events, especially those in the Eastern Theater. Likewise, Charles P. Roland in his *An American Iliad: The Story of the Civil War* asserts:

> The capture of Atlanta was a tremendous Union victory in every sense. It represented a clear tactical victory over one of the two major Confederate armies; it was a strategic victory as a successful part of Grant's comprehensive plan for simultaneous, coordinated offensives against the South; it placed in Union hands and deprived the Confederacy of one of the key communications centers and an important manufacturing center of the lower South. The capture of Atlanta gave a powerful boost to Union morale at a moment when Grant's costly offensive in Virginia seemed indefinitely stopped; conversely, the loss of

---

[31]McMurry, *Atlanta 1864*, 198–203; Castel, *Decision in the West*, 562–63.

[32]Castel, *Decision in the West*, 563; Davis, "Generalship of John Bell Hood," 82.

Atlanta by the Confederates struck a numbing blow to the southern spirit.
Finally, the taking of Atlanta helped assure, if it was not decisive in, the
reelection of Lincoln in the 1864 presidential race in the North.

Despite this powerful declaration, there are eleven pages dedicated to the
Battle of Gettysburg, which did not decide the fate of the war.[33]

Clearly, a strong Eastern Theater bias still exists in textbooks. For a
balanced account, the importance of the Atlanta Campaign to the
outcome of the war must be emphasized. Scholars such as Gary
Gallagher and Kent Masterson Brown have discovered that the
Gettysburg campaign for all its drama did not decide the war nor serve as
the Confederate high tide. In the excellent *This Terrible War: The Civil
War and Its Aftermath,* authors Michael Fellman, Lesley J. Gordon, and
Daniel E. Sutherland declare that Sherman's victory in effect reelected
Lincoln, yet they still devote more space to Gettysburg.[34]

It appears that although textbook authors realize the importance of
the campaign to the outcome of the war, they fail to give it adequate
space and to discuss the campaign in detail. Instead, the overly
romanticized traditional accounts of Gettysburg and the war in the
Eastern Theater garner the lion's share of the attention and text. The fact
that the war was won and lost in the Western Theater and specifically
with the Atlanta Campaign is still to be demonstrated in college-level
textbooks. This is surprising given the evidence.

---

[33]Catton, *Never Call Retreat,* 317–34, 383–87; James McPherson, *Battle Cry of
Freedom: The Civil War Era* (New York: Oxford University Press, 1988) 743–56, 774
(15 pages, but McPherson gives more space to less important events—chap. 13, "The
River War in 1862," is 36 pages, and chap. 21, "Long Remember: The Summer of '63,"
is 40); Charles P. Roland, *An American Iliad: The Story of the Civil War,* 2nd ed. (Boston:
McGraw Hill, 2002) 134–45, 181–85 (quotation on 185).

[34]Kent Masterson Brown *Retreat from Gettysburg: Lee, Logistics, and the
Pennsylvania Campaign* (Chapel Hill: University of North Carolina Press, 2005); Gary
W. Gallagher, "'Lee's Army Has Not Lost Any of Its Prestige': The Impact of
Gettysburg on the Army of Northern Virginia and the Confederate Home Front," in *The
Third Day at Gettysburg and Beyond,* ed. Gary W. Gallagher (Chapel Hill: University of
North Carolina Press, 1994) 1–30; Michael Fellman, Lesley J. Gordon, and Daniel E.
Sutherland, *This Terrible War: The Civil War and Its Aftermath,* 2nd ed. (New York:
Pearson Longman, 2008) 275–78 (While the authors claim that Sherman's victory in
effect reelected Lincoln [278], more space is devoted to the Battle of Gettysburg [234–
38].).

As the nation begins the commemoration of the sesquicentennial, two aspects of the Atlanta Campaign take center stage. First, historians and the general public must come to understand that the struggle for Atlanta and not Gettysburg marks the most important military action of the war. How and when this will become clear depends on the second aspect, the need for more research and analysis into the campaign. While the Atlanta Campaign has attracted some of the best Civil War scholars and some of the most influential scholarship of the past three decades, more needs to be done. New military studies of commanders, battles, strategies, and the fighting men are needed. Likewise, socio-political and economic studies focusing on the civilian population, morale, industry, and a host of other subjects will shed light on the Western Theater and the Atlanta Campaign. After a century and a half of misplaced focus on the East, it is now time to redirect the focus on the true decisive campaign of the war. It will set the historical record straight and do justice to the men who decided the fate of two nations in the red clay hills of Georgia in 1864.

Buttressed Patriarchs and Substitute Patriarchs: Aid to Georgia's Confederate Families during and after the Civil War

by Jennifer Lynn Gross

Like any other young couple, Mariann Green and her husband William Babb embarked on a journey when they married on 7 October 1842. What twists and turns that journey held for them, neither could have anticipated. By 1860, on the eve of the Civil War, Mariann and William's family had grown to include six children: two boys named Walter Tilman (called Tilman) and Lawrence and four girls named Frances, Sarah Jane, Martha, and Virginia. Martha and Virginia were four-year-old twins. William was forty-two when the war erupted and did not enlist immediately. Tilman, the eldest son, enlisted in late July 1863, just before he turned sixteen; this must have weighed heavily on his parents' minds, particularly in light of the devastating losses the Confederacy had just suffered at Vicksburg and Gettysburg. By August 1864, the manpower shortages facing the Confederacy were too much even for a man of forty-six, teetering on the edge of being past his prime, to continue to resist the call. William Babb enlisted in Company B, 3rd Regiment of the Georgia State Troops and was assigned to Andersonville as a prison guard. Though his son returned from the war unscathed, William Babb was not as lucky, contracting chronic dysentery like many of the prisoners he guarded at the Civil War's most infamous prison. Though William survived the war, his illness left him bedridden for much of the rest of his time on earth and eventually claimed his life on 11 July 1876.

When William died, he left a will, unlike many of his economic and regional contemporaries. Perhaps he was spurred by the experience of war, or maybe it was simply the ever-present illness from which he suffered. At any rate, the will was clearly written before he and Mariann had two more children—Charles in 1867 and Anna in 1872. In the will, William bequeathed his entire estate to his six children and his wife, with special instructions regarding its partition. To his wife and his "three youngest daughters"—Sarah Jane, Martha, and Virginia—he specified that their portions of the farm adjoin one another's and encompass the house. To his wife, he left all his personal property including both household items as well as farming implements. He also made Mariann his executor and gave her an additional forty acres in North Georgia with the allowance that she could "dispose of [it] as she deem[ed] proper." After William's death, Mariann and the "three youngest daughters" along with the two children unmentioned in the will, Charles and Anna, continued living on the "William Babb Place." In 1884, they defaulted on the mortgage and lost their portions of the family farm in a sheriff's sale to a neighbor, C. H. Wright. With no land, no income to speak of, and no husbands to support them, the twin sisters Martha and Virginia, along with their younger sister Anna, left their mother in Baldwin County and moved to Macon to find work in the Bibb textile mills. In the winter of 1888–1889, all three sisters died of pneumonia within three weeks of one another. Mariann most likely split her time between the residences of her three married adult children, Tilman, Lawrence, and Frances. In 1890, she began applying for a yearly pension from the state of Georgia, declaring her dependence on the state as a substitute patriarch for her long-dead husband. For almost a decade, Mariann continued to receive her Confederate widow's pension. The journey that Mariann and William had embarked on together in October 1842 finally ended in 1900 when Mariann, a widow for more than twenty years, died.[1]

While the details of the Babbs' life are unique, the larger picture presented by their story is one that many Georgians of the nineteenth century would find familiar. Certainly marriage and children were the norm for Southern men and women before the Civil War. Death, crippling wounds, or chronic illness were not unusual among the men who wore the gray. Widowhood without the possibility of remarriage was a reality for many Confederate soldiers' wives during the postbellum

---

[1]The information in this paragraph was compiled from US Census Records for the years 1850–1910 (excluding 1890, which are not available); Baldwin County GA, Will Book A, pp. 88–89; Confederate Pension Applications, Baldwin County GA; various other records compiled by Eileen Babb McAdams on her website: http://home.windstream.net/eileen99/.

period. So some form of dependence on the state, during the war or after it, became commonplace among Georgia's Confederate families. Through wartime and postwar aid and eventually the Confederate pension system, Georgia's male citizenry via their elected officials buttressed Confederate veterans in their roles as patriarchs and acted as substitute patriarchs for the widows and children of those men who never returned from the war. Confederate aid was not just a thinly veiled attempt to create a social welfare program for the state's "worthiest" citizens.[2] It was paramount in Southerners' efforts to reestablish proper patriarchal gender roles. In the case of aid to families during the war and widows' pensions after, the state took on the role of patriarch in the absence of soldier husbands. Never was the provision the state provided so ample as to preclude any manless woman from choosing remarriage, however. Aid to the state's Confederate dependents was always couched in those terms—aid to deserving individuals who had willingly given their protectors and providers for the cause and were thus in need of a new provider and protector. In the case of artificial limbs and Confederate veterans' pensions, the state's aim was to buttress those men in their role as patriarchs, not replace them. For them, assistance was couched in terms of payment for their service to the state and acknowledgment of their heroic sacrifices. Georgians as a whole were always encouraged to see providing Confederate aid not as charity but as just recompense. By accepting Confederate aid in these terms, they not only created a means to care for such individuals, but also contributed to

---

[2]In her assessment of the Confederate pension system in Florida, Elna Green asserts, "The Lost Cause movement allowed Southern states to create extensive and expensive social welfare programs, without appearing to do so. Indeed, Lost Cause rhetoric disguised these public welfare programs so well that even social welfare historians have largely overlooked their presence." Green's assertions insinuate some covert effort on the part of Southern politicians to create welfare programs against the will of their constituencies under the cover of "Lost Cause" celebrations. Such an assertion ignores many aspects of the aid given to Confederate veterans and widows during and after the war discussed by Lost Cause scholars including myself. See Elna Green, "Protecting Confederate Soldiers and Mothers: Pensions, Gender, and the Welfare State in the U.S. South, A Case Study from Florida," *Journal of Social History* 39/4 (Summer 2006): 1079–1104, and *This Business of Relief: Confronting Poverty in a Southern City, 1740–1940* (Athens: University of Georgia Press, 2003).

the stabilization of the patriarchal gender roles that were threatened by the crisis of the Civil War.[3]

Both during and after the Civil War, the citizens of Georgia agreed that it was their responsibility, through their elected officials, to provide for the welfare of the state's military families. The nonmilitary poor were a distant secondary concern.[4] As Governor Joseph Brown told his state's legislators early in the war, Georgians "from every part of the State fight for the protection of the liberties of the whole people, and the wealth of the whole State. Let our soldiers know that their loved ones at home are provided for." Many of Georgia's volunteers were "almost des-titute of property," he continued, "and their families should be supplied, if need be, at the public expense, with such of the necessaries of life as their labor will not afford them, cost the State what it may."[5] And cost the state, it did.

Not long after the first shots were fired at Fort Sumter, Georgians began taking steps to aid their fellow citizens, particularly the families of

---

[3]Numerous historians have written about the impact of the Civil War on the de-stabilization of the South's gender roles. Some of the best works include Drew Gilpin Faust, *Mothers of Invention: Women of the Slaveholding South in the American Civil War* (New York: Vintage Books, 1996); Gaines M. Foster, *Ghosts of the Confederacy: Defeat, the Lost Cause, and the Emergence of the New South, 1865–1913* (New York: Oxford University Press, 1987); Jean Friedman, *The Enclosed Garden: Women and Community in the Evangelical South, 1830–1900* (Chapel Hill: University of North Carolina Press, 1985); George C. Rable, *Civil Wars: Women and the Crisis of Southern Nationalism* (Urbana: University of Illinois Press, 1989); and LeeAnn Whites, *The Civil War as a Crisis in Gender, Augusta, Georgia, 1860–1890* (Athens: University of Georgia Press, 1995).

[4]Paul D. Escott, "Georgia," *The Confederate Governors*, ed. W. Buck Yearns (Athens: University of Georgia Press, 1985) 73.

[5]Peter Wallenstein, *From Slave South to New South: Public Policy in Nineteenth-Century Georgia* (Chapel Hill: University of North Carolina Press, 1987) 116. Brown and Georgians clearly saw the cause of providing for the state's poor soldiers and their families as the state's responsibility. They also clearly identified where such provision should come from: those who had profited from the war. Georgia Legislature, *Acts of the General Assembly of the State of Georgia Passed in Milledgeville, at an Annual Session in November and December, 1863,* Resolutions: 110–11. Year after year, state and local taxes on income, cotton, and property rose for Georgia's wealthier citizens while the families of yeoman soldiers paid at reduced rates. Wallenstein, *From Slave South to New South*, 99–128. See also, Escott, "Georgia," 77.

soldiers. Initially many of these measures were specific to certain counties. For example, in December 1861, the General Assembly passed legislation that would empower the ordinary of Towns County to shift unused education funds to the county's soldier relief committee.[6] It did not take long, however, for state officials to move toward legislation that applied to the entire state. In a similarly purposed law, legislators authorized the justices of the inferior courts of all the state's counties to issue bonds and borrow money to equip soldiers and to "support the families of indigent volunteers, who are absent in the army, or who may have been killed, or died in the service, or who may have been disabled in the service."[7] During that same legislative session, Georgia's elected officials took an even more broadly based move toward state relief when they authorized the governor to spend $50,000 to encourage the manufacturing of salt within the state to meet citizens' needs.[8] This policy was the first of many such statewide efforts that would be led by the governor's office. While each of these laws provided for a direct form of relief for the state's citizens including soldiers' wives, the General Assembly also passed laws that would provide more indirect relief to the many wives whose husbands were away fighting for the Confederacy. For example, the General Assembly enacted the state's first married women's property law in 1861. Though the motivation was most certainly the many wives whose husbands were away in the military rather than a women's rights agenda, the property law was a rudimentary example of such protectionist measures. It authorized a married woman to deposit money she or her children had earned in any bank chartered by the state "as if she were not a married woman."[9] In the immediate postwar period the legislature enacted a more thorough

[6]Georgia Legislature, *Acts of the General Assembly of the State of Georgia, Passed in Milledgeville, at an Annual Session in November and December, 1861*, part 2. Private and Local Laws, title 7. Education: 107.

[7]Georgia Legislature, *Acts of the General Assembly, 1861*, part 1. Public Laws, title 7. County Regulations: 30.

[8]Georgia Legislature, *Acts of the General Assembly, 1861*, part 1. Public Laws, title 1. Agriculture and Commerce: 7–8. See also Paul D. Escott, "Georgia," 73.

[9]Georgia Legislature, *Acts of the General Assembly, 1861*, part 1. Public Laws, title 14. Banks and Banking: 23.

married woman's property law, perhaps in recognition of what legislators hoped would happen as a result of the sudden widowhood of so many women: high remarriage rates.[10] Of course, with the death of so many men in the war, that would be an unfulfilled hope, and the state would remain in place as a substitute patriarch for the widows and orphans of Georgia's dead Confederate soldiers. Other such indirectly beneficial legislation protected soldiers and their families from having judgments on their property enforced until three months after said soldier was discharged from service.[11] If a soldier died in service, his widow would be entitled to her dower third, free from any encumbrances according to the state's estate laws.

In a groundbreaking move that further indicates Georgians' belief that it was their job to protect a soldier's family in his absence, legislators also authorized the first Confederate widow's pension that same year. After faithfully serving his state as surveyor general, A.J. Boggess enlisted in the ranks of the army, paying his own outfitting expenses. After surviving the Battle of Manassas, he died of a fever in camp August 1861. Desiring to recognize Boggess's "true heroism and self denial," the legislature authorized the governor to draw from the state's coffers the sum of $504.80 to be paid to Boggess's "widow and children who were dependant upon his personal efforts for the means of maintenance and education of which they are now deprived."[12] With this pension, the legislature set a precedent for the future development of their Confederate pension program. Moreover, they established the premises that would guide the distribution of aid to soldiers' families during the war as well as Confederate veterans and their widows after the war. First, such aid was based on the heroism of the soldier. During the war, the fact that a man was away fighting implied his heroism. No proof was required. After the war, a veteran's implied heroism had to be

---

[10]Georgia Legislature, *Acts of the General Assembly, 1866*, part. 1. Public Laws, title 18. Married Women: 146–47.

[11]Georgia Legislature, *Acts of the General Assembly, 1861*, part 1. Public Laws, title 15. Judiciary. I Supreme Courts: 61.

[12]Georgia Legislature, *Acts of the General Assembly, 1861*, part 2. Private and Local Laws, title 12. Relief: 117.

validated by other veterans.[13] Second, and perhaps more important, aid to wives and widows was based on the understanding that women as much as children were legal, economic, and social dependents. If the individual they depend upon is taken away for a limited period of time or forever, a substitute patriarch must step in. Under ordinary circumstances, for example during times of peace, the general route to a new patriarch was remarriage. The war and its aftermath were not "ordinary circumstances," however, and thus required an extraordinary solution. That solution was to render all male citizens of the state, represented by their elected officials, as substitute patriarchs, responsible for the provision and protection of the state's Confederate wives and widows.

By 1862, legislators had begun a statewide program of monetary homefront assistance for the families of soldiers, enacting legislation that gave $100 to the family of any soldier who owned less than $1,000 of taxable property and allowed for a $1,000 exemption on property taxes.[14] The following year, 1863, as inflation ran rampant and various necessities became more and more difficult to acquire, Georgia began a program of relief-in-kind by distributing scarce foodstuffs and goods to the families of indigent soldiers. Citing the effects of the "depredations of the enemy, and the presence and necessities of our own army foraging upon the country," legislators ordered the quartermaster general of the state to purchase and ship, free of charge on the appropriate railroads, some 97,500 bushels of corn to be distributed free among the "families of deceased soldiers" residing in the northern counties of the state and at cost to the rest of the counties' poor.[15] To pay for said corn, the legislature levied taxes upon the "several Banking corporations" of the

---

[13]Significant work has been done on the ins and outs of the Confederate pension system and the possibility that men were deprived of their pensions because of the machinations of other veterans who served on pension boards. See for example Kathleen R. Gorman, "Confederate Pensions as Southern Social Welfare," in *Before the New Deal: Social Welfare in the South, 1830–1930*, ed. Elna C. Green (Athens: University of Georgia Press, 1999).

[14]Escott, "Georgia," 75.

[15]Georgia Legislature, *Acts of the General Assembly, 1863*, part 1. Public Laws, title 17. Relief: 66–68; Georgia Legislature, *Acts of the General Assembly, 1863*, Resolutions: 107.

state.[16] By March 1864, the legislature recognized that the previous year's allotment for corn was insufficient and ordered the Quartermaster to procure and distribute "such amount of corn as the Governor in his discretion may order, not to exceed ten thousand bushels.... said corn is for the use of the citizens...and not for the purpose of speculation or distillation."[17] The distilling of corn and grain into alcohol was as much a problem for Georgia as it was for the other Confederate states, frequently inspiring legislators to legislate against "unlawful distillation" not for "medicinal or mechanical purposes."[18] While much of the early relief-in-kind focused on the northern part of the state, legislators also made provisions for the erstwhile residents of the southern part, especially those of the Sea Islands, exempting refugees' lands from taxes if they were "driven from their homes by the enemy."[19]

By 1864, Governor Brown could accurately claim that Georgia was spending per year "nearly $10,000,000 to feed and clothe the suffering wives, and widows, and orphans."[20] In Georgia, according to Paul Escott, "Welfare costs dominated the budget in the last two years of the war, and by the time of surrender total welfare spending almost equaled the aggregate of military expenditures."[21]

One other piece of wartime legislation that deserves note in the context of aiding Georgia's Confederate citizens and protecting patriarchy is an amendment to Georgia's divorce code. Beginning in 1864, loyal Confederate wives could divorce their husbands for disloyalty to the Confederate cause. Any woman whose husband was serving in the

---

[16]Georgia Legislature, *Acts of the General Assembly, 1863*, part 1. Public Laws, title 18. Soldiers and Their Families: 69–74.

[17]Georgia Legislature, *Acts of the General Assembly of the State of Georgia, Passed in Milledgeville, at the Called Session in March, 1864,* part 1. Public Laws, title 11. Relief: 133.

[18]For example see, Georgia Legislature, *Acts of the General Assembly, 1863*, part 1. Public Laws, title 5. Distillation: 19–23.

[19]Georgia Legislature, *Acts of the General Assembly, 1863*, part 1. Public Laws, title 20. Taxes and Revenue: 82. Such individuals' lands were not entirely exempt; they were charged a nominal tax rate of one cent per acre.

[20]Brown's Annual Message to legislature, 3 November 1864, quoted in Escott, "Georgia," 76.

[21]Escott, "Georgia," 77.

Union military or voluntarily residing "within the lines of the enemy, furnishing them aid and comfort" could request and expect to be granted a divorce by the state legislature.[22] Apparently, in Georgians' view, only loyal Confederate husbands deserved to remain patriarchs. Since divorce was almost universally frowned upon and certainly had not been easily acquired in antebellum Georgia, this revision of the law makes a tremendous statement about Georgians' ideas regarding marriage, proper gender roles, and the state's place in the protection of both.[23]

While Georgians clearly saw the state government as the proper vehicle for fulfilling their responsibility for the welfare of the state's Confederate families, on several occasions it became necessary for the General Assembly to appeal to the Confederate government for relief. In 1863, for example, members of the General Assembly requested that their representatives and senators in the Confederate Congress introduce legislation that would grant free transportation for any Confederate soldiers on furlough. Since the Confederate government had all but nationalized the nation's transportation networks, Georgians had no other choice but to seek relief at the Confederate level. At the same session, Georgia's legislators also sought relief from the "tax in kind" for the families of soldiers within the state, suspension of the "tax in kind" for counties frequently raided by the enemy, and for the appointment of local citizens to the position of Confederate tax-in-kind collector so as to avoid the "gross injustice and oppression" of non-local collectors. All of these efforts were accompanied by a resolution entitled, "Resolutions Express-ive of the Determination of Georgia to Prosecute the Present War with the Utmost Rigor and Energy."[24] While these "requests" can certainly be examined in the context of Georgia's general resistance to the centralization of the Confederate government at the expense of state's

---

[22]Georgia Legislature, *Acts of the General Assembly, 1864*, title 2. Code of Georgia: 123.

[23]To acquire a divorce, one had to petition the legislature. Even then, Southern legislatures did not grant divorces in many cases. See Richard H. Chused, *Private Acts in Public Places: A Social History of Divorce in the Formative Era of American Family Law* (Philadelphia: University of Pennsylvania Press, 1994).

[24]See Resolutions 12–13, and 21–23 in Georgia Legislature, *Acts of the General Assembly, 1863,* Resolutions: 104–5, 109–110.

rights, the coupling of these resolutions with a restatement of the "Resolution of Determination" indicates two things. First, Georgia's legislators wanted to ensure the Confederate Congress saw their request as a valid complaint, not just intransigence toward federal power. Second, the resolutions must be understood as another example of this state's almost herculean efforts to provide aid to their military families and to serve as their substitute patriarch.

Georgian's sense of responsibility for their soldiers and the families of their soldiers did not end with the close of the war. In 1866 four Southern state governments attempted to make special provisions for soldiers who had lost limbs or eyes during the war. Georgia was the first of these four to do so. In the March session of the legislature, Georgians set aside $20,000 to fulfill what they saw as their obligation to the "maimed indigent soldiers and officers" of Georgia. The corresponding Act for the Relief of Maimed Soldiers provided the process by which such men could apply for and receive said artificial limb and also established a fairly stiff punishment for fraudulently taking advantage of the state's largesse—one to three years incarceration in the state penitentiary and a fine of at least $100.[25] Even if a maimed soldier did not apply for assistance, the state wanted to provide it to him, ordering the comptroller general to acquire through his tax collectors "a list of every man in [the] counties, who has lost a leg or legs, or arm or arms, by the casualties of war."[26] Although the original appropriation for artificial limbs was $20,000, only a few months later on 13 December 1866, Georgia legislators set aside an additional $30,000, "or so much as may be necessary," to fulfill their obligations to the state's crippled soldiers, significantly striking the word indigent from the previous

---

[25]Georgia Legislature, *Acts of the General Assembly December 1865, and January, February, and March, 1866,* part 1. Public Laws, title 25. Maimed Indigent Soldiers: 224–25.

[26]Ibid., Resolutions: 320. This list would also help in the state's efforts to discover fraudulent applications. R. B. Rosenburg suggests that many Confederate veterans resisted state aid because they saw it as humiliating. See Rosenburg, "'Empty Sleeves and Wooden Pegs': Disabled Confederate Veterans in Image and Reality," in *Disabled Veterans in History*, ed. David A. Gerber (Ann Arbor: University of Michigan Press, 2000) 222–23.

legislation thereby allowing for a limb (and free transportation to acquire it) to any maimed soldier in need of one or a monetary payment if such a limb "could not be of service" or if a soldier had already "manufactured for himself such an artificial limb suited to his wants." This early effort to provide artificial limbs was certainly an expression of responsibility owed to men who sacrificed not life but limb for the Confederacy, but it must also be understood in the context of the state's role as protector of patriarchy. Making her soldiers whole again, or as close to whole as they could be, contributed to their ability to return to the role of proper patriarch because it, at least in theory, gave them the tools to once again take up the provision and protection of their own families which would then allow the state to step aside as substitute patriarch for the families of soldiers who were lucky enough to come back from the war alive. Not surprisingly, in that same appropriation bill that set aside money for artificial limbs, legislators also allocated $100,000, "or so much thereof as in the opinion of the Governor shall be absolutely necessary," eventually doling out $200,000 for the purchase and distribution of corn and bread to the indigent widows and orphans of Georgia's soldiers, and for whom the state remained a substitute patriarch.[27] Georgia's early efforts to provide aid to her disabled veterans and widows were not limited solely to the level of state government either. In 1866, legislators also authorized individual counties to levy taxes for the support of their local Confederate veterans and widows.[28]

In the immediate postwar years, Georgia legislators found other, perhaps more creative, ways of benefiting the state's Confederate veterans in their bid to re-establish themselves as patriarchs. "Whereas, it is a matter of primary importance that Georgia should have native educated teachers for the instruction of the children of the State; *and whereas*, there are many indigent maimed soldiers in the State…; *and whereas*, it is a holy and patriotic duty to provide in the best manner

---

[27] *Acts of the General Assembly of the State of Georgia, Passed in Milledgeville, at an Annual Session, in November and December, 1866*, part I. Public Laws, title 2. Appropriations, etc.: 10 –11; Georgia Legislature, *Acts of the General Assembly, 1866*, part 1. Public Laws, title 17. Maimed Soldiers: 144. See also Wallenstein, *From Slave South to New South*, 138–39.

[28] Wallenstein, *From Slave South to New South*, 192.

possible for those unfortunate patriots," Georgia's legislators ordered that all indigent maimed soldiers under the age of thirty be provided tuition, books, board, and clothing at any of the state's institutions of higher learning, paying some $100,000 to such schools in 1868 for costs incurred by the program between 1866 and 1868, when the program was repealed by a Republican-dominated legislature. In exchange for this largesse, the soldier-turned-student need only agree to teach somewhere in the state for the same number of years that it took him to earn his degree.[29] At that same legislative session of 1866, Georgia legislators also waived the licensing fee for peddling for disabled soldiers.[30] This proved to be a relatively easy way to aid disabled soldiers, and legislators revisited it numerous times during the postwar period, making more and more professions fee-free for Confederate veterans. Over the years, legislators amended the Georgia code to allow Confederate veterans to be photographic artists, doctors, auctioneers, traveling life insurance agents, and proprietors of parks or race tracks without paying for or otherwise obtaining the normal licenses required to participate in such occupations.[31]

---

[29]Georgia Legislature, *Acts of the General Assembly, 1866*, part 1. Public Laws, title 17. Maimed Soldiers: 143–44; Georgia Legislature, *Acts of the General Assembly of the State of Georgia, 1868*, part 1. Public Laws, title 2. Appropriations: 11. The act was repealed the following year. Georgia Legislature, *Acts of the General Assembly of the State of Georgia, 1869*, part 1. Public Laws, title 5. Education: 22. See also Wallenstein, *From Slave South to New South,* 161.

[30]Georgia Legislature, *Acts of the General Assembly, 1866*, part 1. Public Laws, title 17. Maimed Soldiers: 145–46. There is one last interesting side note to Georgia's efforts to tend to her maimed veterans. In a resolution passed at the same session in 1866, legislators "suggested" that the comptroller general, who determined the viability of various brands of artificial limbs for use by the veterans, "take into consideration...the professional merits of the Eureka leg, invented by Dr. Harvey L. Byrd, of this State, and the arm known as the Byrd and Kolbe arm" and consider adopting both as the State's standard limb offerings. Georgia Legislature, *Acts of the General Assembly, 1866,* Resolutions: 217.

[31]Georgia Legislature, *Acts and Resolutions, 1892*, part 1. Public Laws, title 9. Miscellaneous: 99; *Acts and Resolutions, 1899*, part 1. Public Laws, title 8. Miscellaneous: 99; *Acts and Resolutions, 1891*, part 1. Public Laws, title 4. Code Amendments: 63; *Acts and Resolutions, 1895,* part 1. Public Laws, title 8. Miscellaneous: 92–94; *Acts and Resolutions, 1899*, part 1. Public Laws, title 8. Miscellaneous: 100.

At the same time that Georgia's legislators were appropriating money for the purchase of artificial limbs for disabled veterans and the distribution of food to soldiers' widows, they were also taking care of the state's dead soldiers. In 1866, the General Assembly set aside $6,000 for the Memorial Association of Georgia and other various ladies' memorial associations to aid them in their efforts to properly attend to Georgia's dead Confederates. In 1868 and 1872, another $2,000 and $3,800 respectively was appropriated for the same purpose. Legislators also ordered that the Western and Atlantic Railroad be required to "furnish free transportation for everything required in the performance of this sacred duty."[32] In the 1880s and beyond, as Confederate memorializers began to turn their attention to mass monuments rather than individual graves, Georgia's elected officials fell in step behind them, contributing money to the erection of monuments around the state and creating and funding a State Memorial Board whose job it was to assess historical sites in the state "since the 1st day of January, 1860."[33] While providing funding for such "lost cause" memorialization efforts did not in any way contribute to the material well-being of the state's veterans or widows, it did help to buttress the ideological underpinnings of the same patriarchal gender roles financial aid was meant to support.

---

[32]Georgia Legislature, *Acts of the General Assembly, 1866*, part 1. Public Laws, title 2. Appropriations, etc.: 12; Georgia Legislature, *Acts of the General Assembly, 1868*, Resolutions: 188; Part 1. Public Laws, title 2. Appropriations: 13–14; Georgia Legislature, *Acts and Resolutions of the General Assembly of the State of Georgia, Passed at Its Session in July and August, 1872*, part 2. Local and Private Laws, title 3. Miscellaneous: 487. The legislature appropriated another $5,000 and $1,500 for the Ladies Memorial Associations of Marietta and Resaca respectively. See Georgia Legislature, *Acts and Resolutions of the General Assembly of the State of Georgia, 1908*, part 4. Resolutions. 1002 1003, Georgia Legislature, *Acts and Resolutions of the General Assembly of the State of Georgia, 1910*, part 4. Resolutions: 1270–71.

[33]See Georgia Legislature, *Acts and Resolutions, 1884–1885*, part 3. Local Laws, title 10. Miscellaneous: 652–53; Georgia Legislature, *Acts and Resolutions of the General Assembly of the State of Georgia, 1894*, Part I. Public Laws, title 8. Miscellaneous: 94–95; Georgia Legislature, *Acts and Resolutions of the General Assembly of the State of Georgia, 1895*, part 1. Public Laws, title 1. Appropriations, Taxes, and Public Debt: 11–12; Georgia Legislature, *Acts and Resolutions of the State of Georgia, 1897*, part 1. Public Laws, title 6. Miscellaneous: 103.

After the war's end, state legislators took it upon themselves to appeal three actions taken by the federal government during and immediately after the war, again acting on behalf of their Confederate citizenry in the role of substitute patriarch. Perhaps not surprisingly, the first two appeals occurred during the tumult of Andrew Johnson's Restoration program. Full of self-assurance, Georgia requested that the secretary of war rescind a recent order that authorized the confiscation of all animals branded "U.S." or "C.S." regardless of whether such animals had been legally purchased. They argued that Georgians had bought these animals with the understanding that they were making legal purchases. The recent order overturned already established protocols, thereby violating Georgians' rights and more importantly endangering their ability to provide for themselves. During that same session, Georgia's General Assembly instructed the governor to appeal directly to President Johnson for the return of Sea Island plantations and other confiscated properties then under the control of the Freedman's Bureau.[34]

The final instance in which Georgia's elected officials sought relief from the federal government was less successful than the first two. After the Democrats regained control of the state in 1871, Georgia legislators argued that the tax collected on cotton in the years 1865–1867 was not only unfair and unconstitutional because it was specific only to cotton production, but was also mean-spirited because it was "imposed and collected at a time when the Southern people were prostrated and impoverished by war" as a "mode of meeting retribution upon the vanquished." Georgians made this appeal unsuccessfully in 1871 and again in 1886 and 1897.[35] All three of these efforts, while not directed

---

[34]See resolutions 7 and 16 in Georgia Legislature, *Acts of the General Assembly of the State of Georgia, Passed in Milledgeville, at an Annual Session in December 1865, and January, February, and March, 1866*, resolutions: 314, 317.

[35]Democratic "redemption" began in Georgia in 1871 with the flight of Republican governor Rufus Bullock and the special election of former Confederate General James Milton Smith to finish Bullock's term. Georgia Legislature, *Acts and Resolutions of the General Assembly of the State of Georgia, at a Session in November and December, 1871. Comprising, Also, the Acts and Resolutions Passed at the Session of January, 1872*, Resolutions: 254–55; Georgia Legislature, *Acts and Resolutions of the General Assembly of the State of Georgia, 1886*, part 5. Resolutions: 323–24; Georgia Legislature, *Acts and Resolutions of the General Assembly of the State of Georgia 1897*, part 4. Resolutions:

solely toward the benefit of the state's Confederate veterans or their widows, must still be understood in the context of the state's role in aiding her patriarchs to return to their prewar status. Each appeal implicitly and explicitly addressed the issue of male Georgians' ability to provide for their families and how certain specific actions taken by the federal government could possibly inhibit it and thus the reestablishment of patriarchal gender roles.

Between 1866 and 1871, Georgians continued to try to assist Confederate veterans and widows, but with periods of Republican dominance and military rule in place at varying times after 1867, not all years saw a General Assembly friendly to such legislation. Indeed, the passage of Confederate aid legislation, whether for artificial limbs or burial of the dead, coincided directly with the identity of the General Assembly. In years of Democratic control, such legislation passed with ease. Without Democratic control, it was never a serious consideration. For example, the year before Georgians' first unsuccessful attempt to be repaid for the cotton tax, the Republican-controlled legislature had ratified the 14th and 15th Amendments, steered Georgia back into the Union as a result, and invited then President Ulysses S. Grant to attend the Georgia State Fair.[36]

With the return of Democratic dominance in 1871, there was a renewed effort to provide aid to the state's worthiest citizens, her Confederate veterans, and to step in as substitute patriarch for the state's worthiest dependents, her Confederate widows. In 1871, Georgia's Redeemers immediately reinstituted the artificial limbs program that had initially been established in 1866.[37] In a precedent-setting move, Georgia legislators in 1875 provided for the first Confederate pensions. While

593. In 1899, legislators altered their tune a little and began requesting payment for cotton seized and sold by the US government during the war, see Georgia Legislature, *Acts and Resolutions of the General Assembly of the State of Georgia 1899*, part 4. Resolutions: 529.

[36]Georgia Legislature, *Acts and Resolutions of the General Assembly of the State of Georgia Passed in Atlanta, Georgia, at the Session of 1870*, Resolutions: 501–502. Interestingly, the same legislators also voted to commemorate the death of Robert E. Lee, "the peerless hero and the guileless Christian," the Union's "most gifted pupil and soldier, the South['s] most loved son and peerless chief."

[37]Rosenburg, "Empty Sleeves and Wooden Pegs," 210.

said pensions were distributed by the individual counties rather than the state, they were still pensions. The law required that counties in which veterans resided, who had lost either both eyes or two limbs, tax their citizens to pay such veterans a yearly stipend of $100 provided they owned less than $1,000 of taxable property.[38] In 1885, the state removed the requirement that such veterans not have more than $1,000 of taxable property.[39] These county-based pensions were an attempt to meet the same needs that the statewide pension program would eventually target—the buttressing of disabled Confederate veterans as patriarchs.

When, in 1877, Georgians set about rewriting their constitution in recognition of the official return of home rule, they explicitly reaffirmed their commitment to two things: the subordination of the state's African Americans, most notably through disfranchisement, and the care of their maimed Confederate veterans. Although the state had instituted poll taxes earlier, it made them cumulative in 1877 (to vote one had to pay not only that year's tax, but also back poll taxes to 1871). While the poll tax succeeded in disfranchising roughly half of the state's black voters, it also had the undesirable effect of disfranchising some of the state's white voters, including most importantly former Confederate veterans. In 1882, the legislature addressed that problem by relieving disabled soldiers from paying the poll tax.[40]

In terms of commitment to providing relief for the state's Confederate veterans, Robert Toombs, former Confederate politician and general, led the way, dominating the Constitutional Convention of 1877.[41] Within the constitution itself, Georgians agreed that supplying

---

[38]Georgia Legislature, *Acts and Resolutions of the General Assembly of the State of Georgia, Passed at the Regular January Session, 1875*, part 1. Public Laws, title 9. Maimed Soldiers: 107–108.

[39]Georgia Legislature, *Acts and Resolutions of the General Assembly of the State of Georgia, 1884–85,* part 1. Public Laws, title 11. Miscellaneous: 127.

[40]Georgia Legislature, *Acts and Resolutions of the General Assembly of the State of Georgia. 1882–83,* part 1. Public Laws, title 10. Miscellaneous: 120–21.

[41]After narrowly avoiding arrest by US forces after the Civil War, Toombs fled to Cuba. He returned to the US by way of Canada in 1867. He steadfastly refused to sign the oath of allegiance and never regained his US citizenship. He did, however, maintain a lucrative law practice in Georgia as "an unreconstructed" Southerner. On Toombs's involvement in the Constitutional Convention of 1877, see Walter McElreath, *A Treatise*

"the soldiers who lost a limb, or limbs, in the military service of the Confederate States, with substantial artificial limbs during life" along with public education, paying the principal and interest on the public debt, and suppressing insurrection or repelling invasion were the only legitimate expenditures for which the state could tax her citizens.[42] In 1878, legislators provided for a cash payment "not oftener than once in five years" if a disabled soldier had provided himself with an artificial limb at his own expense.[43] In 1885, they revised that commitment to guarantee disabled soldiers access to artificial limbs for life and "to make suitable provisions for such Confederate soldiers as may have been permanently injured in such service."[44] Though the groundwork had been laid years earlier, this was Georgia's first official pledge to establish a pension system to reward her veterans for their service. Two years later, state legislators followed through on their promise of largess with the 1887 passage of "An Act to carry into effect the last clause of Article VII." With this Act, legislators created the state's first official pension system for Confederate veterans, establishing a fairly complex hierarchy of "reimbursement" for crippling wounds received during the war. Thus, the total loss of sight was worth $100 while the total or partial loss of hearing was worth only $15. While on the surface this disparity may appear to be unfair, it makes sense in the context of the state's motivations for veterans' pensions. The loss of sight would certainly

on the Constitution of Georgia Giving the Origin, History and Development of the Fundamental Law of the State, with all Constitutional Documents Containing such Law, and with the Present Constitution, as Amended to Date, with Annotations (Atlanta: The Harrison Company, 1912) 126.

[42]Art. 7, sec. 1, para. 1 of The Constitution of 1877 in McElreath, A Treatise on the Constitution of Georgia, 1002.

[43]Georgia Legislature, Acts and Resolutions of the General Assembly of the State of Georgia, 1878–79, part 1. Public Laws, title 3. Constitution: 41–42. In 1882, legislators changed the payment to every three years. See Georgia Legislature, Acts and Resolutions, 1882–83, part 1. Public Laws, title 3. Constitution: 44.

[44]Georgia Legislature, Acts and Resolutions, 1884–1885, Part I. Public Laws, title 3. Constitution: 37. Amendment 1071, approved 19 October 1885, ratified 6 October 1886, in McElreath, A Treatise on the Constitution of Georgia, 403.

infringe on one's ability to provide for a family much more than would the loss of hearing.[45]

Two years after the first pensions were granted to Confederate veterans, the state's legislature and citizenry approved amendment 1072 granting pensions to "the widows of such Confederate Soldiers as may have died in the service of the Confederate States, or since, from wounds received therein or disease contracted in the service; provided that this act shall only apply to such persons as were married at the time of such service, and have remained unmarried since the death of such soldier husband." Sixty thousand dollars "or so much thereof as may be necessary" was appropriated to fund pensions for this new class of pensioners. The legislature set each widow's pension at $100 per annum. When the bill passed the legislature, the *Atlanta Constitution* reported simply that the bill had passed, implying a lack of debate or dissension among the legislators. Similarly, the public quickly and easily ratified the amendment the following October.[46] Not long after the ratification of

---

[45]Georgia Legislature, *Acts and Resolutions of the General Assembly of the State of Georgia, 1886–7,* part 1. Public Laws, title 3. Constitution: 27–28. Only a year later, the amount each injury was worth was reevaluated, presumably because the initial amounts were determined to be inadequate or overly adequate for such a maimed individual's living. Georgia Legislature, *Acts and Resolutions of the General Assembly of the State of Georgia, 1888,* part 1. Public Laws, title 1. Appropriations: 16–18. Georgians' understanding that it was their responsibility to look out for the state's unprotected citizens also manifested itself in another interesting way in the 1880s. In 1888, Georgia's legislators passed legislation that required employers in manufacturing, mechanical, or mercantile establishments to supply their female employees with seats "and permit their use when not in active discharge of duty," Georgia Legislature, *Acts and Resolutions, 1888–9,* part 1. Public Laws, title 11. Miscellaneous: 167. Apparently, the legislature's notion of substitute patriarchy was not limited solely to Confederate widows. Not surprisingly, that same legislature also established 19 January as a public holiday honoring Robert E. Lee, the epitome of chivalrous Southern gentlemen. Georgia Legislature, *Acts and Resolutions, 1888–9,* part 1. Public Laws, title 4. Code Amendments: 72–73.

[46]Georgia Legislature, *Acts and Resolutions of the General Assembly of the State of Georgia, 1888–9, Volume II,* part 1. Public Laws, title 3. Constitution: 39–40; Amendment 1072, approved 4 November 1889, ratified 1 October 1890, in McElreath, *A Treatise on the Constitution of Georgia,* 403; Georgia Legislature, *Acts and Resolutions of the General Assembly of the State of Georgia, 1890–'91,* part 1. Public Laws, Title II. Miscellaneous: 202; ibid., Part I. Public Laws, Title I. Appropriations and Public Debt: 17; "The Routine" in Business of the House and Senate section, *Atlanta Constitution,* 19

amendment 1072, the legislature also exempted veterans' and widows' pensions "from garnishment and all other legal process, no matter in who hands the pension or pensions may be" in an effort to protect their investment in patriarchy.[47]

The addition of widows to the pension rolls swelled the amount of state expenditures for pensions from $183,220 to $588,415 in one year. By 1890, Georgia's legislators realized that simply adding widows to the clause providing for veterans' pensions was insufficient to establish a process of applying for such pensions, so they enacted "An Act to allow pensions to certain Confederate widows, and for other purposes." This act restated the previous stipulations that a widow must have been married to her husband at the time of his service and remained unmarried since his death, that her husband must have died during or after the war as a result of wounds received or disease contracted during the war, and that said widow had to be a resident of the state. It also established the application process requiring that a widow provide evidence of her deceased husband's service and death as well as evidence of her status as a resident.[48] During that same session, legislators made allowances so that upon the death of a veteran pensioner his widow would receive his pension for that year.[49] Presumably, from thence forward, she would be required to apply for her own widow's pension. Since such legislation would appear on the surface to be redundant, it is clear that legislators hoped to eliminate any possibility that a widow could suffer without a pension because her husband had the luck to die after the due date to apply for a widow's pension. The last act of the legislature regarding Confederate pensions in 1890 was to protect against fraud by providing

---

December 1890. When responding to Julia Jackson's letter requesting information about pensions to Confederate soldiers' widows and orphans before Amendment 1072 passed the legislature, Ordinary R. T. Ross wrote, "I hope this bill will be passed at the next legislature"—a sentiment evidently felt by many Georgians and desired by many widows (R. T. Ross to Julia Jackson, 13 June 1890, Jackson Family Papers, Georgia State Archives).

[47]Georgia Legislature, *Acts and Resolutions, 1890–'91*, part 1. Public Laws, title 11. Miscellaneous: 203–204.

[48]Georgia Legislature, *Acts and Resolutions, 1890-'91*, part 1. Public Laws, title 11. Miscellaneous: 202–203.

[49]Ibid., 203.

for the examination of the pension rolls by the grand juries of the state to determine the "validity of said claims for pensions," requesting further evidence or proof if the grand jury indicated the claim was "doubtful or illegal."[50]

So strident was Georgians' renewed commitment to serving as substitute patriarchs that when it was discovered that thirty-nine widows had not been paid their pension for 1891 because the appropriated funds were exhausted before their claims were addressed, legislators passed a special resolution to appropriate and distribute the extra $3,900.[51] Unlike other former Confederate states with pension systems, where pension payments were prorated so that the state never paid out more money than had been approved, Georgia always paid the pension amount specified by the law, even if it meant extra appropriations.[52] In response to the recent shortfall and the overwhelming increase in the number of pensioners, state legislators in 1892 decreased the amount of money paid to each widow from $100 to $60.[53] Apparently, while legislators were willing to serve as substitute patriarchs for widows, they did not want to them to become too comfortable in their widowhood. After all, the proper place for women was still marriage. Despite the decrease, the pension rolls continued to expand and the state coffers continued to come up short, necessitating special appropriations for those pensioners the state failed to pay with the initial yearly expenditure.

In the years following the addition of widows to Georgia's pension rolls, the qualifications for becoming a pensioner, whether veteran or

---

[50]Ibid., 204–205.

[51]Georgia Legislature, *Acts and Regulations of the General Assembly of the State of Georgia*, 1892, part 5. Resolutions: 268.

[52]For example, North Carolina prorated pensions for applicants who filed at various times of the year. Georgia came up short with regard to pensions in 1893. Georgia Legislature, *Acts and Resolutions of the General Assembly of the State of Georgia, 1894*, part 1. Public Laws, title 1. Appropriations: 16–17; Georgia Legislature, *Acts and Regulations of the General Assembly of the State of Georgia, 1896*, part 5. Resolutions: 355; Georgia Legislature, *Acts and Regulations of the General Assembly of the State of Georgia, 1899*, part 1. Public Laws, title 1. Appropriations: 20.

[53]James R. Young, "Confederate Pensions in Georgia, 1886–1929," *Georgia Historical Quarterly* 66/1 (Spring 1982): 49; Georgia Legislature, *Acts and Resolutions of the General Assembly of the State of Georgia, 1892*, part 1. Public Laws, title 11. Miscellaneous: 98–99.

widow, grew steadily more liberal, allowing more and more men and women to qualify.[54] In 1893 legislators voted to include veterans "who by reason of age and poverty, or infirmity and poverty, or blindness and poverty, are unable to provide a living for themselves" and, implicitly, their families, among the number of those eligible for pensions. Such veterans received $60 per year, the same amount Confederate widows received.[55] In 1896, the ranks of enrolled pensioners swelled significantly when legislators voted to automatically enroll widows who had been married to veterans who had been pensioners.[56] In 1899, any widow, regardless of how or when her husband died, who was poor by reason of age, infirmity, or blindness, provided she was married to her husband at the time of his service and had remained unmarried since his death, also became eligible to receive a pension.[57] In addition to this general liberalization of eligibility, Georgia's elected officials frequently overruled pension denials if they were appealed to ensure that the state's Confederate veterans and widows were cared for.[58] By 1899, it was clear that the system was only going to continue to expand as veterans and widows aged. Accordingly, legislators created the Commissioner of Pensions to oversee the growing bureaucracy.[59]

In the 1890s, the legislature took several other steps to buttress the state's veterans in their role as patriarchs and to act as substitute

---

[54]This expansion is in keeping with the same kind of liberalization of Federal pensions that was going on at this time.

[55]Georgia Legislature, *Acts and Regulations of the General Assembly of the State of Georgia, 1893*, part 1. Public Laws, title 3. Constitution: 32; Ratified 3 October 1894, see McElreath, *A Treatise on the Constitution of Georgia*, 404.

[56]Georgia Legislature, *Acts and Resolutions of the General Assembly of the State of Georgia, 1895*, part 1. Public Laws, title 8. Miscellaneous: 102.

[57]Georgia Legislature, *Acts and Resolutions, 1899,* part 1. Public Laws, title 3. Amendment to Constitution: 19–20; Ratified 4 October 1890, see McElreath, *A Treatise on the Constitution of Georgia*, 407.

[58]See for example Georgia Legislature, *Acts and Resolutions of the General Assembly of the State of Georgia, 1896*, part 5. Resolutions: 351 and 353. The legislative record is full of such individual pensions.

[59]Georgia Legislature, *Acts and Resolutions of the General Assembly of the State of Georgia, 1895*, part 1. Public Laws, title 2. Constitution: 17–18; Georgia Legislature, *Acts and Resolutions of the General Assembly of the State of Georgia, 1896*, part 1. Public Laws, title 6. Pensions: 65–66.

patriarchs to their Confederate widows. In 1893, Georgians enacted legislation with the intent that "no ex-Confederate soldier of Georgia shall be forced to become an inmate of any Poor House or Poor Farm in this State in order to obtain relief from the authorities of the county in which he may reside." Whereas other poor Georgians who sought assistance from the Poor Funds of their individual counties were compelled to become inmates of the county Poor House or Poor Farm, legislators ordered that county authorities could not force Confederate veterans to do so and must still provide for them from the county Poor Fund "provisions of food and a proper amount of comfortable clothing."[60] This legislation not only set apart the Confederate poor as worthier than the rest of the state's poor, but also helped reinforce patriarchal gender roles as well. A Confederate veteran in the Poor House could not possibly be a proper patriarch. As veterans and widows grew increasingly older, legislators also found it necessary to stipulate punishment for exploitation related to applying for a pension, specifically, "receiving compensation for assisting or representing any one in prosecuting or collecting" a pension.[61] In keeping with the spirit of Confederate pension legislation, legislators hoped to ensure that veterans and widows were able to acquire assistance without being taken advantage of by less patriotic citizens.

In 1908, the Georgia Legislature enacted landmark pension legislation that allowed a pension to any veteran who had served honorably in the Confederacy or any widow of such a veteran. This was the first time that pensions were granted solely based on service not disability acquired while in service. The only stipulations were that the pensioner not own more than $1,500 worth of property and that a widow pensioner had to have been married to her deceased husband prior to 1870. The last clause of the amendment adds that "No widow of a soldier killed during the war shall be deprived of her pension by reason of having subsequently married another veteran who is dead, unless she received a pension on

---

[60]Georgia Legislature, *Acts and Resolutions, 1893*, part 1. Public Laws, title 10. Miscellaneous: 118–19.

[61]Georgia Legislature, *Acts and Resolutions, 1896*, part 1. Public Laws, title 6. Pensions: 66–67.

account of being the widow of such second husband," ensuring that women who had remarried but were presently widowed would still be included under the umbrella of the state's patriarchy.[62] In 1918, pension eligibility requirements grew even more liberal. The qualification that pensioners could not own more than $1500 was stricken from the books, and the year that a widow had to have married her husband by was moved back to 1881—a full sixteen years after the close of the war. The last amendment to the constitution regarding pensions was ratified by the public 8 June 1937. It once more extended the date of marriage for widows. To qualify for a pension after 1937, a widow only had to have been married by 1 January 1920![63]

In the years after Georgia began paying pensions to Confederate veterans or their widows, the percentage of state expenditures for such payments steadily increased so that by 1929 the cumulative percentage was 12.5 percent or around one-eighth of the state's expenditures. From 1886 to 1929, the state expended more than $43 million dollars in

[62]Georgia Legislature, *Acts and Resolutions of the General Assembly of the State of Georgia, 1908*, part 1. Public Laws, title 3. Amendments to Constitution: 34–6; ratified 7 October 1908, see McElreath, *A Treatise on the Constitution of Georgia*, 417.

[63]Amendments ratified 5 November 1918, 2 November 1920, 8 June 1937 respectively (Albert Berry Saye, *A Constitutional History of Georgia* [Athens: University of Georgia Press, 1948] 362, 363, 383). In addition to pension legislation, Georgians also provided for her veterans in one other significant way. Like other former Confederate states, Georgia built a Confederate Soldiers' Home in Atlanta. Having been organized and funded originally by an independent board of trustees, it eventually fell upon hard times when construction costs and delays depleted the subscription fund leaving only $41.01 left to run the home. Between 1891, when it was completed, and 1901, when the state legislature agreed to support the home, it stood largely abandoned, forced into bankruptcy and threatened numerous times with sale on the auction block. In 1901, Georgia legislators passed an appropriation bill for the home, and it opened its doors to forty veterans on 3 June 1901, Jefferson Davis's birthday. Only four months later, however, the home burned down. Strangely enough, the home was rebuilt in a little more than a year with monetary support from the state. It's possible that Confederate veterans who resided in a home were thus not proper patriarchs, defeating the purpose of the pensions. For an examination of Southern efforts to build Confederate Soldiers' Homes, see R. B. Rosenburg, *Living Monuments: Confederate Soldiers' Homes in the New South* (Chapel Hill: University of North Carolina Press, 1993) 46–72; Georgia Legislature, *Acts and Resolutions, 1900*, part 1. Public Laws, title 5. Miscellaneous: 86–89.

Confederate pensions to her veterans and widows.[64] During that same period, education, which was the "single largest expenditure of Georgia," accounted for only 29.3 percent of the state's expenditures. When one takes into account that the liberalization of pension legislation required a constitutional amendment that had to be ratified by the electorate, it becomes clear that white Georgians, at least those Georgians who voted, readily supported the General Assembly's efforts to buttress patriarchy through pensions.[65] As William Glasson writes, the "willingness to vote pensions and constantly increase them under those circumstances [the postwar economy] indicates a popular and deliberate approval of the expenditure and a desire to make it, even on pain of doing without much needed improvements in schools, roads, and other public institutions."[66]

In 1894, a bill was proposed in the US Congress that would have allowed Confederate veterans and widows to receive a pension from the federal government in the same manner that Union pensioners did. Although Southern Congressmen proposed this bill several times during the following decades and in varying forms, it did not pass until 1957.[67] Even so, it engendered a lively debate during the 1890s and early 1900s among Southerners that speaks volumes about the meaning of Confederate pensions for Georgians and other Southerners and their understanding of their role in supporting patriarchy. The effort to add Confederates to the Federal pension rolls had both proponents and opponents in the South. One opponent's response to the proposition

---

[64]Rosenburg, "Empty Sleeves and Wooden Pegs," 219.

[65]The figures in this paragraph were compiled in Young, "Confederate Pensions in Georgia," 49–51; Georgia Legislature, *Acts and Resolutions, 1896*, part 1. Public Laws, title 6. Pensions: 65–66.

[66]William Glasson, "The South's Care for Her Confederate Veterans," *American Review of Reviews* 36/1 (July 1907): 44.

[67]For a full discussion of the effort to give Federal pensions to Confederates, see Jeffrey E. Vogel, "Redefining Reconciliation: Confederate Veterans and the Southern Responses to Federal Civil War Pensions," *Civil War History* 51/1 (March 2005): 67–93. For further discussion of the meaning of federal pensions for Confederates for gender roles, see Jennifer L. Gross, "'Good Angels': Confederate Widowhood and the Reassurance of Patriarchy in the Postbellum South" (Ph.D. diss., University of Georgia, 2001); United States Congress, *Veterans' Benefits Act of 1957*, in *United States Statutes at Large* 72 (1958): 133–34; United States Congress, Committee on the Judiciary, *Veterans' Benefits Act*, in *United States Code*, title 38, 7: sec. 510 (1958) 6240.

reveals what was at stake for some Southerners—predominantly elite, white men—in providing for Confederate veterans and widows. He passionately avowed, "The failure of the Government of the United States to provide for our disabled soldiers has resulted most fortunately for the manhood and womanhood of the South.... Shall we barter this for gold?... No! a thousand times, no!" He continued, "Neither he [the proponent of the bill] nor any Southern representative shall ever, with our consent, place us in any attitude like that of this bill, which is inconsistent with our self-respect, and stains the record, to whose purity we devote and consecrate ourselves, our lives, our fortunes, and our sacred honor."[68] Georgian H. H. Carleton echoed these sentiments declaring that "he and his former comrades would rather...suffer and endure honorable discomfort than become humiliated pensioners.... To make our gallant Confederate veterans dependent for their future...upon piteous charity of a former foe, would not be in keeping with the Southern manhood [he and others] so gallantly and heroically illustrated."[69] Three years later, when the issue again came up in Congress, Confederate Veterans' Camps repeated their vehement objections, claiming that they represented the "united sentiment of the Confederate soldier...[who] simply pleads to be let alone. His own will care for and provide for him." A spokesman for the Pickett-Buchanan camp in Norfolk, Virginia asserted:

> The Confederate soldier is unwilling to be placed on the pension rolls of the United States or to become the recipient of any of its bounties. The time can never come when we would feel honored by any such mistaken generosity, and political art nor sophistry shall place him in this false position. A generation has passed away since Confederate soldiers gave up the fight for separate independence as a nation, but death alone can take away their personal independence as brave and true men.... A Federal pension is worse than Confederate poverty.[70]

---

[68]"Relief of Confederates by National Appropriation, Hon. P. J. Otey's Bill. R. E. Lee Camp, C. V. Protests Against the Consideration of the Bill by Congress," *Southern Historical Society Papers* 23/n.i. (January–December1895): 340–41.

[69]Quoted in Rosenburg, "Empty Sleeves and Wooden Pegs," 221.

[70]"Pensioning of the Confederate Soldier," 312–15.

For opponents of the bill, their pride and very manhood were at stake in refusing a pension from the federal government. For these Confederates, as Senator William Bate of Tennessee attested, it was "a great deal too much [to pay] for Federal pensions."[71]

In contrast to the idea that Confederate poverty was better than a federal pension, proponents of Federal pensions for Confederates generally justified their acceptance of such pensions on the premise that it was reparative for Federal actions during and after Reconstruction and in the interest of national harmony.[72] Always, politicians were careful to emphasize that the willingness of Confederate veterans to accept such pensions was not evidence that they were asking, much less begging, for them. Rather, they were honorable men who had suffered long enough. As John Tillman, a representative from Arkansas, posited, "It is not a

---

[71]"Remarks of Hon. Wm. B. Bate, of Tennessee, on the Resolution of Senator Butler, of North Carolina, to Pension Ex-Confederate Soldiers, in the Senate of the United States," 26 January 1899, Virginia Historical Society, Richmond VA.

[72]There were generally five reasons given citing the reparative nature of such pensions: first, it was a debt owed the South because of the unconstitutional collection of a cotton tax between 1865 and 1868; second, it was a debt owed the South because of the property confiscated by or otherwise forfeited to the federal government during the two years after the close of the war; third, since the end of the war and its readmission to the Union, the South as a whole had paid into the Federal Treasury millions of dollars that went to pay federal pensions to Union soldiers; fourth, in the interest of reconciliation and continued goodwill between the sections, the postwar loyalty of the South to the Union, as shown by her commitment to the Spanish-American war, should be recognized by such a gesture; and fifth, in the simple spirit of humanity and at the behest of Northern veterans who supported such pensions. These five reasons appear consistently along with various justifications of the South's belief in secession at the time of the war, though such justifications were accompanied always by the assertion that it was an issue settled by the war, and clarifications that Confederate soldiers were not traitors because they went to war in the self-defense of their states. These reasons were compiled from various speeches given in support of such pension legislation, such as "Speeches of Hon. Marion Butler, of North Carolina, in the Senate of the United States," in *Congressional Record*, Fifty-Fifth Congress, Third Session (26 and 28 January 1899); Chief Justice Walter Clark, "U.S. Pensions for North Carolina Soldiers," address to Confederate Veterans at Charlotte, North Carolina, 25 January 1909, North Carolina State Archives, Raleigh NC; Benjamin P. Maddox, "An Appeal of the South's Old Soldier to Congress for a Pension by the Government" (Richmond: n.p., 1916), copy located in the Virginia Historical Society, Richmond VA; Hon. John N. Tillman, "Pensions for Confederate Soldiers," speech of Hon. John N. Tillman of Arkansas in the House of Representatives,11 February 1916, North Carolina State Archives, Raleigh NC.

pension that I am asking; it is a payment. It is not a charity, but justice. It is not a gift, but a reparation. It is not an advance; it is a return. It is not largess; it is conscience money."[73] Such assertions affirmed the dire financial situations of many veterans but still allowed for the "masculinity" of the beneficiaries.

Wartime aid to soldiers' families, artificial limbs for disabled veterans, and Confederate pensions for veterans and widows, though they certainly provided much needed assistance, also fulfilled the ideological need of buttressing traditional Southern patriarchy. For Confederate veterans, such assistance was meant to restore them to their proper place as patriarchs. After all, if the epitome of Southern manhood could not be a proper patriarch, how could other Southerners expect to be? For Confederate widows who had been deprived of their traditional protectors and providers by the war, all male Georgians through their elected officials stepped up and served as substitute patriarchs, ideologically restoring them to proper homes. Southerners clearly recognized the value of assistance to their Confederate citizenry both during and after the war, and accordingly, they supported it.

---

[73]Tillman, "Pensions for Confederate Soldiers."

Buried at Savannah:
Confederate Plain Folk Widows, Children,
and the Civil War's Lost Memories

by Mark V. Wetherington

Elizabeth Watson never knew the day her husband Green died. The news came to her by word of mouth when fellow soldiers in his infantry company, the "Pulaski Blues," came home to Pulaski County on furlough in 1862. They told Elizabeth that her husband had "taken sick near Savannah" while at Camp Beaulieu, was sent to a hospital at a nearby village called Montgomery, and died of "brain fever" sometime in June or July. He was buried somewhere "at Savannah."[1]

The news stunned Elizabeth. She had not seen nor heard from Green since his company left Hawkinsville for Savannah in spring 1862, but this was not a cause of concern: neither of them could read nor write, so an exchange of letters was not an option. If anyone in the company had written home and reported his death, no one bothered to get the word to Elizabeth. News of Green's death moved slowly and orally to the home front where such bad tidings had become commonplace and soon lost their sense of urgency. In time, Elizabeth's experience would be repeated for over a quarter million Confederate deaths.

Life had been hard following the marriage of Elizabeth Mitchell to Green Watson in 1850. Elizabeth and Green lived in the remote southwestern corner of the county, about fourteen miles from the county seat at Hawkinsville. Unlike the rich cotton lands to the north, theirs was a poorer neighborhood situated in the longleaf pine forest in the lower county. It was one of the last parts of the county to be settled, mostly by yeomen farmers and livestock herders who owned few slaves. These

---

[1]Confederate Pension Application of Elizabeth Watson, Bibb County GA, microfilm drawer 271, box 32, Georgia Archives, Morrow GA; Lillian Henderson, comp., *Roster of the Confederate Soldiers of Georgia, 1861–1865*, 6 vols. (Hapeville GA: Longina & Porter, 1959–1964) 3:628. On death in the Civil War, see Drew Gilpin Faust, *This Republic of Suffering: Death and the American Civil War* (New York: Alfred A. Knopf, 2008).

"plain folk" made a living running cows, hogs, and sheep on the open wiregrass range and by planting food crops, especially corn, which figured prominently in their diet. During the early 1840s, some of these settlers organized Friendship Baptist Church. This backwoods settlement was typical of rural neighborhoods in the coastal plains south.

One of Friendship's charter members was yeomen farmer William Ridley. In 1850, Green Watson worked on Ridley's place as his farm laborer; that same year Green married Elizabeth Mitchell. What their aspirations were as a couple is hard to say. Like most plain folk, they hoped to raise enough food and livestock to feed themselves and eventually buy their own place, but that dream was elusive. For ten years they worked the farm and Elizabeth washed and cooked, sometimes perhaps for other people. Their household was one of the poorest in the neighborhood. In 1860 they claimed only $28 in personal property to show for over a decade of life together. Moreover, they owned no land. Green gave his occupation as "farming," but he may have rented the place outright or worked it on shares; Elizabeth gave hers as "washer & cook." Together they struggled to feed and clothe their four children, all under the age of eight. As an antebellum farming family, the Watson household led a precarious hand-to-mouth existence on the edge of Georgia's cotton belt.[2]

Then things got worse—much worse. In January 1861, when Green Watson was about thirty-three years old, Georgia seceded from the Union. He did not immediately join the county's eager volunteers who organized three infantry companies and a battery of light artillery by year's end. Instead, he stayed at home with Elizabeth and their children where, on 4 March 1862, he was still listed on the militia roll for the 511th district. It was not until spring 1862 that Green and about thirty others from the county reached the Pulaski Blues in Savannah, a company that left Hawkinsville in the fall of 1861. The timing of their departure, coming as it did with Confederate conscription on the horizon,

---

[2] 1860 US Census, GA, Pulaski County, population, 18 (microfilm), and 1850 US Census, GA, Pulaski County, population, 265 (microfilm); Wallace Leigh Harris, comp., *History of Pulaski and Bleckley Counties, Georgia*, 2 vols. (Macon GA: n.p., 1957) 1:189–92, 2:818.

suggests that Green and other newcomers volunteered rather than be drafted or were outright conscripts. Like other women on the home front, Elizabeth was expected to become a suffering but stoic female patriot. And then, like so many Southern soldiers, Green Watson died of disease, in his case before he even left Georgia.[3]

This story follows the shock waves of a soldier's death back to the home front and explores a number of questions: What choices faced Confederate widows such as Elizabeth Watson? What were the wartime responses by Confederate, state, and local authorities? What was the fate of war widows and their children in the immediate postwar period? What role did families like the Watsons play in remembering the war?

When she heard of Green's death, Elizabeth was about thirty-two years old with four children to feed. She had little money and no one in her household old enough to help farm. At nine, daughter Sarah was the oldest and Nancy was only about seven; both of the boys were under five. It is not known whether she chose to stay at home or move in with family, but without Green's farm labor and soldier's pay her future was bleak. Immediately she was confronted with a new role as head of the household and the domestic confusion that might follow, but at least Green had died a Confederate soldier and her role as a soldier's widow was an honorable one. Her struggle now was to mourn her loss and hold the family together.[4]

Early in 1862, Georgia took steps to provide some care for families such as Elizabeth's, many of which were quickly becoming dependents of the state. Governor Joseph E. Brown ordered each county's inferior court to set up on the militia district level committees of older non-military-aged men to provide oversight of soldiers' families. These men compiled lists of wives, widows, and orphans and reported them to the state. In time these dependents would be eligible to receive corn, cotton cards, salt, and thread from Georgia. In August 1862, Pulaski County's

---

[3]Mark V. Wetherington, *Plain Folk's Fight: The Civil War and Reconstruction in Piney Woods Georgia* (Chapel Hill: University of North Carolina Press, 2005) 86–98, 126; Henderson, comp., *Roster*, 3:620–28. For a treatment of Southern women during the war, see George C. Rable, *Civil Wars: Women and the Crisis of Southern Nationalism* (Urbana: University of Illinois Press, 1991) 5–8 and chap. 3.

[4]1860 US Census, GA, Pulaski County, population, 18; Rable, *Civil Wars*, 62–63.

inferior court found it necessary to levy a tax of 50 percent on the state tax for that year to be collected "and applied as a fund for the relief of the indigent soldiers' families that are in the service from this county."[5]

Although the Watsons' antebellum lives had been far from ideal, the war and its immediate aftermath were traumatic. Elizabeth and the children fell deeper into poverty, along with the widows, wives, and children of many other soldiers in Pulaski County. In fall 1864, Elizabeth's name appeared on the inferior court's list along with almost 350 other soldiers' wives and widows. By the end of January 1865, the number of the county's soldiers' wives, widows, and dependent children had climbed to 1,045. Due to crop failures and chronic food shortages, the inferior court justices reported half of that number "have not nor can they purchase corn for bread." Clearly, the Confederate government and the state could not protect and provide for soldiers' dependents. Indeed, in January 1865, following a disastrous clash between General William T. Sherman's troops and Georgia militia at Griswoldville and Savannah's capture, the county's inferior court decided to withhold foodstuffs from the Confederate government and instead distribute them to soldiers' families at home. The county seat town of Hawkinsville became a source of increasingly scarce food.[6]

At some point during or soon after the war, Elizabeth chose to leave the farm and move her family to Hawkinsville. Her decision was probably influenced by a number of factors, among them her inability to grow enough food to feed five people, the escalating price of virtually everything on the home front, and a growing instability in the remote parts of the county as deserter and anti-Confederate activity increased late in the war. If she resided with relatives in the country, this temporary solution for whatever reasons did not last. Hawkinsville offered protection in numbers for rural refugees and some food supplies. Moreover, the postwar transition from slave to free labor and the emergence of furnishing merchants and the crop lien system placed a premium on male laborers, regardless of color, not widows with young

---

[5]Pulaski County Inferior Court minutes, 30 August 1862, Georgia Department of Archives and History, Morrow GA.
   [6]Ibid., 8 November 1864, 30 January 1865.

daughters. Gradually, landless women such as Elizabeth, with only girls to offer as farmhands, faced a gendered dispossession of farm acreage by landlords.[7]

By summer 1870, the move from countryside to town was complete. While the location of the family shifted from country to town, Elizabeth's role as head of household had not changed. Eight years after her husband's death the war widow, now about forty-two years of age, was still unmarried with slim chances of finding a new husband should she desire one. Although her daughters Sarah and Nancy, aged about seventeen and fifteen, lived in Elizabeth's household, her young sons did not. Instead, two newcomers had appeared, a thirteen-year-old girl named Martha and a twenty-five-year-old man named Madison Sykes, apparently a boarder. Elizabeth gave her occupation as keeping house, but everyone else in her household, the teenage girls and the young man, gave their occupation as "works in factory, cotton." Elizabeth had learned that her girls could bring more into the household economy as textile mill workers than as farm laborers.[8]

Georgia's fall-line towns of Augusta, Columbus, and Macon experienced significant industrialization before and during the Civil War, particularly to meet the needs of the Confederate government for ammunition, clothing, and shoes. However, at more isolated interior towns such as Hawkinsville and throughout the rural South, a lack of railroad service and sufficient capital to build textile mills created significant barriers to industrialization. Moreover, Southern attitudes had traditionally demeaned factory work and favored agricultural pursuits.[9]

Soon after the Civil War, however, circumstances at Hawkinsville changed. Although historians of Southern textile manufacturing have

---

[7]Wetherington, *Plain Folk's Fight*, 172–73, 222–23; Jacquelyn Dowd Hall et al., *Like a Family: The Making of a Southern Cotton Mill World* (Chapel Hill: University of North Carolina Press, 1987) 33. On the transition to postwar crop lien system along the upper Ocmulgee River, see Joseph P. Reidy, *From Slavery to Agrarian Capitalism in the Cotton Plantation South* (Chapel Hill: University of North Carolina Press, 1992); for the lower Ocmulgee, see Mark V. Wetherington, *The New South Comes to Wiregrass Georgia, 1860–1910* (Knoxville: University of Tennessee Press, 1994).

[8]1870 US Census, GA, Pulaski County, population, 9 (microfilm).

[9]Chad Morgan, *Planter's Progress: Modernizing Confederate Georgia* (Gainesville: University Press of Florida, 2005) 3.

rightly emphasized the transition from the antebellum and Civil War era
cotton mills to the larger late-nineteenth-century New South textile
movement, the experience at Hawkinsville represents a local turning
point in attitudes regarding the desirability of factory work. Between
1866 and 1870, Hawkinsville-area businessmen received two charters for
cotton mills, well in advance of investments in cotton mills by the Southern merchant class after 1880.[10] By 1870, the Pulaski Manufacturing
Company was up and running. Its purpose was "manufacturing cotton,
wool and other fibrous substances, into yarns and cloth."[11]

The factory's investors were members of the town's entrepreneurial
class, which included ex-Confederate officer O. C. Horne and veterans,
bankers, and merchants. They were motivated by civic pride,
paternalism, and hopes of financial reward. Given her background as a
poor white widow, it is unlikely that Elizabeth knew these investors well,
if at all. However, Pulaski County's postwar economic recovery was
burdened by a large number of war widows and orphans and indigent
soldiers and their wives. Local boosters hoped to solve this problem in
part by providing factory employment. Thus, Elizabeth Watson and her
children became forerunners of the larger and later migration of white
"female-headed tenant households" to the mills during the 1880s. The
small textile mill was part of the larger agricultural transformation of the
countryside, one that forced women to mill towns in the 1880s. Civil
War deaths helped shape this migration pattern.[12]

Two "operatives houses" soon joined the complex of buildings that
formed the factory grounds. One was described as a two-story building
while the other was single story. Beyond that description little is known
about the structures that became the new homes for widows, single
women, and children. Were they new buildings like the factory or
perhaps older buildings converted to a new residential purpose? How did
the five adjacent households listed in the census with factory workers
actually occupy the two separate buildings? It is certain that for former

[10]*Georgia Acts 1866, I, 87 and 1870*, I, 254–55.

[11]Ibid., 255.

[12]1870 US Census, GA, Pulaski County, population, 12; Hall, et al., *Like a Family*,
31–33; Wetherington, *Plain Folk's Fight*, 191–92.

farm wives like Elizabeth, the close quartering of these households was new and strange.[13]

We know more about the "operatives" even though that information is scanty. The 1870 US Census returns for Pulaski County identified twenty people whose occupation was "works in factory, cotton" or "works in Cotton Factory." More people may have worked there or were dependent in some way on the factory's output, such as the five single women seamstresses between the ages of eighteen and forty-four who lived next door to the factory workers. As might be expected by late antebellum textile employment patterns and by the desire of the owners to put poor women and children to work, 75 percent of the workers were women and children, who normally were paid less than men. Fifty percent of the workers were female, but only 40 percent of them were seventeen years of age or older. The youngest female worker was nine-year-old Julia Johnson while the oldest was twenty-year-old Katy Taylor. Fifteen was the average age for female workers; all of them were born in Georgia. Only one woman worker, Katy Taylor, appears to have been the head of a household, but the five workers between the age of eight and eighteen living in her household appear to be siblings.[14]

One half of the factory workers were male. Fifty percent of them were boys between the ages of eight and sixteen, with an average age of eleven. The youngest male worker was eight-year-old Benjamin Taylor. Despite traditional views among adult Southern white males that factory work in an agricultural economy was beneath them, 50 percent of the male workers were adults. The oldest, thirty-year-old Marion Payne, was employed as the factory's "overseer," while Stephen Mitchell was its clerk. Payne and Mitchell were the only males who headed households. Eighty percent of the males were born in Georgia, with the remainder from Alabama and North Carolina. Well before economic depression, tight credit, and declining crop prices forced them off the land during the

[13]*Hawkinsville Dispatch*, 11 January 1872.
[14]1870 US Census, GA, Pulaski County, population, 9, 17, 21; Michelle Gillespie, "To Harden a Lady's Hand," in *Neither Lady nor Slave: Working Women of the Old South*, ed. Susanna Delfino and Michele Gillespie (Chapel Hill: University of North Carolina Press, 2002) 268–74.

1880s and 1890s, men formed a significant presence at the Hawkinsville mill.[15]

The composition of the workforce suggests a number of things. Since 70 percent of the workers belonged to four families named Ennis, Johnson, Taylor, and Watson, family ties were at the center of the factory's labor force. Continuing a trend noted during the late antebellum period, only 20 percent of factory workers' households were led by women who actually worked in the factory themselves. In the remaining households, women such as Elizabeth Watson had no qualms about sending their children to work in the factory while they stayed at home, allowing them to lead the private life of a "lady" protected from prying eyes and overbearing male supervisors. At forty-two, Elizabeth's entire remaining household worked at the factory while she remained home keeping house, the socially acceptable role for Confederate widows. However, women like Mary Ennis, whose daughter Georgia and son James worked in the factory, had a reason to stay at home because she also had a three-year-old child.[16]

The makeup of the factory workforce suggests that the Civil War had begun to redefine acceptable gender roles for men as well, at least in town. Hawkinsville in 1870 was filled with adult males employed as clerks, laborers, merchants, and skilled and unskilled workers, as it had been in 1860. But the war destabilized the Southern economy. While wage work in a factory might seem emasculating and socially unacceptable by antebellum cultural expectations, young men such as Albert Moore, Washington Osborn, and Madison Sykes may have had little choice but to seek factory work given the postwar reorganization of the Southern economy.

One thing united almost all of the factory workers and their families—the lack of property. None of the female households consisting of factory workers and their parents reported one dollar of real or personal property in 1870. This finding suggests that the workers and

---

[15]Gillespie, "To Harden a Lady's Hand," 269; 1870 US Census, GA, Pulaski County, population, 9, 17, 20.

[16]Gillespie, "To Harden a Lady's Hand," 270–71; 1870 US Census, GA, Pulaski County, population, 9, 17, 20.

their mothers led cramped and marginal lives in the operatives' quarters. Even Marion Payne, the factory's overseer, returned no property. Only Stephen Mitchell, an antebellum Savannah bookkeeper, former Confederate officer, and now the factory's clerk and a stockholder, returned any personal wealth, which was put at $1,500. He had returned to Hawkinsville after the war and married O. C. Horne's daughter, Mary, in 1866.[17]

Much about the factory seemed alien in a small town of several hundred people, which formerly boasted as its largest buildings a few cotton warehouses. In addition to the operatives' quarters, the company owned four lots totaling almost an acre. A main three-story building was soon constructed with a brick first floor, wooden upper floors, and a metal roof. A brick engine house, watch house, and shop soon joined the factory building, which housed 4 Jenks Ring Traveler spinning frames and 204 spindles.[18]

And then in January 1872, Elizabeth Watson's and the other families dependent on the factory learned that it was shutting down immediately. The *Hawkinsville Dispatch* reported that cotton and woolen goods manufactured there had "commanded ready sale in this and other markets." Given the new buildings and machinery, and the fact that similar factories operated successfully at Augusta, Columbus, and Macon, the editor hinted that poor management was the most likely reason for the Pulaski Manufacturing Company's failure. He hoped that "some enterprising company or capitalist" would take over the factory immediately and take advantage of the labor and materials "in abundance right here in sight of the Factory, and at less prices than the same can be had in the North."[19]

What many in the community may not have known was that the factory's Georgia stockholders had borrowed $10,000 from a New Yorker named Daniel H. Baldwin in order to get the mill up and running. Baldwin filed a claim to recover the loan in the Fifth Circuit Court of the

---

[17]1870 US Census, GA, Pulaski County, population, 9, 17, 20; Harris, comp., *History of Pulaski and Bleckley Counties*, 2:770.

[18]*Georgia Acts*, 1870, I, 254–55; *Hawkinsville Dispatch*, 11 January 1872. The town lots were 5, 6, 7, and 8.

[19]*Georgia Acts*, 1870, I, 254–55; *Hawkinsville Dispatch*, 11 January 1872.

United States. He was no stranger to Georgia. Born in Massachusetts, he moved to Savannah at the age of eighteen and clerked in his uncle's mercantile firm. On the eve of the Civil War, he was a partner in the shipping firm of Brigham, Baldwin, and Company, which ran steamboats on Georgia's interior rivers, including the Ocmulgee. During the war, Baldwin served in the Confederate commissary department but after Appomattox immediately left for New York, where he established a cotton commission business called D. H. Baldwin & Company.[20]

Baldwin's actions to recover his loan and the factory's failure forced families like Elizabeth Watson's to again make choices. They could stay in Hawkinsville or leave. For the short term, Elizabeth chose to stay, but perhaps not on terms that she preferred. Four months after the factory closed, Elizabeth's daughter, Nancy, then about seventeen, married a man named Alford Knight. In 1880 she was living in their household, beholden to Alford and Nancy for the roof over her head. Indeed, 1870 was the last time Elizabeth Watson would be considered the head of her own household in the US Census, although, as we shall see, she lived a long life.[21]

Some of the mill workers chose to leave Hawkinsville. James Ennis, who worked in the factory when he was eleven or twelve, settled nearby in East Macon with his mother's family. Like so many of the children employed at the Pulaski Manufacturing Company, including his sister Josephine, he could neither read nor write, suggesting that whatever marginal educational opportunities that had existed in the county had broken down completely during the war. With their employment options limited, James and Josephine, twenty and twenty-two respectively, took their factory work experience to Macon and found mill wages there. Repeating the pattern at Hawkinsville, their widowed mother Mary Ennis Fretwell was, at thirty-eight, still "keeping house" and drawing some small income from another female mill worker who was listed as a

[20]*Hawkinsville Dispatch*, 11 January 1872; William Harden, *A History of Savannah and South Georgia* (Chicago: Lewis Pub. Co., 1913) 608–610.
[21]Harris, comp., *History of Pulaski and Bleckley Counties*, 2:759.

"boarder." Unlike Elizabeth Watson, Mary managed to remain the independent head of her household.[22]

The future was brighter for Stephen Mitchell and Mary Horne Mitchell, but not in Hawkinsville. After the factory closed in 1872, they remained in town for two or three years and then moved to Montgomery, Alabama. There the former clerk of the Pulaski Manufacturing Company found a position in a "mercantile establishment" and prospered.[23]

Twenty-seven years after the factory closed, Stephen Mitchell died in Hawkinsville at home on Merritt Street. Precisely when the Mitchells moved back to Pulaski County from Montgomery is unclear. It may have been a decision made by his wife, Mary, who realized that Bright's disease had taken its toll on her husband. It was time for him to go home to die in the small river town where he had grown up. He was fifty-six years old when he was buried in 1899.[24]

This was not the only time Mary Horne Mitchell returned to Hawkinsville after her departure with Stephen during the economically depressed 1870s. When her beloved father O. C. Horne died in 1882, Mary came home to attend his funeral. It was a big event. Much of her father's career was described in the local newspaper, particularly his Mexican War service in the 1st Regiment, Georgia Volunteers. Relatively little was mentioned about his Civil War days.[25]

The Hawkinsville Mary had known as a sixteen-year-old on the eve of the Civil War was changing. Familiar faces were disappearing as time took its toll on Civil War veterans such as her father and husband. Moreover, during the 1880s many of the antebellum frame structures were destroyed by fire and replaced by new brick buildings. A new agribusiness district of cotton gins and warehouses grew up on the north side of town. When Mary returned during the 1890s with her husband

[22]1880 US Census, GA, Bibb County, population, 49.

[23]Tad Evans, comp., *Pulaski County, Georgia, Newspaper Clippings, V, 1898–1907,* 5 vols. (Savannah: T. Evans, 2000–) 6:49–51.

[24]Ibid.

[25]Ibid., 3:55–56.

Stephen for his final trip home, the antebellum steamboat stop had been transformed into a small New South city.[26]

In time, Mary Horne Mitchell became a leading custodian of Hawkinsville's Confederate memory. Creating that past was deeply influenced by her upbringing in an upper-class Southern white slaveholding family that played a prominent role in local Civil War mobilization. Her father introduced many of the first volunteers in Pulaski County to marching and military life as the local drillmaster. He served as captain of the second infantry company to leave the county for Virginia. And the drillmaster's wife, also named Mary, presented the flag to the Pulaski Volunteers in April 1861, declaring, "Take it, soldiers! and return with it to your homes with honor, or die beneath its folds in defence of Southern Rights and the independence of the Confederate States." At the impressionable age of sixteen, daughter Mary witnessed mother Mary challenge the troops to defend their way of life. Although that patriarchal and segregationist South denied women the right to vote, elite white women such as Mary became the "architects of white historical memory" through membership in voluntary associations.[27]

And so even as her Stephen lay dying, Mary, now in her mid-fifties, organized in their home a local chapter of the United Daughters of the Confederacy on 1 March 1899. It was named in honor of her father, and Mary became the first president of O. C. Horne Chapter 282. She labored in that capacity from 1899 until 1903. By serving as the leader of this movement, Mary and other elite white women related to the Confederate past on personal and family levels and linked themselves to what they remembered, an orderly and stable Old South of their parents even as New South change presented an entirely different reality to them.[28]

This was not the first local step taken to remember the war and give it meaning from the white Confederate perspective. In 1871, one member

---

[26]Wetherington, *New South Comes to Wiregrass Georgia,* 259–62.

[27]Fleming, "Sketch of the Pulaski Volunteers," *Hawkinsville Dispatch,* 10 July 1879; Wetherington, *Plain Folk's Fight,* 101–102; W. Fitzhugh Brundage, *The Southern Past: A Clash of Race and Memory* (Cambridge MA: Harvard University Press, 2005) 15–16.

[28]Daughters of the American Revolution, Hawkinsville Chapter, *History of Pulaski County, Georgia* (Atlanta: Walter W. Brown Pub. Co., 1935) 129; Brundage, *Southern Past,* 15–16.

of the Pulaski Volunteers, a company in the storied "bloody" 8th Georgia Regiment, called for a survivors' reunion. Some of these veterans had wanted to get together two or three years earlier, but it was "declared impolitic under existing affairs," although the purpose of gathering "was a social reunion, and nothing more." Once Reconstruction was over, calls to gather and remember gained momentum. In 1875, members of the Pulaski Light Artillery announced that they would reorganize the company and invited its old members as well as others to join. And then in 1879, D. G. Fleming, a member of the Pulaski Volunteers, published in serial form in the *Hawkinsville Dispatch* his sketch of the company. Such activities by the war's veterans established a foundation for the work of the local UDC chapter, which in time would dwarf the work of men and transform Hawkinsville's civic spaces.[29]

The local UDC chapter soon set out to commemorate the sacrifices of the Confederate veterans by reshaping the public and private landscape. Saturday rummage sales raised enough money to mark the grave of every Confederate soldier and militiaman in the county. The crepe myrtle was adopted as the chapter tree and planted in the front of UDC members' homes and public spaces. The cornerstone for a Confederate monument was laid on the courthouse lawn in September 1903. It would take five years and $3,000 in fundraising before a statue featuring Robert E. Lee and Stonewall Jackson was unveiled during the summer of 1908. Georgian James Longstreet was absent from the monument, perhaps because Lost Cause sentimentalists blamed him for the defeat at Gettysburg.[30]

The creation of Civil War memory was not happenstance. Prominent white families in Hawkinsville took an active role in deciding what commemorative course to take and who would be remembered. For example, Colonel Seaborn Manning, who was mortally wounded in 1862 leading a charge of the 49th Georgia Regiment at the Battle of Cedar

---

[29]D. G. Fleming, "Sketch of the Pulaski Volunteers," 1 June 1871, 21 October 1875, 10, 24, 31 July, 7 August 1879; David W. Blight, *Race and Reunion: The Civil War in American History* (Cambridge MA: Harvard University Press, 2001) 140–44.
[30]Georgia Division of the United Daughters of the Confederacy, *The History of the Georgia Division of the United Daughters of the Confederacy, 1895–1995*, 2 vols. (Atlanta: The Division, 1995) 1:244–45; Blight, *Race and Reunion*, 263–64.

Mountain, Virginia, was all but forgotten in the local Civil War narrative. If Colonel Manning could be forgotten, how much easier was it for Private Green Watson to be lost in public memory? On the other hand, O. C. Horne, who resigned his commission after less than a year of service at the Virginia front, was remembered because daughter Mary organized the local UDC chapter and its name perpetuated her father's memory. The well-placed crepe myrtle in the yard reflected which social and racial groups participated in Confederate memory making. Membership in the chapter eventually reached 659, ranking it third in the entire Georgia Division, a remarkable achievement given the county's relatively sparse population when compared to the state's urban areas. Its members were devoted to the task at hand. At the UDC's state convention in 1920, the O. C. Horne Chapter "won every trophy offered except one" and was known as the "Banner Chapter of the State."[31]

In time the lines between public and private memory blurred. After the completion of a new city auditorium in Hawkinsville in 1906, a project the UDC chapter supported during a bond drive, the city council voted to give the chapter in return for its fundraising assistance the use of a room and kitchenette for "as long as there should be a chapter." The room became a small Lost Cause memorial featuring mementoes, pictures, records, and relics, the most "treasured" being O. C. Horne's two swords. Centered above the auditorium's stage in the position of a keystone is a small Confederate battle flag, which has looked out over audiences for more than a century. Hawkinsville school students too young to have any direct Civil War experiences participated in Confederate Memorial Day programs each year, even as the orphans of local dead soldiers moved away to find their livelihoods as adults. The Confederate monument was decorated as well as each of the 144 Crosses of Honor marking veterans' graves throughout the county. The monument, auditorium, and graves became touchstones for new generations of children long removed from the war itself. Each aging veteran's death became a public cause for reflection and remembrance. In 1915—a half

---

[31]Harris, *History of Pulaski and Bleckley Counties*, 1:235–37; *History of the Georgia UDC*, 1:244–45. This source notes that the O. C. Horne chapter disbanded in 1992. The last chapter report received was in 1987, when membership was given as thirteen.

century after Appomattox—F. H. Bozeman, a local Confederate veteran and adjutant general of the Georgia division of the United Confederate Veterans, wrote of his UCV uniform with three stars: "I want to be buried in it, for no suit that can be bought would do so well as my Confederate Gray Uniform." His original wartime officer's uniform had been stolen in camp at Lovejoy Station.[32]

Ironically, the men who had given their utmost to the Confederate cause, those who died in distant places, went virtually unnoticed as Hawkinsville was remade in the neo-Confederate image. True, men such as Green Watson were collectively represented by the familiar stand-in soldier's statue atop the local monument, but there was no marker at the foot of these men's graves. Indeed, their "final resting places" were largely unmarked and frequently lost because they had been hastily buried, often together in long trenches, on distant battlefields or in hospital graveyards. The Confederates buried at home were those who survived the war and died of old age.[33]

What less fortunate white women such as Elizabeth Watson privately made of all this commemoration of the war that left her husbandless, their children fatherless, and all of them without any means of subsistence beyond their own labor is unknown. However, well before the O. C. Horne chapter began its memorialization and whatever assistance it offered local Confederate veterans and their widows beyond their annual birthday cakes and Christmas packages, Elizabeth had given up on Pulaski County. Like Mary Ennis Fretwell she moved to Bibb County, where Elizabeth began to draw a small Confederate pension in 1891.[34]

In fact, Elizabeth's life after 1880 involved several moves. By 1900, she had left Bibb County and moved to Dooly County. There she lived with her daughter Eugenia and her husband, a machinist named A. C. Barwick. Ten years later Elizabeth, now eighty-one, was back in the

---

[32]Harris, *History of Pulaski and Bleckley Counties*, 1:235–37; "Reminiscences of F. H. Bozeman," 15, Keith Bohannon private papers. I thank Keith Bohannon for making this source available to me.

[33]Wetherington, *Plain Folk's Fight*, 1–2.

[34]Confederate Pension Application of Elizabeth Watson, Bibb County GA; *History of Pulaski County, Georgia*, 130.

household of her fifty-year-old daughter Nancy Knight, who resided in Crisp County. Both mother and daughter were widows. At each new home Elizabeth traveled to the courthouse and filled out a pension application that repeated the few facts she could provide concerning Green Watson's death as a Confederate soldier.[35]

The Civil War was a tremendous watershed for women such as Elizabeth Watson. Owning no real or personal property in 1860, she belonged to a household that existed on the lower margins of antebellum Southern white society. But Green and Elizabeth may have found something akin to self-sufficiency born of their own labor before his death, and this meant some level of independence they may have shared together, however marginal and fleeting. Within a few months of Green's departure, Elizabeth was a widow whose husband had disappeared. She never remarried. After 1862, Elizabeth was dependent on others: state and local government assistance; the good will of daughters and their husbands; and a meager Confederate pension. She may not have been the last Confederate widow alive, but her life of widowhood and dependency lasted for more than a half-century.

The war was also a turning point for her children and those of other Confederate women. Although they lived far from the front and did not fear invasion until late in 1864, white children in Pulaski County felt the excitement of seeing family members off to the front lines as each new company departed for war. Children also mourned soldiers' deaths, saw the war's wounded and disabled, and felt the hardship of dwindling supplies of food and clothing. They led a precarious life and looked to the future with uncertainty.

Without war, Elizabeth's daughters might have grown up like her in a rural setting surrounded by potential husbands from farming backgrounds. The move from countryside to town placed them in new surroundings where they worked indoors with machinery and met future husbands who were themselves often factory workers or machinists.

---

[35] 1900 US Census, GA, Dooly County, 18, and 1910, Crisp County, population, 3; Confederate Pension Application of Elizabeth Watson for Dooly County, Georgia, microfilm drawer 272, box 58, Georgia Archives, and for Crisp County, microfilm drawer 272, box 37.

Thus the war cut them off from a rural past that, while far from ideal, at least represented continuity with the region's majority experience, while their wartime and postwar experiences represented change. This break with rurality was not necessarily bad given the unstable and chaotic circumstances that beset the rural South during Reconstruction and beyond. Odds are a life of tenancy or sharecropping awaited them in the country as both children and adults.[36]

We do not know what one of the war children such as James Ennis would have thought about the relative merits of hand-to-mouth living on the farm or in town. He was, like almost all of the child factory workers at Hawkinsville, illiterate and left no written record. After thirty years in the mills, he had advanced by age forty to the occupation of oiler. In 1900, he lived with his older sister Georgia Johnson in her rented house in Bibb County, along with her son and son-in-law, both mill workers. Georgia gave her occupation as "farmer," one normally associated with independent white men. Twenty years earlier, James had lived with his mother. Ironically, he was as dependent for shelter upon women, first his mother and then his sister, as Elizabeth Watson was dependent on her daughters and their husbands. The postwar world had blurred gender lines and continued to do so long after the shooting stopped.[37]

The stories of plain folk such as Green and Elizabeth Watson and their family, both during the war and long afterward, were largely lost or forgotten. In the violent and unstable postwar era, Elizabeth and her children sought livelihood and shelter where they could find it and left the memory making to those with the inclination and time to glorify the war. The Lost Cause had no use for a past that meted out gendered dispossession from the land, child labor, lifelong illiteracy, and itinerant widows. Historians do not agree on the impact of the Civil War on Southern white women. Some historians argue that the wartime defeat of Southern men expanded opportunities for women, who held families and farms together as best they could. Others suggest that wartime and postwar burdens eroded white women's support for the war as well as

---

[36]James Marten, *The Children's Civil War* (Chapel Hill: University of North Carolina Press, 1998) 6–7.
[37]1900 US Census, GA, Bibb County, population, Vineville district, 6.

their own status. Elizabeth Watson's role certainly changed, and not for the better. As one historian concluded, "Southern women, like their men, had learned to think of success as elusive." But on one point perhaps Elizabeth Watson, the plain folk wife and Confederate widow, would have agreed with F. H. Bozeman, a member of Hawkinsville's elite and an ex-Confederate officer, when he wrote in 1915: "I hope that we may never have to go to war again, for it is a terrible thing."[38]

[38]"Reminiscences of F. H. Bozemen," 15; Margaret Ripley Wolfe, *Daughters of Canaan: A Saga of Southern Women* (Lexington: University Press of Kentucky, 1995) 83–85; Drew Gilpin Faust, *Mothers of Invention: Women of the Slaveholding South in the American Civil War* (New York: Vintage Books, 1996) 256.

Civil War in Georgia
Further Reading

The following bibliography represents only some of the books concerning Georgia during the Civil War. It does not include specialized works or biographies; therefore, it is by no means exhaustive. The works included cover a wide range of general topics and serve as a starting point in the exploration of the state's role in our nation's great calamity. Those interested in delving deeper into Georgia's Civil War past should also examine the many theses, dissertations, and journal articles related to the war and its consequences.

Bailey, Anne J. *Invisible Southerners: Ethnicity in the Civil War.* Athens: University of Georgia Press, 2006.

Bailey, Anne J. and Walter J. Fraser. *Portraits of Conflict: Photographic History of Georgia in the Civil War.* Fayetteville: University of Arkansas Press, 1997.

Boney, F. N. *Rebel Georgia.* Macon: Mercer University Press, 1997.

Bragg, William Harris. *Griswoldville.* Macon: Mercer University Press, 2009.

Brown, Barry L. and Gordon R. Elwell. *Crossroads of Conflict: A Guide to Civil War Sites in Georgia.* Athens: University of Georgia Press, 2010.

Bryan, Thomas Conn. *Confederate Georgia.* Athens: University of Georgia Press, 2009.

Castel, Albert. *Decision in the West: The Atlanta Campaign of 1864.* Lawrence: University Press of Kansas, 1992.

Cimbala, Paul A. *Under the Guardianship of the Nation: The Freedmen's Bureau and the Reconstruction of Georgia, 1865-1870.* Athens: University of Georgia Press, 2003.

Coleman, Kenneth L. *Confederate Athens.* Athens: University of Georgia Press, 2009.

Cozzens, Peter. *This Terrible Sound: The Battle of Chickamauga.* Urbana: University of Illinois Press, 1992.

Davis, Robert Scott. *Requiem for a Lost City: Sallie Clayton's Memoirs of Civil War Atlanta.* Macon: Mercer University Press, 1999.

Davis, Robert Scott. *Andersonville Civil War Prison: Civil War Sesquicentennial Series*. Gloucestershire, Southwest England: The History Press, 2010.

Davis, Stephen. *Atlanta Will Fall: Sherman, Joe Johnston, and the Heavy Yankee Battalions*. Wilmington NC: SR Books, 2001.

Drago, Edmund L. *Black Politicians and Reconstruction in Georgia: A Splendid Failure*. Athens: University of Georgia Press, 1992.

Dyer, Thomas G. *Secret Yankees: The Union Circle in Confederate Atlanta*. Baltimore: Johns Hopkins University Press, 1999.

Freehling, William W. and Craig M. Simpson. *Secession Debated: Georgia's Showdown in 1860*. New York: Oxford University Press, 1992.

Glatthaar, Joseph T. *The March to the Sea and Beyond: Sherman's Troops in the Savannah and Carolinas Campaigns*. New York: New York University Press, 1985.

Harris, J. William. *Plain Folk and Gentry in a Slave Society: White Liberty and Black Slavery in Augusta's Hinterlands*. Baton Rouge: Louisiana State University Press, 1998.

Johnson, Michael P. *Toward a Patriarchal Society: The Secession of Georgia*. Baton Rouge: Louisiana State University Press, 1977.

Jones, Jacqueline. *Saving Savannah: The City and the Civil War*. New York: Alfred A. Knopf, 2009.

Jones, Jacqueline. *Soldiers of Light and Love: Northern Teachers and Georgia Blacks, 1865-1873*. Athens: University of Georgia Press, 2004.

Kennett, Lee. *Marching through Georgia: The Story of Soldiers and Civilians During Sherman's Campaign*. New York: HarperPerennial Publishers, 1995.

Lane, Mills. *"Dear Mother: Don't grieve about me. if I get killed, i'll only be dead": Letters from Georgia Soldiers in the Civil War*. Savannah: Beehive Press, 1977.

Luvaas, Jay and Harold W. Nelson. *Guide to the Atlanta Campaign: Rocky Face Ridge to the Atlanta Campaign*. Lawrence: University Press of Kansas, 2008.

McMurry, Richard M. *Atlanta 1864: Last Chance for the Confederacy*. Lincoln: University of Nebraska Press, 2000.

Miles, Jim. *Civil War Sites in Georgia*. Nashville: Thomas Nelson, 2001.

Mohr, Clarence L. *On the Threshold of Freedom: Masters and Slaves in Civil War Georgia*. Baton Rouge: Louisiana State University Press, 2001.

Morgan, Chad. *Planters' Progress: Modernizing Confederate Georgia.*
Gainesville: University Press of Florida, 2005.

Reidy, Joseph P. *From Slavery to Agrarian Capitalism in the Cotton Plantation South: Central Georgia, 1800-1880.* Chapel Hill: University of North Carolina Press, 1992.

Richards, Samuel P. and Wendy H. Venet. *Sam Richard's Civil War Diary: A Chronicle of the Atlanta Homefront.* Athens: University of Georgia Press, 2009.

Scaife, William R. *Allatoona Pass: A Needless Effusion of Blood.* Cartersville: Etowah Valley Historical Society, 1995.

Scaife, William R. and William Harris Bragg. *Joe Brown's Pets: The Georgia Militia, 1861- 1865.* Macon: Mercer University Press, 2004.

Secrist, Philip L. *The Battle of Resaca: Atlanta Campaign, 1864.* Macon: Mercer University Press, 1998.

Trudeau, Noah Andre. *Southern Storm: Sherman's March to the Sea.* New York: HarperCollins Publishers, 2008.

Turner, Maxine. *Navy Gray: Engineering the Confederate Navy on the Chattahoochee and Apalachicola Rivers.* Macon: Mercer University Press, 1999.

Weitz, Mark A. *A Higher Duty: Desertion Among Georgia Troops During the Civil War.* Lincoln: University of Nebraska Press, 2005.

Wetherington, Mark V. *Plain Folk's Fight: The Civil War and Reconstruction in Piney Woods Georgia.* Chapel Hill: University of North Carolina Press, 2009.

Whites, LeeAnn. *The Civil War as a Crisis in Gender: Augusta, Georgia, 1860-1890.* Athens: University of Georgia Press, 2000.

Wiggins, David N. *Georgia's Confederate Monuments and Cemeteries: Images of Georgia.* Mount Pleasant, South Carolina: Arcadia Publishing, 2006.

Williams, David, Teresa C. Williams, and R. David Carlson. *Plain Folk in a Rich Man's War: Class and Dissent in Confederate Georgia.* Gainesville: University Press of Florida, 2002.

Index